Volumes of A HISTORY OF PHILOSOPHY now available in Image Books:

A History of Philosophy

VOLUME V

Modern Philosophy:
The British Philosophers

PART I

Hobbes to Paley

by Frederick Copleston, S.J.

IMAGE BOOKS
A Division of Doubleday & Company, Inc.
Garden City, New York

Image Books Edition 1964
by special arrangement with The Newman Press
and Burns & Oates, Ltd.
Image Books edition published February, 1964

DE LICENTIA SUPERIORUM ORDINIS:
J. D. Boyle, S.J.
Praep. Prov. Angliae

NIHIL OBSTAT:
J. L. Russell, S.J.
Censor Deputatus

IMPRIMATUR:
☒ Franciscus Archiepiscopus Birmingamiensis
Birmingamiae die 25 Julii 1957

CONTENTS

PREFACE

As I remarked in the preface to the fourth volume of this work, my original intention was to cover the philosophy of the seventeenth and eighteenth centuries, including the system of Kant, in one book. But it did not prove possible to do this. And I have divided the matter between three books, treating each as a separate volume. My original plan has, however, been preserved to this extent, that there is a common introductory chapter and a common Concluding Review for Volumes IV, V and VI. The former has been placed, of course, at the beginning of Volume IV, *Descartes to Leibniz*. The Concluding Review, in which I propose to discuss, not only from an historical but also from a more philosophical point of view, the nature, importance and value of the various styles of philosophizing in the seventeenth and eighteenth centuries, will form the last chapter of Volume VI, *Wolff to Kant*, which will comprise the French Enlightenment, the German Enlightenment, the rise of the philosophy of history, and the system of Kant. The present volume, therefore, *Hobbes to Hume*, which is devoted to British philosophical thought from Hobbes up to and including the Scottish philosophy of common sense and which represents the second part of the originally projected fourth volume, *Descartes to Kant*, does not contain either an introductory chapter or a Concluding Review. As its arrangement differs to this extent from that of the first three volumes, I thought it desirable to repeat here the explanation which has already been offered in the preface to Volume IV.

A HISTORY OF PHILOSOPHY

Volume V   Part I

Chapter One

HOBBES (1)

Life and writings — The end and nature of philosophy and its exclusion of all theology — The divisions of philosophy — Philosophical method — Hobbes's nominalism — Causality and mechanism — Space and time — Body and accidents — Motion and change — Vital motions and animal motions — Good and evil — The passions — Will — Intellectual virtues — Atomic individualism.

1. Thomas Hobbes, author of one of the most celebrated political treatises in European literature, was born at Westport near Malmesbury in 1588. His father was a clergyman. In 1608, when Hobbes went down from Oxford, he entered the service of the Cavendish family and spent the years 1608–10 travelling in France and Italy as tutor to the son of Lord Cavendish, future earl of Devonshire. On his return to England he occupied himself with literary pursuits and translated Thucydides into English, the translation being published in 1628. He had relations with Francis Bacon (d. 1626) and with Lord Herbert of Cherbury; but he had not yet given himself to philosophy.

From 1629 until 1631 Hobbes was again in France, this time as tutor to the son of Sir Gervase Clifton; and it was during a visit to Paris that he made acquaintance with the *Elements* of Euclid. Historians have pointed out that for all his labours Hobbes was never able to acquire that degree of mathematical knowledge and insight which Descartes had attained at a far earlier age. But though he was never a great mathematician, it was this encounter with geometry which supplied him with his lasting ideal of scientific method. During his visit to Paris his attention was also drawn to problems of sense-perception, the relation of sensation to the motions of bodies and the status of secondary qualities.

On returning to England Hobbes again entered the service of the Cavendish family, and from 1634 until 1637 he was once more on the Continent. He met Galileo at Florence, and at Paris he was introduced by Mersenne into philosophical and scientific circles. He thus came to know the Cartesian philosophy, and at Mersenne's invitation he submitted to Descartes his objections against the latter's *Meditations*. This period was of great importance in the development of Hobbes's mind and in determining his philosophical interests. He was already a middle-aged man when he turned his attention to philosophy; but he formulated for himself the idea of a system and projected a presentation of it in three parts. In actual fact his mind was first seriously occupied with social and political problems, and in 1640 he wrote *The Elements of Law, Natural and Politic*, of which two portions appeared in 1650 under the titles *Human Nature or the Fundamental Elements of Policy* and *De corpore politico*. The text of the whole work did not appear until 1889, when it was edited and published by F. Tönnies.

In 1640 Hobbes, thinking that his safety was menaced in England because of his royalist convictions, took refuge in France. In 1642 he published at Paris his work *De cive*, the third part of his projected philosophical system; and it was at Paris that he wrote his famous *Leviathan or the Matter, Form and Power of a Commonwealth, Ecclesiastical and Civil*, which appeared in London in 1651. In 1649 Charles I was beheaded, and one might perhaps expect that Hobbes would have remained in France, especially as he had been for a time mathematical tutor to Charles, Prince of Wales, who was living in exile at Paris. However, he made his peace with the Commonwealth in 1652 and settled down in the household of the earl of Devonshire. Some of the ideas which he was known to have expounded in the *Leviathan* were not acceptable in royalist circles at Paris, and in any case the civil war, which had constituted Hobbes's chief reason for remaining abroad, was over. As will be seen later, his political convictions enabled him to accept any *de facto* government which was in effective control of the State. After the Restoration in 1660 Hobbes enjoyed the favour of Charles II and received a pension.

In 1655 and 1658 Hobbes published the first and second

sections of his philosophical system, the *De corpore* and the *De homine*. And until the end of his life he occupied himself with literary labours, translating the whole of Homer into English and writing a book on the Long Parliament. He was also much engaged in controversy. Thus he conducted a literary debate with Bramhall, bishop of Derry, on the subject of freedom and necessity, in which he maintained a determinist point of view. He was also engaged in controversy with the mathematician Wallis, who published an *Elenchus geometriae hobbinae* in which Hobbes's mathematical errors were subjected to sharp criticism. He was also attacked, particularly by ecclesiastics, on the score of heresy and atheism. However, having successfully weathered both Commonwealth and Restoration, he was not to be killed by verbal polemics, and he survived until the winter of 1679 when he died at the age of ninety-one.[1]

2. Hobbes, like Bacon, stresses the practical purpose of philosophy. 'The *end* or *scope* of philosophy is that we may make use to our benefit of effects formerly seen; or that, by application of bodies to one another, we may produce the like effects of those we conceive in our mind, as far forth as matter, strength and industry will permit, for the commodity of human life. . . . The end of knowledge is power . . . and the scope of all speculation is the performance of some action or thing to be done.'[2] Natural philosophy confers obvious benefits on mankind. But moral and political philosophy also possesses great utility. For human life is afflicted by calamities, of which civil war is the chief, that arise because men do not understand sufficiently the rules of conduct and of political life. 'Now, the knowledge of these rules is moral philosophy.'[3] Both in the sciences and in politics knowledge is power.

But though philosophical knowledge is power, in the sense that its function is to contribute to man's material prosperity and to social peace and security, it does not follow that all knowledge is philosophical. As far as the remote basis of philosophical knowledge is concerned, Hobbes is an empiricist. The philosopher starts with the given, with sense-impressions made on us by external bodies, and with our memories of such impressions. He starts with the empirical data, from what Hobbes calls 'effects' or 'appearances'. But though our immediate awareness of appearances or phenomena and our memory of them constitute knowledge, and though they form the remote basis of philosophy, they are not philosophical knowledge. 'Although sense and memory of things, which are common to man and all living creatures, be knowledge, yet because they are given us immediately by nature, and not gotten by ratiocination, they are not philosophy.'[4] Everyone knows that the sun exists, in the sense that they have the experience which we call 'seeing the sun'; but nobody would say that such knowledge is scientific astronomical knowledge. Similarly, that human actions take place is known by all; but all do not possess a scientific or philosophical knowledge of human actions. Philosophy is concerned with causal relations. 'Philosophy is such knowledge of effects or appearances as we acquire by true ratiocination from the knowledge we have first of their causes or generation. And again, of such causes or generations as may be (had) from knowing first their effects.'[5] The philosopher discovers effects from known causes and causes from known effects. And he does so by 'ratiocination'. He is not concerned with simply stating empirical facts, that this or that is or was a fact, but with the consequences of propositions, which are discovered by reasoning and not by observation.

We can understand, therefore, what Hobbes means when he divides knowledge into knowledge of fact and knowledge of consequence. 'There are of Knowledge two kinds; whereof one is *knowledge of fact:* the other *knowledge of the consequence of one affirmation to another.*'[6] When I see something done or remember seeing it done, I have knowledge of fact. This, says Hobbes, is the kind of knowledge required of a witness in a court of law. It is 'absolute' knowledge, in the sense that it is expressed absolutely or in assertoric form. And the 'register' of knowledge of fact is called history, which may take the form either of natural or of civil history. Knowledge of consequence, on the contrary, is conditional or hypothetical, in the sense that it is knowledge that, for example, if A is true, B is also true. To use Hobbes's example, 'If the figure shown be a circle, then any straight line through the centre shall divide it into two equal parts'.[7] This is scientific knowledge, the kind of knowledge which is required of a philosopher, 'that is to say, of him that pretends to reasoning'.[8] And the 'registers of science' are books containing the demonstrations of the consequences of propositions and 'are commonly called *books of philosophy*'.[9] Scientific or philosophical knowledge can therefore be described as knowledge of consequences. And such knowledge is always conditional: 'if this be, that is; if this has been, that has been; if this shall be, that shall be'.[10]

We have seen that for Hobbes philosophy is concerned with causal explanation. And by causal explanation he means a scientific account of the generative process by which some effect comes into being. From this it follows that if there is anything which does not come into existence through a generative process, it cannot be part of the subject-matter of philosophy. God, therefore, and indeed all spiritual reality, is excluded from philosophy. 'The *subject* of Philosophy, or the matter it treats of, is every body of which we can conceive any generation, and which we may, by any consideration thereof, compare with other bodies, or which is capable of composition and resolution; that is to say, every body of whose generation or properties we can have any knowledge. . . . Therefore it (philosophy) excludes theology, I mean the doctrine of God, eternal, ingenerable, incomprehensible, and in whom there is nothing neither to divide nor compound, nor any generation to be conceived.'[11] History is also excluded, because 'such knowledge is but experience (memory) or authority, and not ratiocination'.[12] And pseudo-sciences, such as astrology, cannot be admitted.

Philosophy, therefore, is concerned with the causes and properties of bodies. And this means that it is concerned with bodies in motion. For motion is the 'one universal cause', which 'cannot be understood to have any other cause besides motion'; and 'the variety of all figures arises out of the variety of those motions by which they are made'.[13] This account of the nature and subject-matter of philosophy may not, Hobbes observes, be acceptable to everyone. Some will say that it is a matter of definition and that anyone is free to define philosophy as he wishes. This is true, 'though I think it no hard matter to demonstrate that this definition of mine agrees with the sense of all men'.[14] Hobbes adds, however, that those who seek another kind of philosophy must adopt other principles. If his own principles are adopted, philosophy will be what he conceives it to be.

Hobbes's philosophy, therefore, is materialistic in the sense that it takes no account of anything but bodies. And in so far as the exclusion of God and of all spiritual reality is simply the result of a freely chosen definition, his materialism can be called methodological. He does not say that there is no God; he says that God is not the subject-matter of philosophy. At the same time it seems to me to be a great mistake to represent Hobbes as saying no more than that according to his use of the word 'philosophy' the existence and nature of God are not philosophical topics. Philosophy and reasoning are for him coextensive; and from this it follows that theology is irrational. To all intents and purposes he identified the imaginable and the conceivable. And from this he drew the conclusion that we can have no idea of the infinite or of the immaterial. 'Whatsoever we imagine is *finite*. Therefore there is no idea or conception of any thing we call infinite.'[15] A term such as *incorporeal substance* is just as contradictory as *incorporeal body* or *round quadrangle*. Terms of this sort are 'insignificant',[16] that is, meaningless. Some people do indeed think that they understand them; but all that they really do is to repeat the words to themselves without any real understanding of their content. For they have no content. Hobbes explicitly asserts that words such as *hypostatical, transubstantiate, eternal-now* and so on 'signify nothing'.[17] 'Words whereby we conceive nothing but the sound are those we call *absurd, insignificant* and *nonsense*. And therefore if a man should talk to me of a *round quadrangle* . . . or *immaterial substances* . . . or of a *free subject* . . . I should not say he were in an error, but that his words were without meaning, that is to say, absurd.'[18] He makes it abundantly clear that theology, if offered as a science or coherent body of true propositions, is absurd and irrational. And to say this is to say very much more than that one proposes to confine one's attention in philosophy to the realm of the corporeal.

At the same time one cannot legitimately conclude without more ado that Hobbes is an atheist. It would indeed appear to follow from his empiricist analysis of the meaning of names that all talk about God is so much gibberish and that belief is simply a matter of emotion, that is, of an emotive attitude. But this is not precisely what Hobbes says. As regards natural religion he says that curiosity or love of the knowledge of causes naturally draws a man to conceive a cause which itself has no cause, 'so that it is impossible to make any profound inquiry into natural causes without being inclined thereby to believe that there is one God eternal; though they (men) cannot have any idea of him in their mind, answerable to his nature'.[19] For 'by the visible things in this world, and their admirable order, a man may conceive there is a cause of them,

which men call God; and yet not have an idea or image of
him in his mind'.[20] In other words, Hobbes emphasizes the
incomprehensibility of God. If a word such as 'infinite' is
predicated of God, it does not stand for any positive idea of
God but expresses our inability to conceive Him. 'And therefore the name of God is used, not to make us conceive him,
for he is incomprehensible; and his greatness and power are
inconceivable, but that we may honour him.'[21] Similarly,
terms such as *spirit* and *incorporeal* are not in themselves intelligible. 'And therefore, men that by their own meditation
arrive to the acknowledgement of one infinite, omnipotent,
and eternal God, choose rather to confess he is incomprehensible and above their understanding than to define his nature by *spirit incorporeal*, and then confess their definition to
be unintelligible: or if they give him such a title, it is not
dogmatically, with intention to make the divine nature *understood*; but *piously*, to honour him with attributes, or significations, as remote as they can from the grossness of bodies
visible.'[22] As for Christian revelation, expressed in the
Scriptures, Hobbes does not deny that there is a revelation,
but he applies the same principles in his interpretation of
the terms used. The word *spirit* either signifies a subtle and
fluid body or is used metaphorically or is purely unintelligible. 'For the nature of God is incomprehensible; that is to say,
we understand nothing of *what he is*, but only *that he is*; and
therefore the attributes we give him are not to tell one another *what he is*, nor to signify our opinion of his nature, but
our desire to honour him with such names as we conceive
most honourable amongst ourselves.'[23]

Some commentators have seen in all this a continuation
and intensification of the tendency, already visible in fourteenth-century thinkers such as Ockham and those who belonged to the movement of which he was the most eminent
representative, to draw a sharp distinction between theology
and philosophy and to relegate all theology, including natural
theology, to the sphere of faith, so that philosophy would
have little or nothing to say about God. And there is certainly
a good deal to be said in favour of this interpretation. As we
have seen, Hobbes makes explicit use of the famous distinction, common enough in the Middle Ages, between knowing
of God *that* He is and knowing *what* He is. But the mediaeval theologians and philosophers who emphasized this distinction believed that God is incorporeal substance and infi-

nite spirit. And this is true both of a writer such as St.
Thomas Aquinas, who combined the use of the distinction
with belief in a philosophical though analogical knowledge of
God, and of a fourteenth-century philosopher such as Ockham, who evidently considered that philosophy is incapable
of telling us much about God. Hobbes, however, seems to
have affirmed the corporeality of God, at least if one can
judge by what he says in the course of his controversy with
Bishop Bramhall. For there he says explicitly that God is 'a
most pure and most simple corporeal spirit' and that 'the
Trinity, and the persons thereof, are that one pure, simple
and eternal corporeal spirit'.[24] The phrase 'simple, corporeal
spirit' seems at first sight to be a contradiction in terms. But
a pure and simple body is said to be 'body of one and the
same kind in every part throughout'.[25] And spirit is said to
be 'thin, fluid, transparent, invisible body'.[26] If, then, the
terms are given these meanings, the contradiction disappears.
But in this case God's corporeality is affirmed. True, this does
not mean that God possesses secondary qualities; but it means
that He possesses magnitude. 'By corporeal I mean a substance that has magnitude.'[27] And magnitude, as will be seen
later, is the same as extension. God, therefore, is infinite, invisible extension. And to make this statement is to say very
much more than that God is incomprehensible and that because of His incomprehensibility philosophy has nothing to
say about Him. However, if Hobbes, who appeals not only to
Tertullian but also to Scripture in support of his theory, is
serious in all this, as presumably he is, he cannot be called an
atheist, unless under the term 'atheist' one includes the man
who affirms God's existence but denies that He is infinite, incorporeal substance. And in Hobbes's opinion to affirm the
latter would be itself atheism; for to say that God is incorporeal substance is to say that there is no God, since substance
is necessarily corporeal.

3. To say, however, that philosophy is concerned exclusively with bodies and their properties and causes is not to
say that it is concerned exclusively with bodies in the ordinary sense and that it is coextensive with what we call the
natural sciences. 'For two chief kinds of bodies, and very different from one another, offer themselves to such as search
after their generation and properties.'[28] The one is called a
natural body, because it is made by nature; the other is called
a *commonwealth*, and 'it is made by the wills and agreement

of men'.[29] Philosophy can thus be subdivided into two parts, natural and civil. Further, civil philosophy can be subdivided. For in order to understand the nature, function and properties of a commonwealth we have first to understand the dispositions, affections and manners of man; and the part of philosophy which treats of this subject is called *ethics*, whereas the part which treats of man's civil duties is called *politics* or takes to itself alone the general term *civil philosophy*. And from this analysis of the subject-matter of philosophy there follows the division of headings which Hobbes adopted for his systematic exposition: *De corpore*, treating of natural bodies, *De homine*, treating of man's dispositions, affections and 'manners', and *De cive*, treating of the commonwealth and of man's civic duties.

This division is not, however, complete. In the dedicatory epistle to the *De cive* Hobbes remarks that just as the British, Atlantic and Indian seas make up the ocean, so do geometry, physics and morals make up philosophy. If we consider the effects produced by a body in motion and confine our attention exclusively to the motion of the body, we see that the motion of a point generates a line, the motion of a line a plane surface, and so on. And from this study there sprang 'that part of philosophy which is called geometry'.[30] We can then consider the effects produced by one moving body on another when the bodies are considered as wholes. And we can thus develop a science of motion. We can also consider the effects produced by the motion of the parts of a body. We can arrive, for example, at knowledge of the nature of secondary qualities and of phenomena such as light. And these 'considerations comprehend that part of philosophy which is called physics'.[31] Finally, we can consider the motions of the mind, such as appetite and aversion, hope, anger and so on, and their causes and effects. And then we have moral philosophy.

The completest division which Hobbes gives of the subject-matter of philosophy is derived from applying the definition of science or philosophical knowledge as the 'knowledge of consequences'.[32] The two main divisions are knowledge of consequences from the accidents of natural bodies and knowledge of consequences from the accidents of political bodies. The former is called natural philosophy, the latter politics or civil philosophy. In politics we study what follows from the institution of commonwealths, first as regards the rights and duties of the sovereign, secondly as regards the duty and rights of subjects. Natural philosophy, however, comprises a considerable number of further divisions and subdivisions. If we study the consequences which follow from the accidents common to all bodies, namely, quantity and motion, we have either 'first philosophy', if it is indeterminate quantity and motion which are being considered, or mathematics, if we are considering the consequences from quantity and motion determined by figure and number, or astronomy or mechanics according to the special kinds of bodies we are considering. If we study the consequences from the qualities of bodies, we have physics. And physics in turn can be subdivided according to the different kinds of bodies considered. For instance, study of the consequences from the passions of men yields ethics, which is classified, therefore, under the general heading of natural philosophy, since a human being is a natural and not an artificial body in the sense in which a commonwealth is an artificial body.[33]

4. The description of philosophical knowledge or science as 'knowledge of the consequences of one affirmation to another', coupled with the assertion that such knowledge is hypothetical or conditional, naturally suggests that Hobbes attached great importance to deduction; that is, to the mathematical method. And some commentators have given the impression that in his opinion philosophy is, or rather should þe, a purely deductive system. 'Rationalism' or reasoning, which is the essential characteristic of philosophy, is described in mathematical terms. 'By *ratiocination* I mean *computation*.'[34] And Hobbes proceeds to say that to compute is to add or subtract, terms which obviously suggest arithmetical operations. The whole system of Hobbes, it has been said, was designed to be a deduction from an analysis of motion and quantity, even though he did not in fact succeed in fulfilling his purpose. In his insistence on the practical function and end of philosophy or science he was akin to Bacon; but his concept of the proper method to be employed in philosophy was very different from Bacon's. The latter stressed experiment, whereas Hobbes took a dim view of the experimenters and upheld an idea of method which clearly resembles that of continental rationalists such as Descartes.

This interpretation of Hobbes's conception of philosophical method contains a great deal of truth. But I think that it is an over-simplified view and stands in need of qualification.

For one thing, Hobbes certainly never imagined that he could start with an abstract analysis of motion and then proceed in a purely deductive manner without the introduction of any empirical material drawn from experience. He was, indeed, a systematizer. He was convinced that there is a continuity between physics, psychology and politics, and that a coherent and systematic view of the different branches of philosophy is possible in the light of general principles. But he was well aware that one cannot deduce man and society from abstract laws of motion. If anything can be deduced, it is the laws governing man's 'motions', not man himself. As we have already seen, there are empirically given data which form the remote subject-matter of philosophy, even though knowledge of these data, considered as mere given facts, is not philosophy.

When Hobbes says that ratiocination means computation, and that computation means addition and subtraction, he goes on to explain that he is using these last-mentioned terms in the sense of 'composition' and 'division or resolution'. 'And the resolutive (method) is commonly called *analytical* method, as the compositive is called *synthetical*.'[35] Philosophical method or ratiocination comprises, therefore, analysis and synthesis. In analysis the mind proceeds from the particular to the universal or to first principles. For example, if a man starts with the idea of gold, he can come by 'resolution' to the ideas of solid, visible, heavy 'and many others more universal than gold itself; and these he may resolve again, till he comes to such things as are most universal. . . . I conclude, therefore, that the method of attaining to the universal knowledge of things is purely *analytical*.'[36] In synthesis, on the contrary, the mind starts with principles or general causes and proceeds to construct their possible effects. The whole process of determining or discovering causal relations and establishing causal explanations, the method of invention as Hobbes calls it, is partly analytical and partly synthetical. To use terms which he borrowed from Galileo, it is partly resolutive and partly compositive. Or, to use terms more familiar to us, it is partly inductive and partly deductive. We can say, I think, that Hobbes envisaged the method of framing explanatory hypotheses and deducing their consequences. The fact that he asserts that the deduced effects are 'possible' effects, at least in what we would call physical science, shows that he had some awareness of the hypothetical character of the explanatory theories concerned.

A distinction is made by Hobbes between the method of invention and the method of teaching or demonstrating. In using the latter method we start with first principles, which stand in need of explanation but not of demonstration, since first principles cannot be demonstrated, and proceed deductively to conclusions. 'The whole method, therefore, of demonstration is *synthetical*, consisting of that order of speech which begins from primary or most universal propositions, which are manifest of themselves, and proceeds by a perpetual composition of propositions into syllogisms, till at last the learner understands the truth of the conclusion sought after.'[37]

It is perhaps this ideal of continuous demonstration which has given the impression that Hobbes aimed at the construction of a purely deductive system. And if we press this point of view, we shall have to say that he failed, at least in part, in his attempt. But in estimating what Hobbes was trying to do it seems reasonable to take into account what he actually says about the method or methods which he in fact employs.

Hobbes certainly emphasizes the debt which science and man owe to mathematics. 'For whatsoever assistance doth accrue to the life of man, whether from the observation of the heavens or from the description of the earth, from the notation of times or from the remotest experiments of navigation; finally, whatsoever things they are in which this present age doth differ from the rude simpleness of antiquity, we must acknowledge to be a debt which we owe to geometry.'[38] The advances in astronomy, for example, were rendered possible by mathematics, and without mathematics there would have been no advance. And the benefits conferred by applied science are also due to mathematics. If moral philosophers took the trouble to ascertain the nature of human passions and actions as clearly as mathematicians understand 'the nature of quantity in geometrical figures'[39] it would be possible to banish war and secure a stable peace.

This suggests that there is a close link between mathematics and physics. And in point of fact Hobbes insists on this link. 'They that study natural philosophy study in vain, except they begin at geometry; and such writers or disputers thereof, as are ignorant of geometry, do but make their readers and hearers lose their time.'[40] But this does not mean that Hobbes endeavoured to deduce from the abstract analysis of motion and quantity and from mathematics the whole of natural philosophy. When he comes to the fourth part of his treatise *Concerning Body*, which he entitles 'Physics or the Phenomena of Nature', he remarks that the definition of philosophy which he gave in the first chapter shows that there are two methods: 'one from the generation of things to their possible effects, and the other from their effects or appearances to some possible generation of the same'.[41] In the foregoing chapters he has followed the first method, affirming nothing but definitions and their implications.[42] He is now about to use the second method, 'the finding out by the appearances or effects of nature, which we know by sense, some ways and means by which they may be, I do not say they are, generated'.[43] He is not now starting with definitions but with sensible phenomena or appearances, and he is seeking their possible causes.

If, therefore, Hobbes asserts a connection between the use of these two methods and his own definition of philosophy, it can reasonably be claimed that his introduction of fresh empirical material is not properly described as a 'failure' to fulfil his aim. And in this case we are not justified in accusing him of inconsistency because he makes, as it were, a fresh start when he comes to psychology and politics. He does, indeed, say that to obtain a knowledge of morals and politics by the synthetical method it is necessary to have first studied mathematics and physics. For the synthetical method involves seeing all effects as conclusions, proximate or remote, from first principles. But I do not think that he means much more by this than following out the exemplification of general principles in progressively particularized subject-matter according to an architectonic scheme. One cannot deduce men from the laws of motion, but one can study first the laws of motion in themselves and their application to body in general, secondly their application to different kinds of natural bodies, inanimate and animate, and thirdly their application to the artificial body which we call the commonwealth. In any case Hobbes observes that it is possible to study moral and political philosophy without previous knowledge of mathematics and physics if one employs the analytical method. Let us suppose that the question is asked whether an action is just or unjust. We can 'resolve' the notion *unjust* into the notion *fact against law*, and the notion of *law* into the notion *com-*

mand of him who has *coercive* power. And this notion of co-ercive power can be derived from the notion of men volun-tarily establishing this power that they may live a peaceful life. Finally we can arrive at the principle that men's appe-tites and passions are of such a kind that they will be con-stantly making war on one another unless they are restrained by some power. And this 'may be known to be so by any man's experience, that will but examine his own mind'.[44] One can then decide, by employing the synthetical method, whether the action in question is just or unjust. And in the total proc-ess of 'resolution' and 'composition' one remains within the sphere of morals and politics without introducing remoter principles. Experience provides the factual data, and the phi-losopher can show systematically how they are connected in a rational scheme of cause and effect without necessarily having to relate the cause or causes to remoter and more general causes. Hobbes doubtless considered that a philosopher should show the connections between natural philosophy and civil philosophy. But the fact that he asserted the relative in-dependence of morals and politics shows clearly enough that he was well aware of the need for fresh empirical data when treating of human psychology and of man's social and politi-cal life. I have no intention of denying the affinity between Hobbes and the continental rationalists. Among English phi-losophers he is one of the few who have tried to create sys-tems. But it is also important to emphasize the fact that he was not a fanatical worshipper of pure deduction.

5. Now, it is obvious that philosophical knowledge, as en-visaged by Hobbes, is concerned with the universal and not simply with the particular. Philosophy aims at a coherent and systematic knowledge of causal relations in the light of first principles or of universal causes. At the same time Hobbes clearly asserts a nominalist position when he is treating of names. The individual philosopher, he says, requires marks to help him to remember or recall his thoughts; and these marks are names. Further, if he is to communicate his thoughts to others, these marks must be able to serve as signs, which they can do when they are connected together in what we call 'speech'. Hence he gives the following definition. 'A *name* is a word taken at pleasure[45] to serve for a mark, which may raise in our mind a thought like to some thought we had be-fore, and which being pronounced to others, may be to them a sign of what thought the speaker had or had not before in his

mind.'[46] This does not mean that every name should be the name of something. The word *nothing* does not connote a special kind of something. But of the names which do designate things some are proper to one thing (such as *Homer* or *this man*), while others are common to many things (such as *man* or *tree*). And these common names are called 'universal'. That is to say, the term 'universal' is predicated of the name, not of the object designated by the name. For the name is the name of many individual things taken collectively. No one of them is a universal; nor is there any universal thing alongside of these individual things. Further, the universal name does not stand for any universal concept. 'This word *universal* is never the name of any thing existent in nature, nor of any idea or phantasm formed in the mind, but always the name of some word or name; so that when *a living creature, a stone, a spirit*, or any other thing, is said to be *universal*, it is not to be understood that any man, stone, etc., ever was or can be universal, but only that the words, living creature, stone, etc., are *universal names*, that is, names common to many things; and the conceptions answering them in our mind are the images and phantasms of several living creatures or other things.'[47] As Hobbes tended to identify the conceivable with the imaginable, he naturally found no place for a universal concept or idea, and he therefore attributed universality to common names only. He gives no very thorough explanation of the justification of our use of common names for sets of individual things, beyond referring to the likeness between things. 'One universal name is imposed on many things, for their similitude in some quality, or other accident.'[48] But his statement of a nominalistic position is unambiguous.

Like Ockham[49] and other mediaeval predecessors, Hobbes distinguishes between names or terms of 'first intention' and names of 'second intention'. Logical terms such as *universal, genus, species* and *syllogism* are, he tells us, 'the names of names and speeches'; they are terms of second intention. Words such as *man* or *stone* are names of first intention. One might expect perhaps that Hobbes would follow Ockham in saying that while terms of second intention stand for other terms, terms of first intention stand for things, universal terms of first intention standing for a plurality of individual things, not, of course, for any universal thing. But this is not what he actually says. He does, indeed, remark that names such as 'a man', 'a tree', 'a stone', 'are the names of things themselves';[50] but he insists that because 'names ordered in speech are signs of our conceptions, it is manifest that they are not signs of the things themselves'.[51] A name such as *stone* is the sign of a 'conception', that is, of a phantasm or image. If John uses this word when speaking to Peter, it is a sign to the latter of John's thought. The general use of speech is to transfer our mental discourse into verbal; or the train of our thoughts into a train of words.'[52] And if the 'thought' or 'conception' is an image, it is obvious that universality can be attributed only to words. But even if a universal word or term signifies directly a mental representation or 'fiction', as Hobbes sometimes puts it, this does not necessarily mean that it has no relation to reality. For it can have an indirect relation, inasmuch as the mental representation is itself caused by things. A 'thought' is 'a representation or appearance of some quality or other accident of a body without us, which is commonly called object. Which object worketh on the eyes, ears, and other parts of a man's body; and by diversity of working produceth diversity of appearances. The original of them all is that which we call *sense*, for there is no conception in a man's mind, which hath not at first, totally or by parts, been begotten upon the organs of sense. The rest are derived from that original.'[53] Thus although universality belongs only to words, which signify 'thoughts', there is an indirect relation between universal statements and reality, even if 'reality' must be here taken to mean the sphere of appearances or phenomena. There is, indeed, a great difference between experience, which Hobbes identifies with memory, and science. 'Experience,' to quote his famous statement, 'concludeth nothing universally.'[54] But science, which does 'conclude universally', is based on sense-experience.

If, therefore, we press the empiricist aspect of Hobbes's philosophy, it is possible to argue that his nominalism is not necessarily infected with scepticism; that is to say, with doubt about the real reference of scientific propositions. It may, indeed, follow that science is concerned with the realm of phenomena. For appearances produce images, and images are translated into words, the connection of which in speech renders science possible. But the conclusions of science, it might be said, are applicable within the realm of phenomena. And of any other realm the philosopher or scientist can say nothing. On a nominalistic basis constructed theories and causal explanations would be, as Hobbes says they are, hypothetical and conditional. But it would be possible to verify, or at least to test, scientific conclusions in experience, though Hobbes, who had no great esteem for the experimental method in science, does not in fact talk about verification.

Hobbes is, of course, very far from being only an empiricist, though there is certainly an important empiricist element in his thought. What he emphasizes when speaking of philosophy and science is deduction of consequences from first principles. As we have seen, he explicitly recognizes the use of the analytical or inductive method in arriving at the knowledge of principles; but what he emphasizes as the mark of scientific procedure is the deduction of the consequences of affirmations. And it is important to notice his clear statement that the principles from which deduction starts are definitions, and that definitions are nothing but the explication of the meanings of words. Definitions are the 'settling of significations' or 'settled significations of words'.[55] More exactly, a definition is 'a proposition, whose predicate resolves the subject, when it may; and when it may not, it exemplifies the same'.[56] Definitions are the sole principles of demonstration, and they are 'truths constituted arbitrarily by the inventors of speech, and therefore not to be demonstrated'.[57]

If this is taken to mean that definitions are no more than arbitrary determinations of the meanings of words, the conclusions derived from such definitions must partake of their arbitrariness. And then we are confronted with a divorce between scientific propositions and reality. There is no guarantee that scientific propositions are applicable to reality. In Hobbes's objections against the *Meditations* of Descartes we find the following remarkable passage. 'But what shall we now say if reasoning is perhaps nothing else but the joining and stringing together of names or appellations by the word *is*? In this case reason gives no conclusions about the nature of things, but only about their names; whether, indeed, or not we join the names of things according to conventions which we have arbitrarily established about their meanings. If this is the case, as it may be, reasoning will depend on names, names on the imagination, and the imagination perhaps, as I think, on the motion of the bodily organs.'[58] Even though Hobbes does not state dogmatically in this passage that reasoning establishes the connections between words only, he certainly suggests it. And it is no matter for surprise that a number of commentators have drawn the conclusion that philosophy or science is, for Hobbes, inevitably affected by subjectivism, and that they have spoken of his nominalistic scepticism.

Sometimes, indeed, it is possible to interpret Hobbes's assertions in a different light. He says, for example, that 'the first truths were arbitrarily made by those that first of all imposed names upon things, or received them from the imposition of others'.[59] But this statement could at any rate be taken to mean that if people had used the terms involved to mean something else than what they have in fact been made to mean, the propositions would not be true.[60] 'For it is true, for example, that *man is a living creature*, but it is for this reason, that it pleased men to impose both those names on the same thing.'[61] If the term *living creature* had been made to mean *stone*, it could not have been true to say that man is a living creature. And this is obviously the case. Again, when Hobbes asserts that it is false to say that 'the definition is the essence of any thing',[62] he is rejecting a form of expression used by Aristotle. And the remark which immediately follows, that 'definition is not the essence of any thing, but a speech signifying what we conceive of the essence thereof', is not by itself a 'sceptical' assertion. For it can be taken to imply that we have some idea or conception of the essence,[63] an idea which is signified by the name that is explained in the definition. Further, it can be pointed out that when Hobbes says that a word is a 'mere name', he does not necessarily mean that the idea signified by the word is without any relation to reality. For example, when he adopts for his own purposes the Aristotelian term 'first matter', he asks what this first matter or *materia prima* is, and he answers that it is a 'mere name'.[64] But he immediately adds, 'yet a name which is not of vain use; for it signifies a conception of body without the consideration of any form or other accident except only magnitude or extension, and aptness to receive form and other accident'.[65] 'First matter' and 'body in general' are for Hobbes equivalent terms. And there is no body in general. 'Wherefore *materia prima* is nothing.'[66] That is to say, there is no thing which corresponds to the name. In this sense the term is a 'mere name'. But it signifies a way of conceiving bodies; and bodies exist. Therefore, even though the name is not the name of any *thing*, it has some relation to reality.

However, even if the statement that Hobbes is a sceptic constitutes an exaggeration, it remains true that whether we proceed from cause to effect or from effect to cause, we attain knowledge only of possible effects or of possible causes. The only certain knowledge we can acquire is knowledge of the implications of propositions. If A implies B, then if A is true, B is true.

It seems to me that in Hobbes's interpretation of philosophy or science there are different strands of thought which he failed to distinguish clearly. The idea that in what we would call 'natural science' explanatory theories are hypothetical in character and that we can at best attain only a very high degree of probability may perhaps be said to represent one strand of thought. The idea that in mathematics we start with definitions and develop their implications, so that in pure mathematics we are concerned only with formal implications and not with the 'real world', represents another strand. And both these ideas reappear in modern empiricism. But Hobbes was also influenced by the rationalist ideal of a deductive philosophical system. For him the first principles of mathematics are 'postulates' and not true first principles, because he considered them to be demonstrable. There are ultimate first principles, antecedent to mathematics and to physics. Now, for a rationalism of the continental type the truth of first principles must be known intuitively, and all the propositions which can be deduced from them will be certainly true. And sometimes Hobbes appears to indicate that this is what he thinks. But at other times he speaks as though the first principles or definitions were 'arbitrary', in the sense in which a modern empiricist might say that mathematical definitions are arbitrary. And then he draws the conclusion that the whole of science or philosophy is nothing but a reasoning about 'names', about the consequences of definitions or meanings which have been arbitrarily established. We are then confronted with a divorce between philosophy and the world which was alien to the spirit of continental rationalism. Further, we can find in Hobbes a monolithic idea of science, according to which there is a progressive development from first principles in a deductive manner, and which, if consistently maintained, would neglect the important differences between, for example, pure mathematics and empirical science. And at the same time we find a recognition of the relative independence of ethics and politics, on the ground that their principles can be known experimentally without reference to the parts of philosophy which logically precede.

If, therefore, these diverse ideas and lines of thought are present together in Hobbes's mind, it is not surprising that different historians have interpreted him in different ways according to the varying degrees of emphasis which they have placed on this or that aspect of his philosophy. As regards the view that he was a 'sceptical nominalist', his nominalism, as we have seen, is clearly stated, and the charge of 'scepticism' is not without support in his writings. But I do not think that anyone who reads his philosophical writings as a whole would naturally form the impression that 'sceptic' is the most appropriate label to give to Hobbes. It is doubtless arguable that nominalism leads, or should lead, to scepticism. But Hobbes happily combined his nominalism with points of view that are scarcely compatible with it. A great deal of the confusion arose, no doubt, from the failure to distinguish adequately between philosophy, mathematics and empirical science. But we can hardly blame Hobbes for this. In the seventeenth century, philosophy and science were not clearly distinguished, and it is no matter for surprise that Hobbes failed to distinguish them adequately. But, of course, by confining philosophy to the study of bodies he made it even more difficult for him to do so than it would have been in any case.

6. Philosophy, as we have seen, is concerned with the discovery of causes. What does Hobbes understand by 'cause'? 'A cause is the sum or aggregate of all such accidents, both in the agents and the patient, as concur to the producing of the effect propounded; all which existing together, it cannot be understood but that the effect existeth with them; or that it can possibly exist if any one of them be absent.'[67] But to understand this definition we must first understand what Hobbes means by 'accident'. He defines the latter as 'the manner of our conception of body'.[68] And this is, he asserts, the same as saying that 'an accident is that faculty of any body by which it works in us a conception of itself'.[69] If, therefore, we choose to call accidents 'phenomena' or 'appearances', we can say that for Hobbes the cause of any given effect is the sum of phenomena, both in the agent and in the patient, which concur in the following way in producing the effect. If the whole set of phenomena is present, we cannot conceive the absence of the effect. And if any one of

the set of phenomena is absent, we cannot conceive the production of the effect. The cause of any thing is thus the sum of all the conditions required for the existence of that thing; the conditions required, that is to say, both in the agent and in the patient. If body A generates motion in body B, A is the agent and B is the patient. Thus if fire warms my hand, fire is the agent and the hand is the patient. The accident generated in the patient is the effect of the action of the fire. And the cause (that is, entire cause) of this effect is to vary the definition slightly, 'the aggregate of all the accidents both of the agents, how many soever they be, and of the patient, put together; which when they are all supposed to be present, it cannot be understood but that the effect is produced at the same instant: and if any one of them be wanting, it cannot be understood but that the effect is not produced'.[70]

Within the 'entire cause', as defined above, Hobbes distinguishes between 'efficient cause' and 'material cause'. The former is the aggregate of accidents in the agent or agents which are required for the production of an effect which is actually produced, while the latter is the aggregate of requisite accidents in the patient. Both together make up the entire cause. We can, indeed, talk about the power of the agent and the power of the patient, or, rather, about the active power of the agent and the passive power of the patient. But these are objectively the same as the efficient cause and the material cause respectively, though different terms are used because we can consider the same things from different points of view. The aggregate of accidents in the agent, when considered in relation to an effect already produced, is called the efficient cause, and when considered in relation to future time, to the effect to be produced later, it is called the active power of the agent. Similarly, the aggregate of actions in the patient is called the material cause when it is considered in relation to the past, to the effect already produced, and the passive power of the patient when it is considered in relation to the future. As for the so-called 'formal' and 'final' causes, these are both reducible to efficient causes. 'For when it is said that the essence of a thing is the cause thereof, *as to be rational is the cause of man*, it is not intelligible; for it is all one, as if it were said, *to be a man is the cause of man*; which is not well said. And yet the knowledge of the *essence* of anything is the cause of the knowledge of the thing itself; for, if I first know that a thing is *rational*, I know from thence that the same is *man;* but this is no other than an efficient cause. A *final cause* has no place but in such things as have sense and will; and this also I shall prove hereafter to be an efficient cause.'[71] For Hobbes final causality is simply the way in which efficient causes operate in man, with deliberation.

In the foregoing account of Hobbes's analysis of causality we can note how he uses Scholastic terms, interpreting them or assigning them meanings in accordance with his own philosophy. To all intents and purposes we are left with efficient causality alone. Now, if the entire efficient cause is present, the effect is produced. Indeed, this statement is necessarily true, once given Hobbes's definition of a cause. For if the effect were not produced, the cause would not be an entire cause. Furthermore, 'in whatsoever instant the cause is entire, in the same instant the effect is produced. For if it be not produced, something is still wanting, which is requisite for the production of it; and therefore the cause was not entire, as was supposed.'[72]

From these considerations Hobbes draws an important conclusion. We have seen that when the cause is present, the effect always and instantaneously follows. Therefore it cannot but be produced, once given the cause. Therefore the effect follows necessarily from the cause. Hence the cause is a necessary cause. The conclusion is, then, that 'all the effects that have been, or shall be produced, have their necessity in things antecedent'.[73] This at once rules out all freedom in man, at least if freedom is taken to imply absence of necessity. If, indeed, to call an agent free is simply to say that he is not hindered in his activity, this way of speaking has a meaning; but if anyone means by the epithet something more than 'free from being hindered by opposition, I should not say he were in error, but that his words were without meaning, that is to say, absurd'.[74] Once given the cause, the effect necessarily follows. If the effect does not follow, the cause (that is, the entire cause) was not present. And that is all there is to it.

Philosophy, therefore, is concerned with necessary causality; for there can be no other. And causal activity consists in the production of motion by an agent in a patient, both agent and patient being bodies. Creation out of nothing, immaterial causal activity, free causes; such ideas have no place in philosophy. We are concerned simply with the action of bodies in motion on contiguous bodies in motion, with the laws of dynamics operating necessarily and mechanically. And this applies to human activity as much as to the activity of unconscious bodies. True, the deliberate activity of rational beings differs from the activity of inanimate bodies; and in this sense the laws operate in different ways. But for Hobbes mechanistic determinism has the last word, in the human as in the non-human sphere. In this respect it can be said that his philosophy is an attempt to see how far the Galilean dynamics can be pushed as an explanatory principle.

7. The fact that Hobbes believed that every effect has a necessary antecedent cause does not mean that he believed that we can determine with certainty what is the cause of a given event. As we have already seen, the philosopher argues from effects to possible causes and from causes to possible effects. And all our knowledge of the 'consequences' of facts is hypothetical or conditional. That this must be so is, indeed, indicated by the use of the word 'accident' in the definition of a cause. For accident is itself defined as 'the manner of our conception of body'. Thus accidents, the aggregate of which form the entire cause, are defined as having a relation to the mind, to our way of looking at things. We cannot attain absolute certainty that causal relations are in fact what we think them to be.

A similar tendency towards subjectivism (I should not care to put it more strongly) can be seen in Hobbes's definitions of space and time. For space is defined as 'the phantasm of a thing existing without the mind simply'[75] and time as 'the phantasm of before and after in motion'.[76] Hobbes does not mean, of course, that the thing existing outside the mind is a phantasm or image: he did not doubt the existence of bodies. But we can have a phantasm or image of a thing 'in which we consider no other accident, but only that it appears without us' (that is, the fact of its externality); and space is defined as being this image. The image has, indeed, an objective foundation, and Hobbes has no intention of denying this. But this does not alter the fact that he defines space in terms of a subjective modification. Time too has an objective foundation, namely, the movement of bodies; but it is none the less defined as a phantasm and so is said to be 'not in the things without us, but only in the thoughts of the mind'.[77]

Given these definitions of space and time, Hobbes naturally answers the question whether space and time are infinite or finite by remarking that the reply depends simply on our imagination; that is, on whether we imagine space and time as terminated or not. We can imagine time as having a beginning and an end, or we can imagine it without any assigned limits, that is, as extending indefinitely. (Similarly, when we say that number is infinite, we mean only that no number is expressed, or that number is an indefinite name.) As for the infinite divisibility of space and time, this is to be taken in the sense that 'whatsoever is divided, is divided into such parts as may again be divided' or as 'the least divisible thing is not to be given, or, as geometricians have it, no quantity is so small, but a less may be taken'.[78]

8. The objective foundation of space is, as we have seen, existent body, which can be considered in abstraction from all accidents. It is called 'body' because of its extension, and 'existing' because it does not depend on our thought. 'Because it depends not upon our thoughts, we say (it) is *a thing subsisting* of itself; as also *existing*, because without us.'[79] It is also called the 'subject', 'because it is so placed in and *subjected* to imaginary space, that it may be understood by reason, as well as perceived by sense. The definition, therefore, of *body* may be this, *a body is that, which having no dependence upon our thought, is coincident or coextended with some part of space.*'[80] Objectivity or independence of human thinking thus enters into the definition of body. But at the same time the latter is defined in relation to our thought, as not dependent upon it and as knowable because subjected to imaginary space. If one takes this idea by itself, it has a remarkably Kantian flavour.

A body possesses accidents. The definition of an accident as 'the manner of our conception of body' has already been given. But some further explanation may be appropriate here. If we ask 'what is hard?', we are asking for the definition of a concrete name. 'The answer will be, hard is that, whereof no part gives place, but when the whole gives place.'[81] But if we ask 'what is hardness?', we are asking a question about an abstract name, namely, why a thing appears hard. And therefore 'a cause must be shown why a part does not give place, except the whole give place'.[82] And to ask this is to ask what it is in a body which gives rise in us to a certain conception of body. According to Hobbes, as has been mentioned before, to say that an accident is the manner in which we conceive a body is the same as to say that an accident is the faculty in a body of producing in us a certain conception of itself. The force of this assertion comes out most clearly in Hobbes's theory of secondary qualities.

A distinction must be made between accidents which are common to all bodies and which cannot perish unless the body also perishes and accidents which are not common to all bodies and which can perish and be succeeded by others without the body itself perishing. Extension and figure are accidents of the first kind, 'for no body can be conceived to be without extension or without figure'.[83] Figure varies, of course; but there is not, and cannot be, any body without figure. But an accident such as hardness can be succeeded by softness without the body itself perishing. Hardness, therefore, is an accident of the second type.

Extension and figure are the only accidents of the first type. Magnitude is not another accident: it is the same as extension. It is also called by some 'real space'. It is not, as is imaginary space, 'an accident of the mind': it is an accident of body. We can say, therefore, if we like, that there is real space. But this real space is the same as magnitude, which is itself the same as extension. Is magnitude also the same as place? Hobbes answers that it is not. Place is 'a phantasm of any body of such and such quantity and figure' and is 'nothing out of the mind'.[84] It is 'feigned extension', whereas magnitude is 'true extension',[85] which causes the phantasm that is place.

Accidents of the second type, however, do not exist in bodies in the form in which they are present to consciousness. Colour and sound, for example, as also odour and savour, are 'phantasms'; they belong to the sphere of appearance. 'The phantasm, which is made by hearing, is sound; by smell, odour; by taste, savour. . . .'[86] 'For light and colour, and heat and sound, and other qualities which are commonly called sensible, are not objects, but phantasms in the sentients.'[87] 'As for the objects of hearing, smell, taste and touch, they are not sound, odour, savour, hardness, etc., but the bodies themselves from which sound, odour, savour, hardness, etc., proceed.'[88] Bodies in motion generate motion in the organs of sense, and thence arise the phantasms which we call colour, sound, savour, odour, hardness and softness, light and so on. A contiguous and moving body effects the outermost part of the organ of sense, and pressure or motion is transmitted to the innermost part of the organ. At the same time, by reason of the natural internal motion of the organ, a reaction against this pressure takes place, an 'endeavour outwards' stimulated by the 'endeavour inwards'. And the phantasm or 'idea' arises from the final reaction to the 'endeavour inwards'. We can thus define 'sense' as 'a phantasm, made by the reaction and endeavour outwards in the organ of sense, caused by an endeavour inwards from the object, remaining for some time more or less'.[89] Colour, for instance, is our way of perceiving an external body, or, objectively, it is that in a body which causes our 'conception' of the latter. And this 'faculty' in the body is not itself colour. In the case of extension, on the contrary, it is extension itself which causes our conception of it.

The world of colour, sound, odour, savour, tactile qualities and light is thus the world of appearance. And philosophy is to a great extent the endeavour to discover the causes of these appearances, that is, the causes of our 'phantasms'. Behind appearances there are, for Hobbes, at least as far as philosophy is concerned, only extended bodies and motion.

9. Motion means for Hobbes local motion. 'Motion is a continual relinquishing of one place and acquiring of another.'[90] And a thing is said to be at rest when for any time it is in one place. It follows, therefore, from these definitions that anything which is in motion has been moved. For if it has not been moved, it is in the same place in which it formerly was. And thus it follows from the definition of rest that it is at rest. Similarly, that which is moved will yet be moved. For that which is in motion is continually changing place. Lastly, whatever is moved is not in one place during any time, however brief. If it were, it would, by definition, be at rest.

Any thing which is at rest will always be at rest, unless some other body 'by endeavouring to get into its place by motion suffers it no longer to remain at rest'.[91] Similarly, if any thing is in motion, it will be always in motion, unless some other body causes it to be at rest. For if there were no other body, 'there will be no reason why it should rest now rather than at another time'.[92] Again, the cause of motion can only be a contiguous and already moving body.

If motion is reduced to local motion, change is also reducible to local motion. 'Mutation can be nothing else but motion of the parts of that body which is changed.'[93] We do not say that any thing is changed unless it appears to our senses otherwise than it did before. But these appearances are effects produced in us by motion.

10. In animals there are two kinds of motion which are peculiar to them. The first is vital motion. This is 'the motion of the blood, perpetually circulating (as hath been shown from many infallible signs and marks by Doctor Harvey, the first observer of it) in the veins and arteries'.[94] Elsewhere Hobbes describes it as 'the course of the blood, the pulse, the breathing, the concoction, nutrition, excretion, etc., to which motions there needs no help of imagination'.[95] In other words, vital motions are those vital processes in the animal organism which take place without any deliberation or conscious effort, such as circulation of the blood, digestion and respiration.

The second kind of motion which is peculiar to animals is 'animal motion, otherwise called voluntary motion'.[96] As examples Hobbes gives, going, speaking, moving the limbs, when such actions are 'first fancied in our minds'.[97] The first internal beginning of all voluntary motions is imagination, while the 'small beginnings of motion within the body of man, before they appear in walking, speaking, striking, and other visible actions are commonly called endeavour'.[98] Here we have the notion of *conatus*, which plays a prominent part in the philosophy of Spinoza.

This endeavour, directed towards something which causes it, is called *appetite* or *desire*. When it is directed away from something ('fromward something', as Hobbes puts it) it is called *aversion*. The fundamental forms of endeavour are thus appetite or desire and aversion, both being motions. They are objectively the same as love and hate respectively; but when we talk of desire and aversion, we think of the objects as absent, whereas in talking of love and hate we think of the objects as present.

11. Some appetites are innate or born with men, such as the appetite for food. Others proceed from experience. But in any case 'whatsoever is the object of any man's appetite or desire, that is it which he for his part calleth *good*: and the object of his hate and aversion, *evil*; and of his contempt, *vile* and *inconsiderable*'.[99]

Good and evil are, therefore, relative notions. There is no absolute good and no absolute evil; and there is no common objective norm, taken from the objects themselves, to distinguish between good and evil. The words 'are ever used with relation to the person that useth them'.[100] The rule for distinguishing good and evil depends on the individual; that is, on his 'voluntary motions', if we consider man as he is apart from the commonwealth or State. In the commonwealth, however, it is the person who represents it; that is, the sovereign, who determines what is good and what is evil.

12. The different passions are different forms of appetite and aversion, with the exception of pure pleasure and pain, which are 'a certain fruition of good or evil'.[101] Consequently, as appetite and aversion are motions, so are the different passions. External objects affect the organs of sense and there arises 'that motion and agitation of the brain which we call conception'.[102] This motion of the brain is continued to the heart, 'there to be called passion'.[103]

Hobbes finds a number of simple passions, namely, appetite, desire, love, aversion, hate, joy and grief.[104] These take different forms; or at least they are given different names according to different considerations. Thus if we consider the opinion which men have of attaining what they desire, we can distinguish hope and despair. The former is appetite with an opinion of attaining the desired object, while the latter is appetite without this opinion. Secondly, we can consider the object loved or hated. And then we can distinguish, for example, between covetousness, which is the desire of riches, and ambition, which is the desire of office or precedence. Thirdly, the consideration of a number of passions together may lead us to use a special name. Thus 'love of one singularly, with desire to be singularly beloved, is called *the passion of love*', whereas 'the same, with fear that the love is not mutual, (is called) *jealousy*'.[105] Finally, we can name a passion from the motion itself. We can speak, for instance, of 'sudden dejection', 'the passion that causeth weeping', and which is caused by events which suddenly take away some vehement hope or some 'prop of power'.[106]

But however many the passions of man may be, they are all motions. And Hobbes speaks in an oft-quoted sentence of delight or pleasure as being 'nothing really but motion about the heart, as conception is nothing but motion in the head'.[107]

13. Hobbes does not overlook the fact that human beings perform some actions with deliberation. But he defines deliberation in terms of the passions. Let us suppose that in a

man's mind desire to acquire some object alternates with
aversion and that thoughts of the good consequences of acquiring it alternate with thoughts of the evil consequences
(that is, undesirable consequences). 'The whole sum of
desires, aversions, hopes and fears continued till the thing be
either done, or thought impossible, is that we call deliberation.'[108] And Hobbes draws the conclusion that beasts also
must be said to deliberate, inasmuch as this alternate succession of appetites, aversions, hopes and fears is found in
them as well as in man.

Now, in deliberation the last appetite or aversion is called
will; that is, the act of willing. 'Will therefore is the last
appetite in deliberating';[109] and the action depends on this
final inclination or appetite. From this Hobbes again concludes that since the beasts have deliberation they must
necessarily also have will.

It follows that the freedom of willing or not willing is no
greater in man than in the beasts. 'And therefore such a
liberty as is free from necessity is not to be found in the
will either of men or beasts. But if by liberty we understand
the faculty or power, not of willing, but of doing what they
will, then certainly that liberty is to be allowed to both and
both may equally have it, whensoever it is to be had.'[110]

14. When treating of the 'intellectual virtues' Hobbes distinguishes between natural and acquired mental capacity or
'wit'. Some men are naturally quick, others slow. And the
principal cause of these differences is 'the difference of men's
passions'.[111] Those, for example, whose end is sensual pleasure, are necessarily less delighted with the 'imaginations'
which do not conduce to this end, and they pay less attention
than others to the means of acquiring knowledge. They suffer
from dullness of mind, which 'proceedeth from the appetite
of sensual or bodily delight. And it may well be conjectured,
that such passion hath its beginning from a *grossness* and
difficulty of the *motion* of the *spirit* about the heart.'[112]
Differences in natural mental capacity are therefore ultimately
caused by differences in motion. As for differences in acquired
'wit', which is reason, there are other causal factors, such as
education, which have to be taken into consideration.

'The passions that most of all cause the difference of wit
are principally the more or less desire of power, of riches, of
knowledge, and of honour. All which may be reduced to
the first, that is, desire of power. For riches, knowledge and

honour are but several sorts of power.'[113] The desire for power is thus the fundamental factor in causing a man to develop his mental capacities.

15. We are presented, therefore, with a multiplicity of individual human beings, each of whom is driven by his passions, which themselves are forms of motion. And it is the appetites and aversions of the individual which determine for him what is good and what is evil. In the next chapter we shall consider the consequences of this state of affairs and the transition from this atomic individualism to the construction of that artificial body, the commonwealth or State.

Chapter Two

HOBBES (2)

The natural state of war — The laws of nature — The generation of a commonwealth and the theory of the covenant — The rights of the sovereign — The liberty of subjects — Reflections on Hobbes's political theory.

1. Men are by nature equal in bodily and mental capacities; not, indeed, in the sense that all possess the same degree of physical strength and of quickness of mind, but in the sense that, by and large, an individual's deficiencies in one respect can be compensated by other qualities. The physically weak can master the physically strong by craft or by conspiracy; and experience enables all men to acquire prudence in the things to which they apply themselves. And this natural equality produces in men an equal hope of attaining their ends. Every individual seeks and pursues his own conservation, and some set their hearts on delectation or pleasure. Nobody resigns himself to making no effort to attain the end to which he is naturally impelled, on the ground that he is not equal to others.

Now, this fact that every individual seeks his own conservation and his own delectation leads to competition and mistrust of others. Further, every man desires that others should value him as he values himself; and he is quick to resent every slight and all signs of contempt. 'So that in the nature of man we find three principal causes of quarrel. First, competition; secondly, diffidence (that is, mistrust); thirdly, glory.'[1]

From this Hobbes draws the conclusion that until such time as men live under a common power, they are in a state of war with one another. 'For *war* consisteth not in battle only, or the act of fighting; but in a tract of time, wherein the will to contend by battle is sufficiently known: and therefore the notion of *time* is to be considered in the nature of war; as it is in the nature of weather. For as the nature of foul weather lieth not in a shower or two of rain; but in an inclination thereto of many days together: so the nature of war consisteth not in actual fighting; but in the known disposition thereto, during all the time there is no assurance to the contrary. All other time is peace.'[2]

The natural state of war, therefore, is the state of affairs in which the individual is dependent for his security on his own strength and his own wits. 'In such condition there is no place for industry; because the fruit thereof is uncertain: and consequently no culture of the earth; no navigation, nor use of the commodities that may be imported by sea; no commodious building; no instruments of moving and removing such things as require much force; no knowledge of the face of the earth; no account of time; no arts; no letters; no society; and, which is worst of all, continual fear and danger of violent death; and the life of man, solitary, poor, nasty, brutish, and short.'[3] In this frequently quoted passage Hobbes depicts the natural state of war as a condition in which civilization and its benefits are absent. The conclusion is obvious, namely, that it is only through the organization of society and the establishment of the commonwealth that peace and civilization can be attained.

The natural state of war is a deduction from consideration of the nature of man and his passions. But if anyone doubts the objective validity of the conclusion, he has only to observe what happens even in a state of organized society. Everyone carries arms when he takes a journey; bars his door at night; he locks up his valuables. And this shows clearly enough what he thinks of his fellow men. 'Does he not there as much accuse mankind by his actions, as I do by my words? But neither of us accuse man's nature in it. The desires and other passions of man are themselves no sin. No more are the actions that proceed from those passions, till they know a law that forbids them; which till laws be made they cannot know: nor can any law be made, till they have agreed upon the person that shall make it.'[4]

This quotation suggests that in the natural state of war there are no objective moral distinctions. And this is precisely Hobbes's view. In this state 'the notions of right and wrong, justice and injustice, have no place. Where there is no common power, there is no law, where no law, no injustice. Force and fraud are in war the two cardinal virtues.'[5] Further, there is 'no dominion, no *mine* and *thine* distinct; but only that to be every man's, that he can get: and for so long as he can keep it'.[6]

Does Hobbes mean that this state of war was an historical fact, in the sense that it universally preceded the organization of society? Or does he mean that it precedes the organization of society only logically, in the sense that if we prescind from what man owes to the commonwealth or State, we arrive by abstraction at this layer, as it were, of atomic individualism, which is rooted in the human passions and which would obtain, were it not for other factors which naturally impel men from the beginning to organize societies and subject themselves to a common power? He means, of course, at least the latter. The state of war was never, in his opinion, universal 'over all the world'; but the idea of this condition of affairs represents the condition which would obtain, were it not for the foundation of commonwealths. There is plenty of empirical evidence for this, apart from *a priori* deduction from the analysis of the passions. We have only to look at the behaviour of kings and sovereigns. They fortify their territories against possible invaders, and even in peace-time they send spies into their neighbours' realms. They are, in fine, in a constant 'posture of war'. Again, we have only to look at what happens when peaceful government breaks down and civil war occurs. This shows clearly 'what manner of life there would be, where there were no common power to fear'.[7] At the same time, the natural state of war is, according to Hobbes, an historical fact in many places, as can be seen in America, where the savages 'live at this day in that brutish manner', if we except the internal government of small families, the harmony of which depends on 'natural lust'.

2. It is obviously in man's interest to emerge from this natural state of war; and the possibility of doing so is provided by nature itself. For by nature men have their passions and their reason. It is, indeed, their passions which bring about the state of war. But at the same time fear of death, desire of such things as are necessary to 'commodious' living, and hope of obtaining these things by industry are passions which incline men to seek for peace. It is not that the passions

simply lead to war, whereas reason counsels peace. Some
passions incline men to peace; and what reason does is to show
how the fundamental desire of self-conservation can be made
effective. It suggests first of all 'convenient articles of peace,
upon which men may be drawn to agreement. These
articles are they, which otherwise are called the Laws of
Nature.'[8]

Hobbes defines a law of nature as 'the dictate of right
reason,[9] conversant about those things which are either to
be done or omitted for the constant preservation of life and
member, as much as in us lies'.[10] Again, 'a law of nature,
lex naturalis, is a precept, or general rule, found out by
reason, by which a man is forbidden to do that which is
destructive of his life or taketh away the means of preserving
the same; and to omit that, by which he thinketh it may
be best preserved'.[11] In interpreting these definitions we
have, of course, to avoid attaching to the word 'law' any
theological or metaphysical significance or reference. A law
of nature in this context is for Hobbes a dictate of egoistic
prudence. Every man instinctively pursues self-preservation
and security. But man is not merely a creature of instinct
and blind impulse; and there is such a thing as rational self-
preservation. The so-called laws of nature state the conditions
of this rational self-preservation. And as Hobbes goes on to
argue that the rational pursuit of self-preservation is what
leads men to form commonwealths or states, the laws of
nature give the conditions for the establishment of society
and stable government. They are the rules a reasonable being
would observe in pursuing his own advantage, if he were
conscious of man's predicament in a condition in which
impulse and passion alone ruled and if he himself were not
governed simply by momentary impulse and by prejudices
arising from passion. Furthermore, Hobbes believed that by
and large man, who is essentially egoistic and self-regarding,
does in fact act according to these rules. For in point of fact
men do form organized societies and subject themselves to
governments. Hence they do in fact observe the dictates of
enlightened egoism. It follows that these laws are analogous
to the physical laws of nature and state the way in which enlightened egoists do in fact behave, the way in which their
psychological make-up determines them to behave. Certainly,
Hobbes frequently speaks as though these rules were teleological principles, and as though they were what Kant would

call hypothetical imperatives; that is, assertoric hypothetical imperatives, since every individual necessarily seeks his own preservation and security. Indeed, Hobbes could hardly avoid speaking in this way. But he is dealing with the interplay of motions and forces which lead to the creation of that artificial body, the commonwealth; and the tendency of his thought is to assimilate the operation of the 'laws of nature' to the operation of efficient causality. The State itself is the resultant of the interplay of forces; and human reason, displayed in the conduct expressed by these rules, is one of these determining forces. Or, if we wish to look at the matter from the point of view of the philosophical deduction of society and government, the laws of nature can be said to represent axioms or postulates which render this deduction possible. They answer the question, what are the conditions under which the transition from the natural state of war to the state of men living in organized societies becomes intelligible. And these conditions are rooted in the dynamics of human nature itself. They are not a system of God-given laws (except, indeed, in the sense that God created man and all that is in him). Nor do they state absolute values; for, according to Hobbes, there are no absolute values.

The list of the laws of nature is given differently by Hobbes in different places. Here I confine myself to the *Leviathan*, where we are told that the fundamental law of nature is the general rule of reason that 'every man ought to endeavour peace, as far as he has hope of obtaining it; and when he cannot obtain it, that he may seek, and use, all helps and advantages of war'.[12] The first part, he asserts, contains the fundamental law of nature, namely, to seek peace and follow it, while the second part contains the sum of natural right, namely, to defend ourselves by all means that we can.

The second law of nature is 'that a man be willing, when others are so too, as far-forth, as for peace and defence of himself he shall think it necessary, to lay down this right to all things; and be contented with so much liberty against other men, as he would allow other men against himself'.[13] To lay down one's right to anything is to divest oneself of the liberty of hindering another from enjoying his own right to the same thing. But if a man lays down his right in this sense, he does so with a view to his own advantage. And it follows from this that there are 'some rights which no man can be understood by any words, or other signs, to have abandoned or transferred'.[14] For example, a man cannot lay down the right to defend his own life, 'because he cannot be understood to aim thereby at any good to himself'.[15]

Hobbes proceeds, in accordance with his declared method, to lay down some definitions. First a contract is defined as 'the mutual transferring of right'.[16] But 'one of the contractors may deliver the thing contracted for on his part, and leave the other to perform his part at some determinate time after, and in the meantime be trusted; and then the contract on his part is called *pact* or *covenant*'.[17] This definition is of importance because, as will be seen presently, Hobbes founds the commonwealth on a social covenant.

The third law of nature is 'that men perform their covenant made'.[18] Without this law of nature 'covenants are in vain, and but empty words; and the right of all men to all things remaining, we are still in the condition of war'.[19] Further, this law is the fountain of justice. When there has been no covenant, no action can be unjust. But when a covenant has been made, to break it is unjust. Indeed, injustice can be defined as 'the not performance of covenant. And whatsoever is not unjust, is *just*.'[20]

It may appear to be an instance of gross inconsistency on Hobbes's part if he now talks about justice and injustice when earlier he has asserted that such distinctions do not obtain in the state of war. But if we read carefully what he says, we shall see that on this point at least he is not guilty of contradicting himself. For he adds that covenants of mutual trust are invalid when there is fear of non-performance on either part, and that in the natural condition of war this fear is always present. It follows, therefore, that there are no valid covenants, and hence no justice and injustice, until the commonwealth is established; that is, until a coercive power has been established which will compel men to perform their covenants.

In the *Leviathan* Hobbes states nineteen laws of nature in all; and I omit the rest of them. But it is worth noting that after completing his list he asserts that these laws, and any others which there may be, bind in conscience. And if we take this statement in a moral sense, we can only conclude that Hobbes has suddenly adopted a point of view very different from the one which he has hitherto expressed. In point of fact, however, he appears to mean simply that reason, considering man's desire for security, dictates that he should (that is, if he is to act rationally) desire that the laws should be observed. The laws are only improperly called 'laws', Hobbes tells us; 'for they are but conclusions or theorems concerning what conduceth to the conservation and defence of themselves (men); whereas law, properly, is the word of him, that by right hath command over them'.[21] Reason sees that the observance of these 'theorems' conduces to man's self-preservation and defence; and it is therefore rational for man to desire their observance. In this sense, and in this sense alone, they have an 'obligatory' character. 'The laws of nature oblige *in foro interno*; that is to say, they bind to a desire they should take place: but *in foro externo*; that is, to the putting them in act, not always. For he that should be modest, and tractable, and perform all he promises, in such time and place where no man else should do so, should but make himself a prey to others, and procure his own certain ruin, contrary to the ground of all laws of nature, which tend to nature's preservation.'[22] It is clear that there is no question of a categorical imperative in the Kantian sense. Study of the laws of nature is, indeed, declared by Hobbes to be 'the true moral philosophy',[23] which is the science of good and evil. But, as we have already seen, 'private appetite is the measure of good and evil';[24] and the only reason why the laws of nature are to be called good or, as Hobbes puts it, 'moral virtues', is that men's private appetites happen to agree in desiring security. 'All men agree on this, that peace is good; and therefore also the way or means of peace.'[25]

3. Philosophy deals with generative causes. Hence it includes a study of the causes which generate the artificial body which is known as the 'commonwealth'. We have already considered the remote generative causes. Man seeks self-preservation and security, but he is unable to attain this end in the natural condition of war. The laws of nature are unable to achieve the desired end by themselves alone, that is, unless there is coercive power able to enforce their observance by sanctions. For these laws, though dictates of reason, are contrary to man's natural passions. 'And covenants, without the sword, are but words, and of no strength to secure a man at all.'[26] It is necessary, therefore, that there should be a common power or government backed by force and able to punish.

This means that a plurality of individuals 'should confer

all their power and strength upon one man, or upon one assembly of men, that may reduce all their wills, by plurality of voices, unto one will'.[27] That is to say, they must appoint one man, or assembly of men, to bear their person. This done, they will form a real unity in one person, a person being defined as 'he whose words or actions are considered, either as his own, or as representing the words or actions of another man, or of any other thing, to whom they are attributed, whether truly or by fiction'.[28] If the words and actions are considered as the person's own words and actions, we have a 'natural person'. If, however, they are considered as representing the words or actions of another man or of other men, we have a 'feigned or artificial person'. In the present context we are concerned, of course, with an artificial person, with a representer. And it is 'the unity of the representer, not the unity of the represented, that maketh the person one'.[29]

How does this transfer of rights take place? It takes place 'by covenant of every man with every man, in such manner, as if every man should say to every man, I *authorize and give up my right of governing myself, to this man, or to this assembly of men, on this condition that thou give up thy right to him, and authorize all his actions in like manner.* This done, the multitude so united in one person, is called a Commonwealth, in Latin *Civitas*. This is the generation of that great Leviathan, or rather, to speak more reverently, of that *mortal god*, to which we owe under the *immortal God*, our peace and defence.'[30]

It is to be noted that when Hobbes speaks of the multitude being united in one person he does not mean that the multitude constitute this person. He means that the multitude are united in the person, whether individual or assembly, to whom they transfer their rights. He therefore defines the essence of the commonwealth as 'one person, of whose acts a great multitude, by mutual covenants one with another, have made themselves every one the author, to the end he may use the strength and means of them all, as he should think expedient, for their peace and common defence'.[31] This person is called the *sovereign*. Everyone else is his subject.

The proximate cause, therefore, of the generation of the commonwealth is the covenants made with one another by the individuals who on the establishment of the commonwealth become the subjects of the sovereign. This is an important point. For it follows that the sovereign is not himself a party to the covenant. And Hobbes says as much in explicit terms. 'Because the right of bearing the person of them all is given to him they make sovereign, by covenant only of one to another, and not of him to any of them; there can happen no breach of covenant on the part of the sovereign.'[32] The commonwealth is certainly instituted for a specific purpose, namely, for the peaceful security of those who are party to the social covenant. And this point, too, has its importance, as will be seen later. But Hobbes's insistence that the covenants are made between the subjects, or more accurately future subjects, and not between the subjects and the sovereign, enables him to emphasize more easily the undivided nature of sovereign power. In his opinion it is by the centralization of authority in the person of the sovereign that the evil which he particularly dreaded, namely, civil war, can be avoided.

Further, this view of the matter enables Hobbes to avoid, at least in part, a difficulty which would inevitably arise if he made the sovereign a party to the covenant. For he has already said that covenants without the sword are but words. And if the sovereign were himself a party to the covenant and at the same time possessed all the authority and power which Hobbes proceeds to attribute to him, it would be difficult to see how the covenant could be valid and effective on his part. As it is, however, the parties to the covenant are simply the individuals who, on making the covenant, immediately become subjects. It is not that they first make a covenant setting up a society and then afterwards choose a sovereign. For in this case a similar difficulty would arise. The covenant would be but words: it would be a covenant within the natural condition of war. It is rather that on the covenant being made sovereign and society come into existence together. From the abstract and theoretical point of view, therefore, we can say that no period of time elapses between the making of the covenant and the setting up of sovereign authority. The covenant, therefore, cannot be made without there immediately coming into existence a power capable of enforcing the covenant.

Although, however, the sovereign is not himself a party to the covenant, his sovereignty derives from the covenant. Hobbes's doctrine lends no support to the theory of the divine right of kings; and he was in fact attacked by those who favoured this theory. In the statement of the covenant he mentions indifferently 'this man' and 'this assembly of men'. He was, as we have seen, a royalist; and he favoured monarchy as conducing to greater unity, and for certain other reasons. But as far as the origin of sovereignty is concerned, the covenant may establish monarchy, democracy or aristocracy. The main point is not what form of constitution is set up, but that wherever sovereignty lies, it must be entire and indivisible. 'The difference between these three kinds of commonwealth consisteth not in the difference of power; but in the difference of convenience or aptitude to produce the peace and security of the people; for which end they were instituted.'[33] But the sovereign's power is absolute, whether the sovereign be an individual or an assembly.

One obvious objection to the covenant theory of the generation of the State is that it bears little relation to historical fact. But, of course, it is not at all necessary to suppose that Hobbes thought that, as a matter of historical facts, States originated through an explicit covenant. He is concerned with a logical or philosophical deduction of the State, not with tracing the historical developments of States. And the theory of the covenant enables him to make the transition from the condition of atomic individualism to organized society. I do not mean to imply that for Hobbes men are less individualistic after the covenant, if one may so speak, than before. Self-interest, according to him, lies at the basis of organized society; and self-interest, in an egoistic sense, rules in organized society just as much as it did in the hypothetical state of war. But in organized society the centrifugal tendencies of individuals and their proneness to self-destructive mutual enmity and war are checked by fear of the sovereign's power. The theory of the covenant is, in part at least, a device to exhibit the rational character of subjection to the sovereign and of his exercise of power. Hobbes is a utilitarian in the sense that the basis of the commonwealth is for him utility; and the covenant-theory is an explicit recognition of this utility. The theory is doubtless open to serious objections; but any fundamental criticism of Hobbes must be directed against his account of human nature rather than against the details of the theory of the covenant.

Hobbes makes a distinction between a commonwealth 'by institution' and a commonwealth 'by acquisition'. A commonwealth is said to exist by institution when it has been established in the manner mentioned above, namely, through the covenant of every member of a multitude with every other member. A commonwealth is said to exist by acquisition when the sovereign power has been acquired by force; that is to say, when men 'for fear of death or bonds do authorize all the actions of that man or assembly that hath their lives and liberty in his power'.[34]

In the case of a commonwealth by institution a multitude of men subject themselves to a chosen sovereign from fear of one another. In the case of a commonwealth by acquisition they subject themselves to him of whom they are afraid. Thus 'in both cases they do it for fear'.[35] Hobbes is quite explicit in his statement that sovereign power is based on fear. There is no question of deriving the commonwealth and the legitimacy of sovereign power from either theological or metaphysical principles. Of course, the fear, whether of men for one another or of subjects for their sovereign, is rational, in the sense that it is well-grounded. And the commonwealth by acquisition can be defended for the same utilitarian reasons as the commonwealth by institution. Thus when Hobbes says that all commonwealths are founded on fear, he does not mean to say anything in depreciation of the commonwealth. Given human nature as Hobbes describes it, the commonwealth must in any case be founded on fear. The theory of the covenant glosses over this fact to some extent, and it is perhaps designed to impart some show of legality to an institution which does not rest on legality. In this sense it does not fit in well with the rest of Hobbes's political theory. But at the same time he is quite frank about the part played by fear in politics.

4. This distinction between two kinds of commonwealth does not affect the rights of the sovereign. 'The rights and consequences of sovereignty are the same in both.'[36] Hence in examining these rights we can disregard the distinction.

Sovereignty, Hobbes insists, is not and cannot be conferred conditionally. Hence the subjects of a sovereign cannot either change the form of government or repudiate the authority of the sovereign and return to the condition of a disunited multitude: sovereignty is inalienable. This does not mean, for example, that a monarch cannot legitimately confer executive power or consultative rights on other individuals or on assemblies; but if the sovereign is a monarch, he cannot alienate part of his sovereignty. An assembly, such as a parliament, can have no rights independent of the monarch, if we suppose that the monarch is sovereign. It does not follow, therefore, from Hobbes's position that a monarch cannot make use of a parliament in governing a nation; but it does follow that the parliament does not enjoy part of the sovereignty and that in the exercise of its delegated powers it is necessarily subordinate to the monarch. Similarly, if an assembly which is not coextensive with the people is sovereign, the people do not and cannot enjoy part of the sovereignty. For they must be considered as having conferred unlimited and inalienable sovereignty on that assembly. Hence sovereign power cannot be forfeited. 'There can happen no breach of covenant on the part of the sovereign; and consequently none of his subjects, by any pretence of forfeiture, can be freed from his subjection.'[37]

By the very institution of sovereignty every subject becomes the author of all the sovereign's actions; and 'it follows that whatsoever he (the sovereign) doth, it can be no injury to any of his subjects; nor ought he to be by any of them accused of injustice'.[38] No sovereign can justly be put to death or in any way punished by his subjects. For, inasmuch as every subject is author of all the sovereign's actions, to punish the sovereign would be to punish another for one's own actions.

Among the prerogatives of the sovereign which are enumerated by Hobbes is that of judging what doctrines are fit to be taught. 'It belongeth therefore to him that hath the sovereign power, to be judge or constitute all judges of opinions and doctrines, as a thing necessary to peace; thereby to prevent discord and civil war.'[39] And among the diseases of the commonwealth he lists the doctrines that 'every private man is judge of good and evil actions'[40] and that 'whatsoever a man does against his conscience, is sin'.[41] In the state of nature, it is true, the individual is judge of what is good and what is evil, and he has to follow his own reason or conscience, because he has no other rule to follow. But this is not the case in the commonwealth. For there the civil law is the public conscience, the measure of good and evil.

It is no matter for surprise, therefore, if in the third and fourth parts of the *Leviathan* Hobbes defends a thoroughgoing Erastianism. To be sure, he does not deny Christian revelation or the validity of the idea of a Christian commonwealth, wherein 'there dependeth much upon supernatural revelations of the will of God'.[42] But he completely subordinates Church to State. He makes it abundantly clear that he interprets the struggle between Church and State simply in terms of power. The Church has tried to arrogate to itself an authority which belongs to the civil sovereign; and Hobbes, in a famous passage, likens the Papacy to the ghost of the Roman empire. 'And if a man consider the original of this great ecclesiastical dominion, he will easily perceive that the Papacy is no other than the *ghost* of the deceased *Roman empire*, sitting crowned upon the grave thereof. For so did the Papacy start up on a sudden out of the ruins of that heathen power.'[43] But though Hobbes regards the Catholic Church as providing the chief example in the religious sphere of an attempt to steal from the sovereign his rightful authority, he makes it clear that his primary concern is not with anti-Catholic polemics. He is concerned to reject any claim, whether by pope, bishop, priest or presbyter, to possess spiritual authority and jurisdiction independently of the sovereign. Similarly, he rejects any claim on the part of private individuals to be independent channels of divine revelations or of divinely inspired messages.

A Church is defined as 'a company of men professing Christian religion, united in the person of one sovereign, at whose command they ought to assemble'.[44] There is no such thing as a universal Church; and within the national Church the Christian sovereign is the fount, under God, of all authority and jurisdiction, and he alone is the final judge of the interpretation of the Scriptures. In his answer to Bishop Bramhall, Hobbes asks, 'If it be not from the king's authority that the Scripture is law, what other authority makes it law?'[45] And he remarks that 'there is no doubt but by what authority the Scripture or any other writing is made a law, by the same authority the Scriptures are to be interpreted or else they are made in vain'.[46] Again, when Bramhall remarks that on Hobbes's Erastian principles the authority of all general councils is destroyed, Hobbes admits that this is the case. If Anglican prelates pretend that general councils possess authority independently of the sovereign, they to this extent detract from the latter's inalienable authority and power.

5. The power of the sovereign being thus to all intents and purposes unlimited, the question arises, what freedom, if any, is possessed by the subjects or ought to be possessed by

them. And in discussing this question we have to presuppose
Hobbes's theory of 'natural liberty'. As we have already seen,
natural liberty means for him simply the absence of external
hindrances to motion; and it is perfectly consistent with necessity, that is, with determinism. A man's volitions, desires
and inclinations are necessary in the sense that they are the
results of a chain of determining causes; but when he acts
in accordance with these desires and inclinations, there being
no external impediment to prevent him from so acting, he
is said to act freely. A free man is thus 'he that in those
things which by his strength and wit he is able to do, is not
hindered to do what he has a will to do'.[47] This general
conception of liberty being presupposed, Hobbes inquires
what is the liberty of subjects with regard to the artificial
bonds or chains which men have forged for themselves by
the mutual covenants which they have made with one another in handing over their rights to the sovereign.

It is scarcely necessary to say that Hobbes has no sympathy
with any demand for freedom from law. For law, backed by
sanctions, is the very means which protects a man from the
caprice and violence of other men. And to demand exemp-
tion from law would be a demand for a return to the state
of nature. The liberty which is exalted in the histories and
philosophies of the ancient Greeks and Romans is, he says,
the liberty of the commonwealth, not of particular men. 'The
Athenians and Romans were free; that is, free commonwealths: not that any particular men had the liberty to resist
their own representative; but that their representative had
the liberty to resist or invade other people.'[48] It is true that
many people have found in the writings of the ancients an
excuse for favouring tumults and 'licentious controlling the
actions of their sovereigns . . . with the effusion of so much
blood, as I think I may truly say, there was never any thing
so dearly bought, as these western parts have bought the
learning of the Greek and Latin tongues'.[49] But this comes
from failure to distinguish between the rights of individuals
and the rights of sovereigns.

At the same time it is clear that in no commonwealth are
all actions regulated by law; nor can they be. Hence subjects
enjoy liberty in these matters. 'The liberty of a subject lieth
therefore only in those things which, in regulating their
actions, the sovereign hath praetermitted: such as is the
liberty to buy and sell, and otherwise contract with one an-

other; to choose their own abode, their own diet, their own trade of life, and institute their children as they themselves think fit, and the like.'[50]

So far as Hobbes is not simply making the tautological pronouncement that actions unregulated by law are unregulated by law, he is here drawing attention to the actual state of affairs, namely, that in a very wide field of human activity subjects can, as far as the law is concerned, act according to their will and inclination. And such liberty is found, he tells us, in all forms of commonwealth. The further question arises, however, whether there are any cases in which the subject is entitled to resist the sovereign.

The answer to this question can be obtained by considering the purpose of the social covenant and what rights cannot be transferred by the covenant. The covenant is made with a view to peace and security, the protection of life and limb. It follows, therefore, that a man does not and cannot transfer or lay down his right to save himself from death, wounds and imprisonment. And from this it follows that if the sovereign commands a man kill or maim himself, or to abstain from air or food, or not to resist those who assault him, 'yet hath that man the liberty to disobey'.[51] Nor is a man obliged to confess his own crimes. Nor is a subject obliged to kill any other man at command or to take up arms, unless refusal to obey frustrates the end for which sovereignty was instituted. Hobbes does not mean, of course, that the sovereign may not punish a subject for refusing to obey: he means that subjects, having made mutual covenants with one another, and having thus instituted sovereignty with a view to self-protection, cannot legitimately be considered as having bound themselves by covenant to injure themselves or others simply because the sovereign commands it. 'It is one thing to say, *Kill me, or my fellow, if you please;* another thing to say, *I will kill myself or my fellow.*'[52]

A point of greater importance is that subjects are absolved from their duty of obedience to the sovereign, not only if the latter relinquishes his sovereignty, but also if he has, indeed, the will to retain his power but cannot in fact protect his subjects any longer. 'The obligation of subjects to the sovereign is understood to last as long, and no longer, than the power lasteth, by which he is able to protect them.'[53] According to the intention of those who institute it, sovereignty may be immortal; but in actual fact it has in itself 'many

seeds of a natural mortality'.[54] If the sovereign is conquered
in war and surrenders to the victor, his subjects become subjects of the latter. If the commonwealth is torn asunder by
internal discord and the sovereign no longer possesses effective power, the subjects return to the state of nature, and a
new sovereign can be set up.

6. A good deal has been written about the significance of
Hobbes's political theory and about the comparative importance of the various points which he makes. And different
estimates are possible.

The point which is most likely to strike modern readers
of the *Leviathan* is, very naturally, the power and authority
attributed to the sovereign. This emphasis on the sovereign's
position was, in part, a necessary counterbalance in Hobbes's
political theory to his theory of atomic individualism. If
according to Marxists the State, the capitalist State at least,
is the means of binding together conflicting economic interests and classes, the State for Hobbes is the means of
uniting warring individuals; and the State cannot perform
this function unless the sovereign enjoys complete and unlimited authority. If men are naturally egoistic and always
remain so, the only factor which can hold them together
effectively is centralized power, vested in the sovereign.

This is not to say that Hobbes's insistence on the power
of the sovereign was simply and solely the result of an inference from an aprioristic theory of human nature. He was
also undoubtedly influenced by contemporary events. In the
civil war he saw a revelation of man's character and of the
centrifugal forces operative in human society. And he saw in
strong and centralized power the only remedy for this state
of affairs. 'If there had not first been an opinion received of
the greatest part of England, that these powers (of legislating, administering justice, raising taxes, controlling doctrines
and so on) were divided between the King, and the Lords,
and the House of Commons, the people had never been
divided and fallen into this civil war; first between those
that disagreed in politics; and after between the dissenters
about the liberty of religion. . . .'[55] Hobbes's absolutism
and his Erastianism were greatly strengthened by his reflections on concrete political and religious dissensions.

At this point it may be advisable to remark that it is authoritarianism rather than 'totalitarianism' in a modern sense
which is characteristic of Hobbes's political theory. Of

course, there are certainly obvious elements of what we call totalitarianism in his theory. For example, it is the State, or more precisely the sovereign, that determines good and evil. In this sense the State is the fount of morality. Against this interpretation it has been objected that Hobbes admits 'natural laws' and that he allows also that the sovereign is responsible to God. But even if we are prepared to concede that he accepts the notion of natural law in any sense which is relevant to the matter under discussion, it remains true that for him it is the sovereign who interprets the natural law, just as it is the Christian sovereign who interprets the Scriptures. On the other hand, Hobbes did not envisage the sovereign as controlling all human activities; he thought of him as legislating and controlling with a view to the maintenance of peace and security. He was not concerned with exalting the State as such and in subordinating individuals to the State because it is the State; he was concerned, first and last, with the interests of individuals. And if he advocated centralized power and authority, this was because he saw no other way of promoting and preserving the peace and security of human beings, which constitute the purpose of organized society.

But though authoritarianism is certainly a prominent feature of Hobbes's political philosophy it should be emphasized that this authoritarianism has no essential connection with the theory of the divine right of kings and with the principle of legitimacy. Hobbes certainly speaks as though the sovereign is in some sense the representative of God; but in the first place monarchy is not for him the only proper form of government. For the word 'sovereign' in Hobbes's political writings we are not entitled simply to substitute the word 'monarch'; but the principle on which he insists is that sovereignty is indivisible, not that it should necessarily be vested in one man. And in the second place sovereignty, whether vested in one man or in an assembly of men, is derived from the social covenant, not from appointment by God. Further, this fiction of the social covenant would justify any *de facto* government. It would justify, for example, the Commonwealth no less than the rule of Charles I, as long, that is to say, as the latter possessed the power to rule. It is therefore easy to understand the charge brought against Hobbes that he wrote the *Leviathan* when he had a mind to go home and that he wished to win the favour of Cromwell.

Thus Dr. John Wallis declared that the *Leviathan* 'was written in defence of Oliver's title, or whoever, by whatsoever means, can get to be upmost; placing the whole right of government merely in strength and absolving all his Majesty's subjects from their allegiance, whenever he is not in a present capacity to force obedience'.[56] Hobbes roundly denied that he had published his *Leviathan* 'to flatter Oliver, who was not made Protector till three or four years after, on purpose to make way for his return',[57] adding 'it is true that Mr. Hobbes came home, but it was because he would not trust his safety with the French clergy'.[58] But though Hobbes was justified in saying that he had not written his work to flatter Oliver Cromwell and that he had not intended to defend rebellion against the monarch, it remains true that his political theory is favourable neither to the idea of the divine right of kings nor to the Stuart principle of legitimacy. And commentators are right in drawing attention to the 'revolutionary' character of his theory of sovereignty, an aspect of his thought which is apt to be overlooked precisely because of his authoritarian conception of government and his personal predilection for monarchy.

If one had to find an analogy to Hobbes's theory of the State in mediaeval philosophy, it might perhaps be suggested that it is provided by St. Augustine much more than by St. Thomas Aquinas.[59] For St. Augustine regarded the State, or at least tended to do so, as a consequence of original sin; that is, as a necessary means of restraining man's evil impulses which are a result of original sin. And this view bears at any rate some likeness to Hobbes's conception of the State as the remedy for the evils consequent on man's natural condition, the war of all against all. Aquinas, on the other hand, adhering to the Greek tradition, regarded the State as a natural institution, the primary function of which is to promote the common good and which would be necessary even if man had not sinned and possessed no evil impulses.

This analogy is, of course, only partial, and it should not be pressed. St. Augustine certainly did not believe, for instance, that the sovereign determines moral distinctions. For him there is an objective moral law, with transcendent foundations, which is independent of the State and to which all sovereigns and subjects are morally obliged to conform their conduct. For Hobbes, however, there is no such moral law. It is true that he allowed that the sovereign is responsible to

God and that he did not admit that he had eliminated any idea of objective morality apart from the sovereign's legislation. But at the same time philosophy, according to his own assertion, is not concerned with God, and he explicitly asserted that it is the sovereign who determines what is good and what is evil. In the state of nature good and evil are simply relative to the desires of individuals. On this point Hobbes gets rid of all metaphysical and transcendental theories and ideas.

He acts in a similar way with regard to the State considered as an institution. For Aquinas the State was demanded by the natural law, which was itself a reflection of the eternal law of God. It was therefore divinely willed, irrespective of man's sin and of his evil impulses. But this transcendent foundation of the State disappears in Hobbes's theory. In so far as we can speak of him as deducing the State, he deduces it simply from the passions of man, without reference to metaphysical and transcendental considerations. In this sense his theory is thoroughly naturalistic in character. If Hobbes devotes a considerable part of the *Leviathan* to religious and ecclesiastical questions and problems, he does so in the interests of a defence of Erastianism, not in order to supply a metaphysical theory of the State. A great deal of the importance of Hobbes's theory is due to the fact that he tries to set political philosophy on its own feet, so to speak, connecting it, indeed, with human psychology and, in intention at least, with his general mechanistic philosophy, but cutting it adrift from metaphysics and theology. Whether this was a profitable step is open to dispute; but it was certainly a step of considerable importance.

Hobbes's deduction of the State from a consideration of the passions of man goes a long way towards explaining his authoritarianism and his insistence on the power of the sovereign. But we have seen that his authoritarian ideas were not simply the result of a philosophical deduction; for they were greatly strengthened by his reflections on concrete historical events in his own country and by his fear and hatred of civil war. And, in general, he can be regarded as having discerned the great part played by power in the dynamics of political life and history. In this respect he can be called a 'realist'. And we can link him up with the Renaissance writer, Machiavelli.[60] But whereas the latter had been primarily concerned with political mechanics, with the means of attaining and preserving power, Hobbes provides a general political theory in which the concept of power and its function plays a supremely important part. Much in this theory is dated, historically conditioned, as is indeed inevitable in any political theory which goes beyond principles which can be considered 'eternal', that is, of lasting applicability, precisely because they are too general and abstract to be intrinsically related to a given epoch. But his conception of the role of power in human affairs is of lasting significance. To say this is not to subscribe to his theory of human nature (which, in its nominalistic aspects, connects him with fourteenth-century nominalism) or to pronounce adequate his account of the function of the State and of sovereignty. It is simply to say that Hobbes recognized very clearly factors which have undoubtedly helped to determine the course of human history as we know it up to date. In my opinion, Hobbes's political philosophy is one-sided and inadequate. But precisely because it is one-sided and inadequate it throws into clear relief features of social and political life of which it is important to take account.

Chapter Three

THE CAMBRIDGE PLATONISTS

Introductory remarks — Lord Herbert of Cherbury and his theory of natural religion — The Cambridge Platonists — Richard Cumberland.

1. Francis Bacon[1] had admitted a philosophical or natural theology, which treats of God's existence and of His nature, so far as this is manifested in creatures. Hobbes, however, excluded from philosophy all consideration of God, since he regarded philosophy as concerned with bodies in motion. Indeed, if by the term 'God' we mean an infinite spiritual or immaterial Being, reason can tell us nothing at all about Him; for terms such as 'spiritual' and 'immaterial' are not intelligible, unless they are used to connote invisible body. But this attitude was not common among the seventeenth-century British philosophers. The general tendency was rather to hold that reason can attain to some knowledge of God, and at the same time to maintain that reason is the judge of revelation and of revealed truth. Associated with this outlook we find in a number of writers the tendency to play down dogmatic differences and to belittle their importance in comparison with the general truths which are attainable by reason alone. And those who thought in this way were obviously more inclined towards a certain broadness of outlook and towards the promotion of toleration in the field of dogmatic religion than were the theologians of the diverse schools and traditions.

This general point of view may be said to have been characteristic of John Locke and his associates. But in this chapter I intend to treat of the group of writers who are known as the Cambridge Platonists. They fit in well enough at this point because, though some of them refer little or not at all to Hobbes, Ralph Cudworth regarded the latter as the principal enemy of true religion and of a spiritualist philosophy and consciously endeavoured to combat his influence. To say this is not to say, however, that the Cambridge Platonists should be estimated simply in terms of a reaction to Hobbes. For they represent a positive and independent current of thought which is not without interest, even though none of them were philosophers of the first rank.

But before treating of the Cambridge Platonists I wish to say something about an earlier writer, Lord Herbert of Cherbury. He is, indeed, generally regarded as the predecessor of the eighteenth-century deists, who will be mentioned in a later chapter; but his philosophy of religion can be dealt with briefly here. On certain points his philosophical ideas have an affinity with those of the Cambridge Platonists.

2. Lord Herbert of Cherbury (1583–1648) was the author of *Tractatus de Beritate* (1624), *De causis errorum* (1645) and *De religione gentilium* (1645; complete version 1663). In his view in addition to the human cognitive faculties we must postulate a number of 'common notions' (*notitiae communes*). These 'common notions', to use the Stoic term employed by Lord Herbert, are in some sense at least innate truths, characterized by 'apriority' (*prioritas*), independence, universality, certainty, necessity (that is, necessity for life) and immediacy. They are implanted by God and are apprehended by 'natural instinct', being the presuppositions, not the products, of experience. The human mind is not a *tabula rasa*; rather does it resemble a closed book which is opened on the presentation of sense-experience. And experience would not be possible without these 'common notions'.

On this last point Lord Herbert, as commentators have pointed out, anticipated in some degree a conviction which at a much later date was defended by Kant. But Lord Herbert does not provide any systematic deduction of these *a priori* notions or truths; nor does he attempt to tell us what they all are. That he does not attempt to give any exhaustive list of them is not, however, surprising if we bear in mind the fact that in his view there are impediments (for example, lack of talent) which prevent men from recognizing more than a fraction of them. In other words, to say that these truths are implanted by God or by nature is not to say that they are all consciously and reflectively apprehended from the start. When recognized, they win universal consent; so that universal consent is a mark of a recognized 'common notion'. But there can be growth in insight into these virtually innate ideas or truths; and many of them come to light only in the process of discursive thought. Hence one cannot give a complete list of them *a priori*. If men follow the path of reason alone, unhampered by prejudice and passion, they will come to a fuller reflective apprehension of the ideas implanted by God.

Another reason why Lord Herbert does not attempt to list the 'common notions' is that he is primarily interested in those which are involved in religious and moral knowledge. According to him there are five fundamental truths of natural religion; that there is a supreme Being, that this supreme Being ought to be worshipped, that a moral life has always been the principal part of divine worship, that vices and crimes should be expiated by repentance, and that in the next life our deeds on earth are rewarded or punished. In his *De religione gentilium* Lord Herbert tried to show how these five truths are recognized in all religions and form their real essence, in spite of all accretions due to superstition and fantasy. He does not deny that revelation is capable of supplementing natural religion; but he insists that alleged revelation must be judged at the bar of reason. And his reserved attitude towards dogma is evident. His interest, however, lies in defending the rationality of religion and of a religious outlook rather than in purely negative criticism of the different positive religions.

3. The first word in the name 'Cambridge Platonists' is due to the fact that the group of men to whom it is applied were all associated with the University of Cambridge. Benjamin Whichcote (1609–83), John Smith (1616–52), Ralph Cudworth (1617–88), Nathaniel Culverwel (c. 1618–c. 1651) and Peter Sterry (1613–72) were all graduates of Emmanuel College, while Henry More (1614–87) was a graduate of Christ's College. Some of them were also Fellows of their college; and all were Anglican clergymen.

In what sense were these men 'Platonists'? The answer is, I think, that they were influenced by and drew inspiration from Platonism as being a spiritualist and religious interpretation of reality. But Platonism did not mean for them simply the philosophy of the historic Plato: it meant rather the whole tradition of spiritualist metaphysics from Plato to Plotinus. Moreover, though they utilized Platonism in this sense and referred to philosophers such as Plato and Plotinus, and though they regarded themselves as continuing the Platonic tradition in contemporary thought, they were concerned to expound a religious and Christian philosophy in opposition to materialistic and atheistic currents of thought rather than to propound the philosophy of Plato or that of Plotinus, between which, indeed, they made no clear distinction. Cudworth in particular was a determined opponent of Hobbes. But though Hobbes was the chief enemy, the Cambridge Platonists also rejected Descartes' mechanistic view of nature. They did not perhaps give sufficient weight to the fact that Cartesianism possesses another and different aspect; but his views of nature seemed to them to be incompatible with a spiritual interpretation of the world and to pave the way for the more radical philosophy of Hobbes.

Emmanuel College was, in effect, a Puritan foundation and a stronghold of Calvinism. The Cambridge Platonists, however, reacted against this narrow Protestant dogmatism. Whichcote, for example, rejected the Calvinist (and, one might add, Hobbesian) view of man. For man is an image of God, gifted with reason, which is 'the candle of the Lord, lighted by God, and leading us to God'; and he should not be belittled or denigrated. Again, Cudworth rejected the doctrine that some men are predestined to hell and eternal torment antecedently to any fault of their own. His study of the ancient philosophers and of ethics liberated him from the Calvinism in which he had been educated and which he had brought with him to the university. It would, indeed, be inaccurate if one asserted that all the Cambridge Platonists rejected Calvinism and liberated themselves from its influence. Culverwel certainly did not do so. While agreeing with Whichcote in extolling reason, he at the same time emphasized the diminution of its light and the weakness of the human mind in a way which shows the influence of the Calvinist theology. None the less one can say in general that the Cambridge Platonists disliked the Calvinist denigration of human nature and its subordination of reason to faith. In fact, they were not concerned with supporting any one dogmatic system. They aimed rather at revealing the essential elements of Christianity; and they regarded a good deal in the Protestant systems as being little more than matter of opinion. With regard to dogmatic differences they thus tended to adopt a tolerant and 'broad' outlook and were known as 'Latitudinarians'. This is not to say that they rejected the idea of revealed truth or that they refused to admit 'mysteries'. They were not rationalists in the modern sense. But they strongly objected to insistence on obscure doctrines, the relevance of which to the moral life was not clear. The essence of Christianity, and indeed of all religion, they found in the moral life. Doctrinal disputes and disputes about ecclesiastical government and institution they regarded as being of secondary importance in comparison with a sincerely moral and Christian life. Religious truth is of value if it reacts on life and produces practical fruit.

By saying this I do not mean to imply that the Cambridge Platonists were pragmatists. They believed in the power of the human reason to attain to objective truth about God and to give us insight into absolute and universal moral laws. But they insisted on two points; first, that a sincere attempt to lead a moral life is a necessary condition for obtaining insight into truth about God and, secondly, that the truths which are of most importance are those which form the clearest basis for a Christian life. In their dislike for sectarian wrangling and bitter controversy about obscure theoretical problems they bear some resemblance to those fourteenth-century writers who had deplored the wrangling of the schools and all preoccupation with logical subtleties to the neglect of the 'one thing necessary'.

At the same time the Cambridge Platonists emphasized the contemplative attitude. That is to say, although they stressed the close connection between moral purity and the attainment of truth, they emphasized the understanding of reality, the personal appropriation and contemplation of truth, rather than the manipulation of reality. In other words, their attitude was different from the attitude insisted on by Francis Bacon and summed up in the aphorism 'Knowledge is power'. They had little sympathy with the subordination of knowledge to its scientific and practical exploitation. For one thing, they believed, whereas Bacon had not, that rational knowledge of supersensible reality is attainable; and this knowledge cannot be exploited scientifically. Nor, for the matter of that, had they much sympathy with the Puritan subordination of knowledge of religious truth to 'practical' purposes. They emphasized rather the Plotinian idea of the conversion of the mind to the contemplation of divine reality and of the world in its relation to God. As historians have pointed out, they were not in tune with either the empiricist or the religious movements of their time and country. It may very well be true that, as Ernst Cassirer has argued,[2] there is a historical connection between the Platonism of the Italian renaissance and the Platonism of the Cambridge divines; but as Cassirer also argues, this Cambridge Platonism stood apart from the dominant movements in contemporary British philosophical and theological thought. The Cambridge men were neither empiricists nor Puritans.

The Cambridge Platonists, therefore, were concerned with defending a spiritualist interpretation of the universe as a foundation for the Christian moral life. And the most elaborate defence of such an interpretation of the universe is given by Ralph Cudworth in his work *The True Intellectual System of the Universe* (1678). It is a tedious piece of writing, because the author discusses at length the views of different ancient philosophers to the detriment of a clear statement of his own position. But behind the welter of quotations and of expositions of Greek philosophers there appears clearly enough the figure of Hobbes, whom Cudworth interprets as a sheer atheist. In answer to Hobbes he argues that we do in fact possess an idea of God. He reduces materialism to sensationalism and then observes that sense-perception is not knowledge, thus reaffirming the position of Plato in the *Theaetetus*. Moreover, it is evident that we have ideas of many things which are not perceptible by the senses. It follows, therefore, that we cannot legitimately deny the existence of a being simply because it cannot be perceived by the senses; nor are we entitled to say that a name which purports to connote an incorporeal object is necessarily devoid of significance. 'Were existence to be allowed to nothing, that doth not fall under corporeal sense, then must we deny the existence of soul and mind in ourselves and others, because we can neither feel nor see any such thing. Whereas we are certain of the existence of our own souls, partly from an inward consciousness of our own cogitations, and partly from that principle of reason, that nothing cannot act. And the existence of other souls is manifest to us, from their effects upon their respective bodies, their motions, actions, and discourse. Wherefore since the Atheists cannot deny the existence of soul or mind in men, though no such thing fall under external sense, they have as little reason to deny the existence of a perfect mind, presiding over the universe, without which it cannot be conceived whence our imperfect ones should be derived. The existence of that God, whom no eye hath seen nor can see, is plainly proved by reason from his effects, in the visible phenomena of the universe, and from what we are conscious of within ourselves.'[3] Nor can we argue validly from the fact that even the theists admit the incomprehensibility of God to the conclusion that God is altogether inconceivable and that the term 'God' has no meaning. For the statement that God is incomprehensible means that the finite mind cannot have an adequate idea of Him, not that it can have no idea of Him at all. We cannot comprehend the divine perfection; but we can have an idea of absolutely perfect Being. This can be shown in various ways. For example, 'that we have an idea or conception of perfection, or a perfect Being, is evident from the notion that we have of imperfection, so familiar to us; perfection being the rule and measure of imperfection, and not imperfection of perfection . . . : so that perfection is first conceivable, in order of nature, as light before darkness, a positive before the privative or defect'.[4] And the same applies to the idea of the infinite. Further, it is useless to assert that the idea of God is a construction of the imagination, like the idea of a centaur, or that it is implanted in the mind by lawgivers and politicians for their own ends. For a finite and imperfect mind could not have constructed the idea of an infinitely perfect Being. 'Were there no God, the idea of an absolutely or infinitely perfect Being could never have been made or feigned, neither by politicians, nor by poets, nor philosophers, nor any other.'[5] 'The generality of mankind in all ages have had a prolepsis or anticipation in their minds concerning the real and actual existence of such a being.'[6] And it is possible to demonstrate the existence of God by means of the idea of God. For example, 'because we have an idea of God, or a perfect Being, implying no manner of contradiction in it, therefore must it needs have some kind of entity or other, either an actual or possible one; but God, if he be not, is possible to be, therefore he doth actually exist'.[7]

The influence of Descartes on Cudworth's mind is evident from what has just been said about the idea of the perfect. Cudworth does, indeed, give other lines of argument. For example, he argues that from nothing there can come nothing, so that 'if once there had been nothing, there could never have been any thing'.[8] There must, therefore, be something which existed from all eternity, itself unmade; and this something must exist by the necessity of its own nature. But there is nothing which exists necessarily and eternally save an absolutely perfect Being. Hence either God exists or nothing at all exists. But though Cudworth gives a variety of arguments, the influence of Descartes is undeniable. Nor does Cudworth attempt to deny it. He criticizes Descartes' use of our knowledge of God's existence on the ground that it involves us in a scepticism from which we can never escape. Interpreting Descartes as saying that we cannot be sure of anything, even of the trustworthiness of our reason, until we have proved that God exists, he argues that the attainment of such a proof is rendered impossible, because it presupposes the very fact which it is afterwards used to establish, namely, that we can trust our reason and the first principles of reason. But this does not alter the fact that Cudworth drew inspiration from the writings of Descartes.

However, though Cudworth was certainly influenced by Descartes, he viewed with sharp disfavour the latter's mechanistic theory of the material world. Descartes belongs to the class of those who have 'an undiscerned tang of the mechanic Atheism hanging about them', because of 'their so confident rejecting of all final and intending causality in nature, and admitting of no other causes of things, as philosophical, save the material and mechanical only'.[9] Cudworth calls the Cartesians 'mechanic Theists' and rejects Descartes' contention that we should not claim the power of discerning God's purposes in nature. That eyes were made for seeing and ears for hearing is so plain that 'nothing but sottish stupidity or atheistic incredulity can make any doubt thereof'.[10] Cudworth argues also against the notion that animals are machines and favours attributing to them sensitive souls. 'If it be evident from the phenomena that brutes are not mere senseless machines or automata, and only like clocks or watches, then ought not popular opinion and vulgar prejudice so far to prevail with us, as to hinder our assent to that which sound reason and philosophy clearly dictate, that therefore they must have something more than matter in them.'[11]

Cudworth thus rejects altogether the sharp dichotomy made by Descartes between the spiritual and material worlds.

I do not mean by this that he postulated an evolutionary continuity between inanimate matter, plants, sensitive life and rational life. On the contrary, he denied that life can proceed from inanimate matter, and he denounced Hobbes's account of consciousness and thought in materialist terms. 'There is nothing in body or matter, but magnitude, figure, site, and motion or rest: now it is mathematically certain, that these, however combined together, can never possibly compound, or make up life or cogitation.'[12] Moreover the rational soul of man is naturally immortal, whereas the sensitive souls of brutes are not. There are, therefore, essential differences of degree in nature. 'There is a scale, or ladder of entities and perfections in the universe, one above another, and the production of things cannot possibly be in way of ascent from lower to higher, but must of necessity be in way of descent from higher to lower.'[13] But precisely because there are these various degrees of perfection in nature we cannot make a simple division between the spiritual sphere on the one hand and, on the other, the material sphere, from which final causality is banished and where vital phenomena are interpreted in purely mechanistic terms.

A more pronounced hostility towards the Cartesian dualism was shown by Henry More. In his younger days he had been an enthusiastic admirer of Descartes. Thus in a letter to Clerselier, written in 1655, he remarks not only that Cartesianism is useful for promoting the highest end of all philosophy, namely, religion, but also that the reasoning and method of demonstration concerning God and man is soundest if it is based on Cartesian principles. Indeed, if exception is made perhaps for Platonism, there is no system of philosophy besides Cartesianism, properly understood, which so stoutly bars the way to atheism.[14] But in his *Enchiridion metaphysicum* (1671) More depicted the Cartesian philosophy as an enemy of religious belief. Inclined as he was to mysticism and theosophy he found Descartes' intellectualism repugnant. The notion of a material world sharply separated from spiritual reality and consisting of extension which can be adequately treated in terms of mathematics was unacceptable to a man who regarded nature as permeated by vitality, by soul. In nature we see the creative activity of the world-soul, a vital dynamic principle, not to be identified with God but operating as the divine instrument. Cudworth, too, speaks of 'Plastic Nature', which, as the instrument of

God, is the immediate agent in producing natural effects. In other words, Cudworth and More turned their backs on the Cartesian interpretation of nature and on its developments and attempted to reinstate a philosophy of nature of the type which was popular at the time of the Renaissance.

What has been said about Cudworth's theory of the idea of the perfect as being prior to the idea of imperfection indicates clearly enough his opposition to empiricism. Indeed, he does not hesitate to declare that the statement that the human mind is originally 'a mere blank or white sheet of paper that hath nothing at all in it, but what was scribbled upon it by the objects of sense',[15] implies that the human soul is generated from matter or that it is 'nothing but a higher modification of matter'.[16] He is, of course, interpreting the statement as meaning that the mind is merely the passive recipient of sense-impressions. But in his writings he makes it clear that he intends to reject the empiricist principle even when it is not interpreted in this narrow sense. Thus in the *Treatise concerning eternal and immutable Morality*[17] he states that there are two kinds of 'perceptive cogitations' in the soul. The first kind consists of passive perceptions of the soul, which may be either sensations or images (or phantasms). The other kind consists of 'active perceptions which rise from the mind itself without the body'.[18] And these are called 'conceptions of the mind' or νοήματα. They include not only ideas such as those of justice, truth, knowledge, virtue and vice but also propositions such as 'Nothing can be and not be at the same time' or 'Out of nothing there can come nothing'. These conceptions of the mind are not abstracted from phantasms by any active intellect (a view which, according to Cudworth, has been erroneously attributed to Aristotle). The idea that they are so abstracted is due to the fact that they are 'most commonly excited and awakened occasionally from the appulse of outward objects knocking at the door of our senses',[19] and men have failed to distinguish between the outward occasion of these conceptions and their active, productive cause. In reality 'they must needs arise from the innate vigour and activity of the mind itself',[20] which is a created image of the divine mind. These virtually innate ideas are imprinted on the human mind by God. And by them we know not only immaterial objects and eternal truths but also material things. This is not to deny that sense and imagination have a part to play in our knowledge of material things. But sensation cannot give us knowledge of the essence of any thing or of any scientific truth. We cannot have scientific knowledge of the material world save by the activity of the mind producing 'conceptions' from within itself by virtue of its God-given power.

The criterion of theoretical truth is 'the clearness of the apprehensions themselves'.[21] 'Clear intellectual conceptions must of necessity be truths, because they are real entities.'[22] Cudworth accepts, therefore, the Cartesian criterion of truth, clarity and distinction of idea; but he rejects the use of the hypothesis of the 'evil genius' and Descartes' device to escape from the possibility of error and deception. Men are, indeed, sometimes deceived and imagine that they clearly understand what they do not clearly understand. But, says Cudworth, it does not follow that they can never be certain that they do clearly comprehend some thing. We might just as well argue that 'because in our dreams we think we have clear sensations we cannot therefore be ever sure, when we are awake, that we see things that really are'.[23] Cudworth evidently thought that it was absurd to suggest that waking life might be a dream.

The mind, therefore, can perceive eternal essences and immutable truths. And it can do this, as has already been mentioned, because it derives from and depends on the eternal mind 'which comprehends within itself the steady and immutable *rationes* of all things and their verities'.[24] It can therefore discern eternal moral principles and values. Good and evil, just and unjust, are not relative conceptions, as Hobbes imagined. Even if it is possible to have varying degrees of insight into moral values and principles, these are none the less absolute. Cudworth had therefore no sympathy with the view, which he ascribes to Descartes, that moral and other eternal truths are subject to the divine omnipotence and therefore, in principle, variable. Indeed, he goes so far as to say that 'if any one did desire to persuade the world, that Cartesius, notwithstanding all his pretences to demonstrate a Deity, was indeed but an hypocritical Theist, or personated and disguised Atheist, he could not have a fairer pretence for it out of all his writings than from hence; this being plainly to destroy the Deity, by making one attribute thereof to devour and swallow up another; infinite will and power, infinite understanding and wisdom'.[25]

This belief in the mind's power of discerning immutable truths, which bear the evidence of their truth within themselves and which are in some sense imprinted on the mind, was shared by other Cambridge Platonists. Whichcote, for example, spoke of 'truths of first inscription', of which we have knowledge 'by the light of first impression'. 'For God made man to them (moral truths of first inscription), and did write them upon the heart of man, before he did declare them upon Mount Sinai, before he engraved them upon the tables of stone, or before they were writ in our Bibles: God made man to them, and wrought his law upon men's hearts; and as it were, interwove it into the principles of our reason. . . . (We possess) principles that are *concreated*. . . . Things of natural knowledge, or of first impression in the heart of man by God, these are known to be true as soon as ever they are proposed. . . .'[26] Such are, for example, the principles of reverence for the Deity and the fundamental principles of justice.

Similarly, Henry More, in his *Enchiridion ethicum* (1668) enumerates twenty-three moral principles which he calls *Noemata moralia*. According to him, they are 'the fruit of that faculty which is properly called *Nous*',[27] and their truth is immediately evident. The first of them is that 'good is that which is pleasing, agreeable and fitting to some perceptive life, or to a degree of this life, and which is conjoined with the conservation of the percipient'.[28] Another is that 'what is good should be chosen; but evil should be avoided. The greater good should be chosen in preference to the latter, while a lesser evil should be tolerated lest we undergo a greater.'[29] But More evidently did not think that his list of twenty-three fundamental moral principles was exhaustive; for he speaks of 'these propositions and their like'.[30] This laying-down of a large number of 'undeniable' principles links More with Lord Herbert of Cherbury and anticipates the procedure of the later 'Scottish School'.

The Cambridge Platonists, as we have seen, were not much in sympathy with the prevailing philosophical and religious movements of their country and time. Though they certainly did not deny the part played by experience in human knowledge, they were not in sympathy with the restricted and narrow concept of experience which was becoming characteristic of what we call 'empiricism'. And though they were far from denouncing science, they showed little understanding of the development and method of contemporary mathematical physics. They tended to look back to 'Platonic' philosophies of nature rather than to attempt a forward-looking synthesis or harmonization of physics with metaphysics. Further, their devotion to a Platonic and Christian humanism led them to hold aloof from, and to adopt a critical attitude towards, the theological controversy of the time. It is understandable, therefore, that their influence was comparatively slight, particularly if one bears in mind the unattractive literary presentation of their ideas. This is not to say, of course, that they exercised no influence at all. For example, in his *Enchiridion metaphysicum* Henry More argued that the Cartesian geometrical interpretation of nature leads us to the idea of absolute space, indestructible, infinite and eternal. These attributes cannot, however, be the attributes of material things. Absolute space must be, therefore, an intelligible reality which is a kind of shadow or symbol of the divine presence and immensity. More was primarily concerned with arguing that the mathematical interpretation of nature, which separated the corporeal from the spiritual, ought logically to lead to the linking of the one to the other; in other words, he was concerned with developing an *argumentum ad hominem* against Descartes. But his argument appears to have exercised an influence on the Newtonian conception of space. Again, Shaftesbury, who will be considered in connection with ethics, was certainly influenced by Cambridge Platonists such as Cudworth, More and Whichcote. Yet though Cambridge Platonism did exercise some influence, it obviously stands apart from what is generally considered to be the chief development in British philosophy of the period, namely, empiricism.

4. The theory of innate ideas and principles was criticized by Richard Cumberland (1632–1718), who died as bishop of Peterborough. In the introduction to his *De legibus naturae* (1672) he makes it clear that in his opinion it is an unjustifiable short-cut if in order to defend the moral order one simply postulates innate ideas. To build natural religion and morality on a hypothesis which has been rejected by the majority of philosophers and which can never be proved is, he says, an ill-advised procedure.

But though Cumberland rejected the Cambridge Platonists' hypothesis of innate ideas, he was at one with Cudworth in his zeal to refute the philosophy of Hobbes. Laws of nature, in the moral sense, were for him 'propositions of unchangeable truth, which direct our voluntary actions about choosing good and evil; and impose an obligation to external actions even without civil laws, and laying aside all consideration of those compacts which constitute civil government'.[31] The moral law does not depend, therefore, on civil law or on the sovereign's will. And the word 'good' has an objective meaning, signifying that which preserves, develops and perfects the faculties of one or more things. But the point which Cumberland especially emphasizes is that the good of the individual is inseparable from that of others. For man is not, as Hobbes depicted him, a human atom, entirely and incurably egoistic: he is a social being, and he possesses altruistic and benevolent, as well as egoistic, inclinations. There is, therefore, no contradiction between the promotion of one's own good and the promotion of the common good. Indeed, the common good comprises within itself the good of the individual. It follows, therefore, that 'the common good is the supreme law'.[32] And the laws of nature prescribe those actions which will promote the common good, 'and by which only the entire happiness of particular persons can be obtained'.[33]

Cumberland does not work out his ideas in any very precise way. But because he lays down the promotion of the common good as the supreme law, in relation to which all other moral rules should be determined, he has been called the precursor of utilitarianism. It should be noted, however, that promotion of the common good includes for him not only promotion of benevolence and love of other men but also love of God. For perfection of our faculties, even if Cumberland does not define 'perfection', certainly involves for him the conscious appropriation and expression of our relationship to God. Moreover, the law of benevolence is itself an expression of the divine will and is furnished with sanctions, even though disinterested love of God and man provides a higher motive for obedience to the law than is provided by a self-regarding consideration of sanctions.

In view of the emphasis which is customarily, and rightly, placed on the development of empiricism in British philosophy, it is as well not to forget the existence of men such as the Cambridge Platonists and Richard Cumberland. For they represent what Professor J. H. Muirhead called 'the Platonic tradition in Anglo-Saxon Philosophy'. If we wish to use the term 'idealism' in the very wide sense in which the Marxists are accustomed to use the word, we can speak of the Cambridge Platonists and kindred thinkers as representing one phase of the idealist tradition in British philosophy, the tradition which found an eminent expression (combined with empiricism) in the writings of Berkeley and which flourished in the latter part of the nineteenth century and in the first two decades of the twentieth. On the Continent British philosophy is often supposed to be inherently and constantly empiricist and even naturalistic in character. The existence of another tradition needs, therefore, to be emphasized if we are to form a balanced view of the development of British thought.

Chapter Four

LOCKE (1)

Life and writings — Locke's moderation and common sense — The purpose of the Essay — *The attack on innate ideas — The empiricist principle.*

1. John Locke was born at Wrington, near Bristol, in 1632. His father was a country attorney, and he was educated at home until he went in 1646 to Westminster School, where he remained until 1652. In that year he entered the university of Oxford as a junior student of Christ Church. After taking in due course the B.A. and M.A. degrees, he was elected in 1659 to a senior studentship at Christ Church. In the following year he was made a lecturer in Greek, and later he was appointed Reader in rhetoric and Censor of Moral Philosophy.

When Locke started studying philosophy at Oxford, he found there a debased and rather petrified form of Scholasticism for which he conceived a great distaste, regarding it as 'perplexed' with obscure terms and useless questions. No doubt, like some other Renaissance and modern philosophers who revolted against Aristotelian Scholasticism, he was more influenced by it than he himself was aware; but his interest in philosophy was aroused by his private reading of Descartes rather than by what was then being taught at Oxford. This is not to say that Locke was ever a Cartesian. But on certain points he was influenced by Descartes, and in any case the latter's writings showed him that clear and orderly thinking is as possible inside as it is outside the sphere of philosophy.

Locke's studies at Oxford were not confined to philosophy. As a friend of Sir Robert Boyle and his circle, he interested himself in chemistry and physics, and he also pursued studies in medicine, though it was not until a later date (1674) that he obtained his medical degree and a licence to practise. He did not, however, take up the practice of medicine as a regular career, nor did he continue his academic life at Oxford. Instead he became involved, in a minor way, in public affairs.

In 1665 Locke left England as secretary to a diplomatic mission, headed by Sir Walter Vane, to the Elector of Brandenburg. Two years later, after his return to England, he entered the service of Lord Ashley, afterwards the first earl of Shaftesbury, acting as medical adviser to his patron and as tutor to the latter's son. But Shaftesbury evidently held a higher opinion of Locke's abilities; for when he became Lord Chancellor in 1672, he appointed his friend to the post of secretary for the presentation of ecclesiastical benefices. In 1673 Locke was made secretary to the council of trade and plantations; but Shaftesbury's political fortunes suffered a reverse, and Locke retired to Oxford, where he still held his studentship at Christ Church. Ill-health, however, led him to go to France in 1675, and he remained there until 1680. During this period he met Cartesians and anti-Cartesians and was influenced by the thought of Gassendi.

On his return to England Locke re-entered the service of Shaftesbury. But the latter was engaged in intrigue against King James II, then Duke of York, and he was finally forced to take refuge in Holland, where he died in the January of 1683. Locke, believing that his own safety also was menaced, fled to Holland in the autumn of the same year. Charles II died in 1685, and Locke's name was placed on a list of people wanted by the new government in connection with Monmouth's rebellion. He therefore lived under an assumed name and did not return to England even when his name had been removed from the list of wanted persons. However, as Locke was aware, plans were afoot for placing William of Orange on the throne of England, and shortly after the revolution of 1688 Locke returned to his own country, the Dutchman having been safely installed in London.

For reasons of health Locke declined the proffered post of ambassador to the Elector of Brandenburg; but he retained a minor office in London until in 1691 he retired to Oates in Essex, where he lived as guest of the Masham family, though from 1696 until 1700 his duties as Commissioner of

Trade forced him to spend part of the year in the capital. He died in October 1704, while Lady Masham was reading the Psalms to him. Incidentally, this lady was the daughter of Ralph Cudworth, the Cambridge Platonist, with whom Locke had been acquainted and with some of whose views he was in sympathy.

Locke's principal work is his *Essay concerning Human Understanding*.[1] In 1671 he was engaged in philosophical discussion with five or six friends when it occurred to him that they could not make further progress until they had examined the mind's capacities and seen 'what objects our understandings were, or were not, fitted to deal with'.[2] Locke prepared a paper on the subject, and this formed the nucleus of the two early drafts of the *Essay*. He continued work on the treatise during the following years, and the first edition was published in 1690 (preceded in 1688 by a French abstract for Le Clerc's *Bibliothèque universelle*). Three further editions were published during Locke's lifetime.

In 1690 there also appeared Locke's *Two Treatises of Civil Government*. In the first he attacked the theory of the divine right of kings as expounded by Sir Robert Filmer, while in the second he developed his own political theory. According to Locke in his preface to the *Treatises* his motive in writing was to justify the revolution of 1688 and make good the title of William of Orange to occupy the throne of England. But this does not mean that his political principles had been hurriedly conceived with a view to achieving this practical purpose. Moreover, his expression of his political theory remains one of the most important documents in the history of liberal thought, just as the *Essay* remains one of the most important documents in the history of empiricism.

In 1693 Locke published *Some Thoughts concerning Education* and in 1695 *The Reasonableness of Christianity*. In 1689 he published in Latin, and anonymously, his first *Letter on Toleration*; and this was followed, in 1690 and 1693, by two other letters on the same subject. An incomplete fourth letter appeared posthumously in 1706, together with his discourse on miracles, his examination of Malebranche's opinion about seeing all things in God, the uncompleted work on *The Conduct of the Understanding*, his memoirs of Shaftesbury, and some letters. Other material has been subsequently published.

2. Locke, as is evident from his writings, was very much a man of moderation. He was an empiricist, in the sense that he believed that all the material of our knowledge is supplied by sense-perception and introspection. But he was not an empiricist in the sense that he thought that we can know only sense-presentations. In his own modest fashion he was a metaphysician. He was a rationalist in the sense that he believed in bringing all opinions and beliefs before the tribunal of reason and disliked the substitution of expressions of emotion and feeling for rationally grounded judgments. But he was not a rationalist in the sense of one who denies spiritual reality or the supernatural order or the possibility of divine revelation of truths which, while not contrary to reason, are above reason, in the sense that they cannot be discovered by reason alone and may not be fully understandable even when revealed. He disliked authoritarianism, whether in the intellectual or in the political field. And he was one of the earlier exponents of the principle of toleration. But he was far from being a friend of anarchy; and there were limits to the extent to which he was willing to apply the principle of toleration. He was a religious man; but he had no sympathy with fanaticism or with intemperate zeal. One does not look to him for brilliant extravaganzas or for flashes of genius; but one finds in him an absence of extremes and the presence of common sense.

One or two commentators have objected against over-emphasizing Locke's 'common sense'. And it is true, for example, that his theory of an occult substrate in material things is not a common-sense view, if by this one means a view spontaneously held by a man who is innocent of all philosophy. But when one speaks of Locke's common sense, one does not mean to imply that his philosophy is no more than an expression of the spontaneously held views of the ordinary man. One means rather that he endeavoured to reflect on and analyse common experience, that he did not strive after originality by producing far-fetched theories and one-sided, if brilliant, interpretations of reality, and that the theories which he did produce were, in his opinion, required by rational reflection on common experience. To those who expect from a philosopher startling paradoxes and novel 'discoveries' he inevitably appears as pedestrian and unexciting. But he gives throughout the impression of being an honest thinker. In reading him one is not forced to ask oneself constantly whether he can possibly have believed what he was saying.

In his writings Locke employs ordinary English, apart from a few technical terms; and he is to this extent easy to follow. But, as far as the *Essay* at any rate is concerned, terms are not always employed in the same sense; and he is to this extent difficult to follow. In his 'Epistle to the Reader' Locke makes open acknowledgement of the fact that the *Essay* was 'written by incoherent parcels; and after long intervals of neglect, resumed again, as my humour or occasions permitted'. This serves to explain defects in arrangement and a certain repetitiveness; 'the way it has been writ in, by catches, and many long intervals of interruption, being apt to cause some repetitions'. The reason for leaving the results as they are is provided by Locke himself. 'But to confess the truth, I am too lazy, or too busy to make it shorter.' He might, however, have profitably cleared up some major inconsistencies and fixed more definitely the meaning of certain terms. For example, sometimes he speaks as though what we know is our ideas and the relations between ideas, and, indeed, he defines the idea as the object of the understanding when a man thinks. But at other times he implies that we know at least some things directly. In other words, he sometimes implies a representationist view of knowledge, while on other occasions he implies the opposite. Again, in what he has to say about universal ideas there are several different strands or tendencies of thought. Sometimes he speaks in a nominalist fashion, but at other times he implies what the Scholastics call 'moderate realism'. And the result of all this is that under the *prima facie* simplicity and clarity of Locke's writing there is a certain amount of ambiguity and confusion. It is not that Locke was incapable of clearing up these obscurities of thought: he has himself provided what is doubtless the true explanation, namely, that he was either too lazy or too busy to do so.

3. We have seen that Locke undertook to institute an inquiry concerning human knowledge. Other philosophers before him had, of course, reflected on and written about human knowledge. In the Greek world both Plato and Aristotle had done so and, from a very different point of view, the sceptics. St. Augustine had reflected on this subject, and the leading mediaeval philosophers all considered it in one connection or another. In post-Renaissance philosophy Des

cartes had treated the problem of certainty, and in England both Francis Bacon and Hobbes had written about human knowledge. But Locke was really the first philosopher to devote his main work to an inquiry into human understanding, its scope and its limits. And we can say that the prominent place occupied in modern philosophy by the theory of knowledge is in large measure due to him, even though it was the influence of Kant which subsequently led to this branch of philosophical inquiry usurping to all intents and purposes the whole field of philosophy; that is to say, among those thinkers who adhered more or less closely to the position of Kant himself. The mere fact, therefore, that Locke devoted a large-scale treatise to an inquiry into human understanding and knowledge has a peculiar importance of its own.

Now it has already been mentioned that in his 'Epistle to the Reader', prefaced to the *Essay*, Locke says that he considered it necessary to inquire, with what objects are our understandings fitted to deal, with what objects are they not fitted to deal. That he asked such a question is understandable. For he thought that men not infrequently wasted their energies on problems which could not be solved by the human mind. And he also considered that this procedure is an occasion for scepticism in others. If we confined our attention to matters which fall within the scope of the human intellect, we should make progress in knowledge, and less occasion would be given for scepticism. But though it is understandable that he asked the question, its formulation, as given above, is unfortunate. For how, it may be asked, can we distinguish between the objects with which the mind is capable of dealing and those with which it is incapable of dealing without passing beyond the scope of the mind? Or the objection can be expressed in this way. If we can mention any object with which the human mind is incapable of dealing, have we not implicitly stated that the mind is capable of saying something about it and so 'dealing' with it to a certain extent?

Further, Locke defines an idea as 'whatever is meant by phantasm, notion, species, or whatever it is which the mind can be employed about in thinking'.[3] Here he tells us that the objects of the mind are ideas. And it would appear that the mind is fitted to deal with all its ideas. We could not say, with what objects the mind is not fitted to deal. For if we could say this, we should have ideas of these objects. And in this case we could deal with them, since an idea is defined as that about which the mind can be employed in thinking.

In his introduction to the *Essay* Locke says that his purpose is 'to inquire into the original, certainty, and extent of human knowledge; together with the grounds and degrees of belief, opinion, and assent'.[4] He thus makes no clear distinction between the psychological question concerning the origin of our ideas and epistemological questions such as the nature of certain knowledge and the sufficient grounds for 'opinion'. But this could hardly be expected at the time. Before speaking of the method which he proposes to employ, he remarks that it is worth while 'to search out the bounds between opinion and knowledge; and examine by what measures, in things, whereof we have no certain knowledge, we ought to regulate our assent, and moderate our persuasions'.[5] Here we have a more or less epistemological programme. But the first point of the method of inquiry which Locke then gives is to inquire 'into the origin of those ideas, notions, or whatever else you please to call them, which a man observes, and is conscious to himself he has in his mind; and the ways, whereby the understanding comes to be furnished with them'.[6] Here we have a psychological inquiry.

This inquiry into our ideas covers the first and second books of the *Essay*. In the first book Locke argues against the theory of innate ideas, while in the second he gives his own theories about our ideas, their origin and nature. But, as one might expect when an idea is defined as whatever is the object of the understanding when a man thinks, discussion of ideas is sometimes discussion of our ideas of things and sometimes of the things of which we have ideas.

The third book treats of words. It is closely connected with the preceding book, because 'words in their primary or immediate signification stand for nothing but the ideas in the mind of him that uses them'.[7] Ideas represent things, and words stand for ideas.

The second and third points in Locke's method are 'to show what knowledge the understanding hath by those ideas; and the certainty, evidence, and extent of it' and to inquire 'into the nature and grounds of faith, or opinion'.[8] These subjects, knowledge and opinion, are dealt with in the fourth book.

4. With a view to clearing the ground in preparation for laying the empiricist foundations of knowledge Locke first disposes of the theory of innate ideas. He understands this theory as being the doctrine that 'there are in the understanding certain innate principles; some primary notions, κοιναὶ ἔννοιαι, characters, as it were stamped upon the mind of man, which the soul receives in its very first being; and brings into the world with it'.⁹ Some of these principles are speculative. Locke gives as examples 'whatsoever is, is' and 'it is impossible for the same thing to be and not to be'. Others are practical, that is to say general moral, principles. In the course of his discussion of this theory Locke makes explicit mention of Lord Herbert of Cherbury's theory of 'common notions'.¹⁰ But he says that he consulted the latter's De veritate 'when I had writ this' (the foregoing part of the discussion). Hence he did not set out to attack Lord Herbert specifically; and he does not tell us which philosopher or philosophers he had in mind when he started to attack the theory of innate ideas. His remarks about this theory being 'an established opinion amongst some men' and about there being 'nothing more commonly taken for granted' suggest perhaps that he was simply writing in general against the theory, without intending to direct his criticism against any individual in particular, Descartes, for example, or against a particular group, such as the Cambridge Platonists. He includes in a global fashion all the upholders of the theory.

The chief argument, according to Locke, which is customarily adduced in favour of the theory is universal consent. Because all men agree about the validity of certain speculative and practical principles, it needs must be, it is argued, that these principles are originally imprinted on men's minds and that they brought them into the world with them 'as necessarily and really as they do any of their inherent faculties'.¹¹

Against this theory Locke argues in the first place that even if it were true that all men agree about certain principles this would not prove that these principles are innate, provided that some other explanation can be given of this universal agreement. In other words, if the agreement of all mankind about the truth of these principles can be explained without introducing the hypothesis of innate ideas, the hypothesis is superfluous, and the principle of economy should be applied. Locke was, of course, convinced that the origin of all our ideas can easily be explained without postulating innate ideas.

And for this reason alone he was prepared to exclude the theory.

Secondly, Locke argues that the argument which is brought in favour of the theory of innate ideas is worthless. For there is no universal consent about the truth of any principle. Children and idiots have minds, but they have no knowledge of the principle that it is impossible for the same thing to be and not to be. Yet if this principle were really innate, it must be known. 'No proposition can be said to be in the mind, which it never yet knew, which it was never yet conscious of.'[12] Moreover, 'a great part of illiterate people, and savages, pass many years, even of their rational age, without ever thinking on this and the like general propositions'.[13] The general principles of the speculative order are 'seldom mentioned in the huts of Indians, much less are they to be found in the thoughts of children, or any impression of them on the minds of naturals'.[14] As for the practical or moral principles, 'it will be hard to instance any one moral rule, which can pretend to so general and ready an assent as, "What is, is" or to be so manifest a truth as this, that "it is impossible for the same thing to be, and not to be"'.[15] Where is the moral rule to which all men assent? The general principles of justice and of observing contracts seem to be the most generally received. But it is difficult to believe that those who habitually infringe these rules have received them at birth as innate principles. It may be urged that these people assent in their minds to rules which they contradict in practice. But 'I have always thought the actions of men the best interpreters of their thoughts'.[16] And 'it is very strange and unreasonable to suppose innate practical principles, that terminate only in contemplation'.[17] We have, indeed, natural tendencies; but natural tendencies are not the same thing as innate principles. If moral principles were really innate, we should not find those differences in moral outlook and practice in different societies and in different epochs which we do in fact find.

It may be objected that all this presupposes that principles, to be innate, must be consciously apprehended from the beginning of life, and that this presupposition is unwarranted. For they may be innate, not in the sense that infants in arms consciously apprehend them, but in the sense that they are apprehended when people come to the use of reason. They may even be innate simply in the sense that if and when a man comes to understand the meaning of the relevant terms, he necessarily sees the truth of the proposition in question.

If to apprehend the truth of a principle when one reaches the age of reason means apprehending its truth when one reaches a certain determinate age, Locke did not believe that there are any principles which a man necessarily apprehends when he has passed a certain time in this world. Indeed, he thought, as we have seen, that there are men who apprehend no general abstract principles at all. As for the view that those principles are innate the truth of which is seen when the meaning of the terms is known, Locke did not deny that there are principles of this kind, but he refused to admit that there is any adequate reason for calling them 'innate'. If immediate assent to a proposition once the terms are understood is a certain sign that the proposition is an innate principle, people 'will find themselves plentifully stored with innate principles'.[18] There will be 'legions of innate propositions'.[19] Moreover, the fact that the meanings of the terms have to be learned and that we have to acquire the relevant ideas is a sure sign that the propositions in question are not in fact innate.

If, therefore, we take 'innate' to mean explicitly innate, Locke objects that all the available evidence goes to show that there are no explicitly innate principles. If, however, 'innate' is taken to mean implicitly or virtually innate, Locke asks what is really signified by the statement that there are innate principles in this sense. 'It will be hard to conceive what is meant by a principle imprinted on the understanding implicitly; unless it be this, that the mind is capable of understanding and assenting firmly to such propositions.'[20] And nobody denies that the mind is capable of understanding and assenting firmly to, for example, mathematical propositions. Why, then, call them innate? By the addition of this epithet nothing is explained and nothing further is said.

In view of the facts that the theory of innate ideas is not a theory which counts in contemporary thought and that in any case the Kantian theory of the *a priori* superseded the older theory of innate ideas, it may seem that I have given too much space to an outline of Locke's treatment of the subject. But his discussion of the theory serves at least to illustrate Locke's common-sense attitude and his constant recourse to the available empirical evidence. Moreover, the purpose of a history of philosophy is not simply that of mentioning theories which have an importance also today. And in Locke's time the theory of innate ideas was influential. To a certain extent he may have been tilting at a windmill; for it is hard to think of anyone who believed that infants in arms apprehend explicitly any innate propositions. But, as we have seen, Locke also attacked the theory of implicitly or virtually innate ideas and principles; the theory in this form was held by men of the calibre of Descartes and Leibniz.

5. Setting aside, therefore, the hypothesis of innate ideas, how does the mind come to be furnished with ideas? 'Whence has it all the materials of reason and knowledge? To this I answer, in one word, from *experience*. In that all our knowledge is founded, and from that it ultimately derives itself.'21 But what does Locke understand by experience? His theory is that all our ideas are ultimately derived from sensation or from reflection; and that these two make up experience. 'Our senses, conversant about particular sensible objects, do convey into the mind several distinct perceptions of things, according to the ways wherein those objects do affect them . . . when I say the senses convey into the mind, I mean, they from external objects convey into the mind what produces there those perceptions.'22 This is sensation. The other source of ideas is the perception of the operations of our own minds, such as perceiving, thinking, doubting, believing and willing. This source is reflection, 'the ideas it affords being such only as the mind gets by reflecting on its own operations within itself'.23 All our ideas come from one or other of these sources.

Attention may be drawn in passing to the ambiguous use of the term 'idea' to which allusion has already been made. Locke frequently speaks, for example, of our ideas of sensible qualities, while at other times the sensible qualities are spoken of as ideas. Further, as will be shown later, he uses the term 'idea' not only for sense-data but also for concepts and universal ideas. And though it is doubtless possible to make out what Locke really wishes to say on a given occasion, this careless use of the term 'idea' scarcely serves the cause of clarity.

In any case, however, Locke is convinced that experience is the fountain of all ideas. If we observe children, we see how their ideas are formed, develop and increase in number together with their experience. The human being's attention is primarily directed outwards, and sensation is thus the chief source of ideas. 'Growing up in a constant attention to outward sensation, (men) seldom make any considerable reflection on what passes within them till they come to be of riper years; and some scarce ever at all.'[24] But though reflection or introspection is not generally developed to the same extent as sensation, we have no ideas of psychical activities such as thinking and willing save by actual experience of these activities. If the words are used when we have had no experience at all of the corresponding activities, we do not know what the words mean. Locke's conclusion is, therefore, that 'all those sublime thoughts which tower above the clouds, reach as high as heaven itself, take their rise and footing here: in all that good extent wherein the mind wanders, in those remote speculations, it may seem to be elevated with, it stirs not one jot beyond those ideas which sense or reflection have offered for its contemplation'.[25]

Locke's general principle, that all our ideas are grounded in experience and depend on it, was basic in classical British empiricism. And in view of the fact that rationalist philosophers such as Descartes and Leibniz believed in virtually innate ideas, we can speak of it as the 'empiricist principle'. But this should not be taken to mean that Locke invented it. To take but one example, St. Thomas Aquinas in the thirteenth century maintained that all our natural ideas and knowledge are grounded in experience, and that there are no innate ideas. Moreover, Aquinas admitted sense-perception and introspection or reflection as 'fountains' of ideas, to use Locke's way of talking, though he subordinated the latter to the former, in the sense that attention is directed first to external material objects. Aquinas was not, of course, what is generally called an 'empiricist'. Nor, for the matter of that, was Locke himself a pure 'empiricist', if by pure empiricism we mean a philosophy which excludes all metaphysics. But I do not wish to institute any comparison between Aquinas and Locke. My object in mentioning the former is simply to point out that it is a mistake to suppose that Locke invented the theory that our ideas originate in experience and to speak as though the doctrine of innate ideas had held undisputed sway in the Middle Ages. Quite apart from the fourteenth-century philosophers of the Ockhamist current of thought, a metaphysician of the thirteenth century such as Aquinas, who adhered more closely than did philosophers such as St. Bonaventure to the Aristotelian way of thinking, had no belief in the hypothesis of innate ideas. Locke's assertion of the empiricist principle was of great historical importance, but it was not a novelty in the sense that nobody before him had maintained anything of the kind.

Chapter Five

LOCKE (2)

*Simple and complex ideas — Simple modes; space, dura-
tion, infinity — Mixed modes — Primary and secondary
qualities — Substance — Relations — Causality — Identity
in relation to inorganic and organic bodies and to man
— Language — Universal ideas — Real and nominal essences.*

1. What was said in the final section of the last chapter about
the origin of our ideas may suggest that in Locke's view the
mind is purely passive; that is, that ideas are 'conveyed into
the mind' and lodged there, and that in the formation of
ideas the mind plays no active part at all. But this would be
an erroneous interpretation of Locke's theory, if it were taken
to be an adequate account. For he made a distinction between simple and complex ideas. And while the mind receives the former passively, it exercises an activity in the production of the latter.

As examples of simple ideas Locke first gives the coldness
and hardness of a piece of ice, the scent and whiteness of a
lily, the taste of sugar. Each of these 'ideas' comes to us
through one sense only. Thus the idea of whiteness comes to
us only through the sense of sight, while the idea of the scent
of a rose comes to us only through the sense of smell. Locke
calls them, therefore, 'ideas of one sense'. But there are other
ideas which we receive by more than one sense. Such are
'space or extension, figure, rest, and motion. For these make
perceivable impressions, both on the eyes and touch; and we
can receive and convey into our minds the ideas of the extension, figure, motion and rest of bodies, both by seeing and
feeling.'[1]

Both these classes of simple ideas are ideas of sensation.

But there are also simple ideas of reflection, the two principal ones being the ideas of 'perception or thinking, and volition or willing'.[2] Further, there are other simple ideas 'which convey themselves into the mind by all the ways of sensation and reflection, viz. pleasure or delight, and its opposite, pain or uneasiness; power; existence; unity'.[3] Thus pleasure or pain, delight or uneasiness, accompanies almost all our ideas, both of sensation and reflection, while 'existence and unity are two other ideas that are suggested to the understanding by every object without, and every idea within'.[4] So also we obtain the idea of power both by observing the effects which natural bodies produce on one another and by observing in ourselves our own power of moving the members of our bodies at will.

We have, therefore, four classes of simple ideas. And a common characteristic of all these ideas is that they are passively received. 'For the objects of our senses do, many of them, obtrude their particular ideas upon our minds whether we will or not; and the operations of our minds will not let us be without at least some obscure notions of them. No man can be wholly ignorant of what he does when he thinks.'[5] Moreover, once the mind has these simple ideas it cannot alter or destroy them or substitute new ones at will. 'It is not in the power of the most exalted wit, or enlarged understanding, by any quickness or variety of thought, to invent or frame one new simple idea in the mind, not taken in by the ways aforementioned: nor can any force of the understanding destroy those that are there.'[6]

On the other hand the mind can actively frame complex ideas, using simple ideas as its material. A man can combine two or more simple ideas into one complex idea. He is not confined to bare observation and introspection, but he can voluntarily combine the data of sensation and reflection to form new ideas, each of which can be considered as one thing and given one name. Such are, for example, 'beauty, gratitude, a man, an army, the universe'.[7]

Locke's general notion of a complex idea presents no great difficulty. For example, we combine the simple ideas of whiteness, sweetness and hardness to form the complex idea of a lump of sugar. In what sense Locke's simple ideas can properly be called 'simple' is doubtless disputable, just as it is open to question in what sense they can properly be termed 'ideas'. Still, the general notion is clear enough, as long as we do not scrutinize it too closely. But Locke complicates matters by giving two classifications of complex ideas. In the original draft of the *Essay* he divided complex ideas into ideas of substances (for example, the idea of a man or of a rose or of gold), of collective substances (for example, of an army), of modes or modifications (of figure, for example, or of thinking or running) and of relations, 'the considering of one idea with relation to another'.[8] And this classification reappears in the published *Essay*, being reduced for convenience to the three heads of modes, substances and relations. It is a classification in terms of objects. But he includes another threefold classification in the published *Essay*, and puts it in the first place. This is a classification according to the mind's activities. The mind may combine simple ideas into one compound one, 'and thus all complex ideas are made',[9] a remark which seems at first sight to restrict complex ideas to ideas of this type. Secondly, the mind can bring together two ideas, whether simple or complex, and compare them with one another without uniting them into one. And thus it obtains its ideas of relations. Thirdly, it can separate ideas 'from all other ideas that accompany them in their real existence; this is called abstraction: and thus all its general ideas are made'.[10] Having given this classification in the fourth edition of the *Essay*, Locke then proceeds to give his original classification. In the ensuing chapters he follows the latter, treating first of modes, then of substances, and afterwards of relations.

Once given the general theory of simple and complex ideas, it is incumbent on Locke to justify it. It is his business to show how abstract ideas which seem to be extremely remote from the immediate data of sensation and reflection are in fact explicable in terms of the compounding or comparing of simple ideas. 'This I shall endeavour to show in the ideas we have of space, time and infinity, and some few others, that seem the most remote from those originals.'[11]

2. We have seen that complex ideas are divided by Locke into the ideas of modes, substances and relations. Modes are defined as 'complex ideas which, however compounded, contain not in them the supposition of subsisting by themselves, but are considered as dependencies on or affections of substances; such as are ideas signified by the words triangle, gratitude, murder, etc.'[12] And there are two kinds of modes, namely, simple and mixed. Simple modes are 'variations or different combinations of the same simple idea, without the

mixture of any other, (while mixed modes are) compounded of simple ideas of several kinds, put together to make one complex one'.[13] For example, if we suppose that we have the simple idea of one, we can repeat this idea or combine three ideas of the same kind to form the complex idea of three, which is a simple mode of one. According to Locke's definition it is a simple mode, because it is the result of combining ideas 'of the same kind'. The idea of beauty, however, is the idea of a mixed mode. It is the idea of a mode and not of a substance, because beauty does not subsist of itself but is an affection or mode of things. It is the idea of a mixed mode, because it consists 'of a certain composition of colour and figure, causing delight in the beholder',[14] that is to say, it consists of ideas of different kinds.

Examples of simple modes discussed by Locke are space, duration, number, infinity, modes of motion and modes of sound, colour, taste and smell. Thus 'to slide, roll, tumble, walk, creep, run, dance, leap, skip' and so on are 'all but the different modifications of motion'.[15] Similarly, blue, red and green are variations or modifications of colour. And some indication has been given above of the way in which Locke regarded distinct numbers as simple modes of number. But it is not so easy to see how he could think of space, duration and infinity as simple modes, and a brief explanation must be given here.

The simple idea of space comes to us through two senses, sight and touch. 'This space considered barely in length between any two beings, without considering anything else between them, is called distance; if considered in length, breadth and thickness, I think it may be called capacity. The term extension[16] is usually applied to it in what manner soever considered.'[17] Now, 'each different distance is a different modification of space; and each idea of any different distance or space is a simple mode of this idea'.[18] And we can repeat or add to or expand a simple idea of space until we come to the idea of a common space, for which Locke suggests the name of 'expansion'. The complex idea of this common space, in which the universe is thought of as extended, is thus due to combining or repeating or enlarging simple ideas of space.

The ultimate foundation of our idea of time is our observation of the train of ideas succeeding one another in our minds. 'Reflection on these appearances of several ideas, one after another, in our minds, is that which furnishes us with the idea of succession; and the distance between any parts of that succession, or between the appearances of any two ideas in our minds, is that we call duration.'[19] We thus obtain the ideas of succession and duration. And by observing certain phenomena occurring at regular and apparently equidistant periods we get the ideas of lengths or measures of duration, such as minutes, hours, days and years. We are then able to repeat ideas of any length of time, adding one to another without ever coming to the end of such addition; and so we form the idea of eternity. Lastly, 'by considering any part of infinite duration, as set out by periodical measures, we come by the idea of what we call time in general'.[20] That is to say, time in general, in one of the possible meanings of the term, is 'so much of infinite duration as is measured by and coexistent with the existence and motions of the great bodies of the universe, so far as we know anything of them: and in this sense time begins and ends with the frame of this sensible world'.[21]

Finite and infinite, says Locke, seem to be modes of 'quantity'. It is true that God is infinite; but He is at the same time 'infinitely beyond the reach of our narrow capacities'.[22] For present purposes, therefore, the terms 'finite' and 'infinite' are attributed only to things which are capable of increase or diminution by addition or subtraction; 'and such are the ideas of space, duration and number'.[23] And the question is, how the mind obtains the ideas of finite and infinite as modifications of space, duration and number. Or, rather, the question is, how the idea of infinity arises, since the idea of the finite is easily explicable in terms of experience.

Locke's answer is what we would expect from the foregoing paragraphs. We can continue adding to any idea of a finite space, and, however long we go on adding, we are no nearer the limit beyond which no addition is possible. We thus obtain the idea of infinite space. It does not follow that there is such a thing as infinite space; for 'our ideas are not always proofs of the existence of things';[24] but we are concerned simply with the origin of the idea. Similarly, by repeating the idea of any finite length of duration, we arrive, as has already been seen, at the idea of eternity. Again, in the addition or increase of number we can set no bound or limit.

An obvious objection to the foregoing account of the origin of the idea of the infinite is that Locke slurs over the gap between, say, the ideas of progressively larger finite spaces and the idea of infinite space. But it should be noted that he does not claim that we have or can have a positive idea of the infinite. 'Whatsoever positive ideas we have in our minds of any space, duration or number, let them be ever so great, they are still finite; but when we suppose an inexhaustible remainder, from which we remove all bounds, and wherein we allow the mind an endless progression of thoughts, without ever completing the idea, there we have our idea of infinity.'[25] He can say, therefore, with regard to number, that 'the clearest idea it (the mind) can get of infinity is the confused incomprehensible remainder of endless addible numbers, which affords no prospect of stop or boundary'.[26] In an idea of the infinite there is, of course, a positive element, namely, the idea of 'so much' space or duration of 'so great' a number; but there is also an indefinite or negative element, namely, the indefinite ideas of what lies beyond, conceived as boundless.

Commentators have drawn attention to the crudeness and inadequacy of Locke's description of the genesis of our idea of the infinite and to the fact that his account of infinite number would certainly not satisfy the modern mathematician. But whatever may be the defects of Locke's analysis, whether from the psychological or from the mathematical point of view, his main endeavour, of course, is to show that even those ideas, such as the ideas of immensity or boundless space, of eternity and of infinite number, which seem to be very remote from the immediate data of experience, can nevertheless be explained on empiricist principles without recourse to the theory of innate ideas. And on this point many, who criticize his analysis on other grounds, would agree with him.

3. Mixed modes, says Locke, consist of combinations of simple ideas of different kinds. These ideas must be compatible, of course; but, apart from this condition, any simple ideas of different kinds can be combined to form a complex idea of a mixed mode. This complex idea will then owe its unity to the mind's activity in effecting the combination. There may, indeed, be something in nature corresponding to the idea, but this is by no means necessarily the case.

As examples of mixed modes Locke gives, for instance,

obligation, drunkenness, hypocrisy, sacrilege and murder. No one of these is a substance. And each one (or, more accurately, the idea of each one) is a combination of simple ideas of different kinds. Can they be said to exist, and, if so, where? Murder, for example, can be said to exist externally only in the act of murder. Hence its external existence is transient. It has, however, a more lasting existence in men's minds, that is, as an idea. But 'there too they (mixed modes) have no longer any existence than whilst they are thought on'.[27]

They appear to have their most lasting existence in their names; that is, in the words which are used as signs for the relevant ideas. In the case of mixed modes, indeed, we are very prone, according to Locke, to take the name for the idea itself. The name plays an important role. Because we have the word 'parricide', we tend to have the corresponding complex idea of a mixed mode. But because we have no one name for the killing of an old man (who is not the murderer's father) as distinct from the killing of a young man, we do not combine the relevant simple ideas into a complex idea, nor do we regard the killing of an old man, as distinct from a young man, as a specifically different type of action. Locke was well aware, of course, that we could choose to form this complex idea as a distinct idea and attach a separate name to it. But, as will be seen presently, he believed that one of the principal ways in which we come to have complex ideas of mixed modes is through the explanation of names. And where there is no name, we are apt not to have the corresponding idea.

There are three ways in which we come to have complex ideas of mixed modes. First, 'by experience and observation of things themselves. Thus, by seeing two men wrestle or fence, we get the idea of wrestling or fencing.'[28] Secondly, by voluntarily putting together several simple ideas of different kinds: 'so he that first invented printing, or etching, had an idea of it in his mind, before it ever existed'.[29] Thirdly, 'which is the most usual way, by explaining the names of actions we never saw, or notions we cannot see'.[30] What Locke means is clear enough. A child, for example, learns the meanings of many words not by actual experience of the things signified but by having the meanings explained to him by others. He may never have witnessed sacrilege or murder, but he can obtain the complex ideas of these mixed modes if someone explains the meanings of the words in terms of ideas with which he is already familiar. In Locke's terminology, the complex idea can be conveyed to the child's mind by resolving it into simple ideas and then combining these ideas, provided, of course, that the child already has these simple ideas or, if he has not got them, that they can be conveyed to him. As a child has the idea of man and most probably also possesses the idea of killing, the complex idea of murder can easily be conveyed to him, even though he has never witnessed a murder. Indeed, the majority of people have never witnessed a murder, but they none the less have the complex idea of it.

4. It will be remembered that Locke divides complex ideas into the ideas of modes, of substances and of relations. And after treating of his distinction between simple and complex ideas I have gone on to deal with the complex ideas of simple and mixed modes, in order to illustrate more easily the application of his theory that all our ideas are derived ultimately from sensation and reflection; that is, from experience, without there being any need to postulate the hypothesis of innate ideas. But before proceeding to discuss the ideas of substance and of relation I wish to say something about his theory of primary and secondary qualities. He treats of this matter in a chapter entitled 'Some further considerations concerning our simple ideas', before, that is to say, proceeding to speak of complex ideas.

Locke makes a distinction between ideas and qualities. 'Whatsoever the mind perceives in itself or is the immediate object of perception, thought or understanding, that I call idea; and the power to produce any idea in our mind I call quality of the subject wherein that power is.'[31] Taking the example of a snowball, he explains that the snowball's powers of producing in us the ideas of white, cold and round are called by him 'qualities', while the corresponding 'sensations or perceptions' are called 'ideas'.

A further distinction must now be made. Some qualities are inseparable from a body, whatever changes it undergoes. A grain of wheat has solidity, extension, figure and mobility. If it is divided, each part retains these qualities. 'These I call original or primary qualities of body, which I think we may observe to produce simple ideas in us, viz. solidity, extension, figure, motion or rest, and number.'[32] Besides these primary qualities there are also secondary qualities. The latter are 'nothing in the objects themselves but powers to produce various sensations in us by their primary qualities'.[33] Such are colours, sounds, tastes and odours. Locke also mentions tertiary qualities, namely, the powers in bodies of producing, not ideas in us, but changes of bulk, figure, texture and motion in other bodies, so that the latter operate on our senses in a different way from the way in which they previously operated. 'Thus the sun has a power to make wax white, and fire to make lead fluid.'[34] But we can confine our attention to primary and secondary qualities.

Locke supposes that in the production of our ideas both of primary and of secondary qualities 'insensible particles' or 'imperceptible bodies' emanate from objects and act on our senses. But there is this great difference between our ideas of primary and those of secondary qualities. The former are resemblances of bodies, 'and their patterns do really exist in the bodies themselves; but the ideas produced in us by these secondary qualities have no resemblance of them at all. There is nothing like our ideas existing in the bodies themselves. They are, in the bodies we denominate from them, only a power to produce those sensations in us; and what is sweet, blue or warm in idea is but the certain bulk, figure and motion of the insensible parts in the bodies themselves, which we call so.'[35] Thus our idea of figure, for example, resembles the object itself which causes the idea in us: the object really has figure. But our idea of, say, red does not resemble the rose considered in itself. What corresponds in the rose to our idea of red is its power of producing in us the idea of red through the action of imperceptible particles on our eyes. (In modern terminology we would speak, of course, of the action of light-waves.)

It is not terminologically accurate to say that according to Locke secondary qualities are 'subjective'. For, as we have seen, what he calls secondary qualities are powers in objects of producing certain simple ideas in us. And these powers are really in the objects. Otherwise, of course, the effect would not be produced. But the ideas of secondary qualities, that is to say, the simple ideas of colours, sounds and so on, which are produced in us are not copies, as it were, of colours and sounds in the objects themselves. Obviously, we can say that the ideas of secondary qualities are subjective; but then so are the ideas of primary qualities, if we mean by 'subjective' existing in the percipient subject. Locke's point is, however, that the latter resemble what is in the object, whereas the former do not. 'The particular bulk, number, figure and motion of the parts of fire or snow are really in them, whether any one's senses perceive them or no; and therefore they may be called real qualities, because they really exist in those bodies. But light, heat, whiteness or coldness are no more really in them than sickness or pain is in manna.'[36] 'Why are whiteness and coldness in snow, and pain not, when it produces the one and the other idea in us; and can do neither, but by the bulk, figure, number and motion of its solid parts?'[37] 'Let us consider the red and white colours in porphyry: hinder light from striking on it, and its colours vanish, it no longer produces any such ideas in us; upon the return of light, it produces these appearances on us again.'[38] Again, 'Pound an almond, and the clear white colour will be altered into a dirty one, and the sweet taste into an oily one. What real alteration can the beating of the pestle make in any body, but an alteration of the texture of it?'[39] Such considerations show us that our ideas of second-ary qualities have no resembling counterparts in bodies.

This theory about secondary, as distinct from primary, qualities was not Locke's invention. It had been held by Galileo[40] and Descartes, and something of the kind had been maintained by Democritus[41] many centuries before. And at first sight at least it may appear to be a perfectly reasonable conclusion, perhaps the only reasonable conclu-sion, to be drawn from the available scientific data. Nobody, for instance, would wish to question the fact that our sen-sations of colour depend on certain differences in the wave-lengths of the light rays which affect our eyes. But it is possible to maintain that there is no necessary connection at all between admitting the scientific data which are more or less established and saying that it is improper to speak, for instance, of an object as crimson or blue. If two men argue about the physical events involved in sensation, the argument is a scientific and not a philosophical argument. If they are in agreement about the scientific data, they can dispute about the propriety or impropriety of speaking of roses as white or red, and of sugar as sweet and of tables as hard. And it might well be maintained that the scientific data provide no cogent reasons for saying anything else but what we are accustomed to say. But it would not be appropriate

to discuss the problem here for its own sake. I wish instead
to point out the very difficult position in which Locke places
himself.

That Locke's way of expressing himself is confused and
careless is scarcely open to denial. Sometimes he speaks of
'the ideas' of white and black. And it is clear enough that
if the term 'idea' were taken in the ordinary sense, these
ideas can only be in the mind. If an idea can be said to be
somewhere, where else can it be said to be but in the mind?
True, he tells that what he here calls 'ideas' are sensations
or perceptions. But, again, that our sensations are our sensations and not the object's which produces them is an obvious
truism. And Locke does not raise the question whether, if
the object is not crimson or sweet, the sensation is to be
spoken of as crimson or sweet. He simply says that we have
an idea or sensation of crimson or sweet. However, these
questions left aside, the main difficulty which arises on
Locke's premisses arises from the fact that for him an idea
is 'the immediate object of perception, thought or understanding'.[42] We do not know things immediately but me-
diately, by means of ideas. And these ideas (in the present
context we can substitute sense-data, if we like) are regarded
as representing things, as signs of them. Ideas of primary
qualities really resemble things; ideas of secondary qualities
do not. But if what we know immediately are ideas, how
can we ever know whether these ideas do or do not resemble
things? How, for the matter of that, can we be certain that
things other than our ideas even exist? For if we know only
ideas immediately, we are in no position to compare ideas
with things and ascertain whether the former resemble the
latter or not, or even to establish whether there are any
things other than ideas. On Locke's representative theory of
perception he has no means of establishing the validity of
his distinction between primary and secondary qualities.

Locke was not unaware of this difficulty. As will be seen
later on, he fell back on the notion of causality to show that
there are things which correspond to our ideas. When we
observe constantly recurring collections of simple ideas,
which are conveyed to us without choice on our part (except,
of course, for the choice not to shut one's eyes and stop one's
ears), it is at least highly probable that there are external
things which cause these ideas, at least during the time when
the latter are being passively received by our minds. And

from the common-sense point of view this inference is reliable. But, apart from any intrinsic difficulties in this theory,
it would scarcely be sufficient to warrant his distinction between primary and secondary qualities. For this seems to
require further knowledge than the knowledge that there is
'something out there'.

Berkeley, as will be shown later in connection with the
latter's philosophy, maintained that Locke's arguments to
show that colour, taste, odour and so on are ideas in our
minds and not real qualities of objects, could just as well be
employed to show that the so-called primary qualities are
ideas in our minds and not real qualities of objects. And
there is obviously a great deal to be said in favour of this
point of view. According to Locke, primary qualities are inseparable from bodies. But this is true only if he is speaking
of determinable and not of determinate primary qualities.
To take one of his own examples, the two parts of a divided
grain of wheat certainly possess extension and figure; but
they do not possess the determinate extension and figure of
the whole grain of wheat. One can also say, however, of a
pounded almond that even if, as Locke asserts, it has not the
same colour as the unpounded almond, it still possesses colour. And do not the perceived size and shape of an object
vary with the position of the percipient subject and with
other physical conditions just as much as secondary qualities
vary?

The foregoing considerations are not, of course, intended
to express doubt concerning the scientific data which can be
used to support Locke's position. They are intended to show
some of the difficulties which arise on Locke's theory when
this is presented as a philosophical theory and thus as something more than an account of scientific data. His representationist theory of perception is a particular source of difficulty. To be sure, he sometimes forgets this theory and
speaks in common-sense terms, implying that we know objects immediately; but his prevalent and, so to speak, official
position is that ideas are, in Scholastic language, the *media
quae*, or immediate objects, of knowledge. And matters are
further complicated because, as has already been noted, he
uses the term 'idea' in different senses on different occasions.

5. Mention has been made above of 'collections' of simple
ideas. We find certain groups of similar sense-data constantly recurring or tending to recur. For example, a certain

colour and a certain shape may be associated with a certain scent and with a certain softness or hardness. This is a matter of common experience. If I go into the garden on a summer day I see certain patches of colour (say, the petals of a red rose) of definite shapes and I perceive a certain scent. I can also have certain experiences through the sense of touch, by performing the action which we call touching the rose. There is thus a given constellation or cluster or collection of qualities which appear to accompany one another and which are associated together in my mind. If I go into the same garden in the dark, I do not see the colour patches, but I perceive the scent and I can have similar experiences of touch to those which I had in the daylight. And I am confident that if there were sufficient light I should see the colours which appear to go with the scent and texture. Again, certain sounds may be associated in my experience with certain colours and with a certain shape. For instance, what we call the song of the blackbird is a succession of sounds which appear to go together with the presence of certain colours and with a certain figure or shape.

There are, therefore, collections or clusters of qualities or, as Locke puts it, 'ideas'. And 'not imagining how these simple ideas can subsist by themselves, we accustom ourselves to suppose some substratum wherein they do subsist and from which they do result; which therefore we call substance'.[43] This is the idea of substance in general, namely, 'a supposition of he knows not what support of such qualities, which are capable of producing simple ideas in us; which qualities are commonly called accidents'.[44] The mind supplies the idea of a substratum, a support for qualities. More accurately, the mind supplies the idea of a substratum or support in which the primary qualities inhere and which has the power of producing in us, by means of the primary qualities, simple ideas of secondary qualities. The general idea of substance is 'nothing but the supposed but unknown support of those qualities we find existing, which we imagine cannot subsist *sine re substante*, without something to support them, (and) we call that support *substantia*, which, according to the true import of the word, is in plain English "standing under" or "upholding" '.[45]

It is important to understand that Locke is talking about the origin of our idea of substance. Bishop Stillingfleet of Worcester at first understood him to mean that substance is nothing but the figment of men's fancies. To this Locke replied that he was discussing the idea of substance, not its existence. To say that the idea is grounded in our custom of supposing or postulating some support for qualities is not to say that this supposition or postulate is unwarranted and that there is no such thing as substance. In Locke's view the inference to substance is justified; but this does not alter the fact that it is an inference. We do not perceive substances; we infer substance as the support of 'accidents', qualities or modes, because we cannot conceive the latter as subsisting by themselves. And to say that the general idea of substance is the idea of an unknown substratum is to say that the only characteristic note of the idea in our minds is that of supporting accidents; that is, of being the substratum in which the primary qualities inhere and which possesses the power of causing simple ideas in us. It is not to say that substance is a mere figment of the imagination.

This general idea of substance, which is not clear and distinct, must be distinguished from our distinct ideas of particular substances. These are 'nothing but several combinations of simple ideas. . . . It is by such combinations of simple ideas, and nothing else, that we represent particular sorts of substances to ourselves.'[46] For example, we have a number of simple ideas (of red or white, of a certain odour, a certain figure or shape, and so on) which go together in experience, and we call the combination of them by one name, 'rose'. Similarly, 'the idea of the sun, what is it but an aggregate of those several simple ideas, bright, hot, roundish, having a constant regular motion, at a certain distance from us, and perhaps some other?'[47] In fine, 'all our ideas of the several sorts of substances are nothing but collections of simple ideas, with a supposition of something to which they belong, and in which they subsist; though of this supposed something we have no clear distinct idea at all'.[48]

The simple ideas which we unite to form the complex idea of a particular substance are obtained through sensation or reflection. Thus our idea of the spiritual substance of the soul is obtained by combining together simple ideas of thinking, doubting and so on, which are obtained by reflection, with the vague and obscure notion of a substratum in which these psychical operations inhere.

It may be as well to remark at once that by 'spiritual substance' in this connection Locke means simply a substance

which thinks. In the fourth book of the *Essay*, when discussing the extent of our knowledge he declares that 'we have
the ideas of matter and thinking, but possibly shall never
be able to know, whether any mere material being thinks
or no'.[49] For all we know, divine omnipotence might be
able to confer the faculty of thinking on a material thing.
Dr. Stillingfleet, bishop of Worcester, objected that in this
case it is impossible to prove that there is in us a spiritual
substance. To this Locke replied that the concept of substance is vague and indeterminate, and that the addition of
thinking makes it a spiritual substance. That there is a spiritual substance in us can thus be shown. But if Dr. Stillingfleet means by 'spiritual substance' an immaterial substance,
the existence of such a substance in us cannot be strictly
proved by reason. Locke does not say that God can confer
the faculty of thinking on a material thing, but rather that
he does not see that it is inconceivable that God should do
so. As for the implications with regard to immortality, to
which the bishop draws attention, our certainty on this matter is derived from faith in revelation rather than from strict
philosophical demonstration.

Further, 'if we examine the idea we have of the incomprehensible Supreme Being, we shall find that we come by
it in the same way, and that the complex ideas we have both
of God and separate spirits are made up of the simple
ideas we receive from reflection'.[50] When we frame the idea
of God we enlarge to infinity the ideas of those qualities
'which it is better to have than to be without'[51] and combine
them to form one complex idea. In Himself God is simple
and not 'compounded'; but our idea of Him is complex.

Our distinct ideas of corporeal substances are made up of
the ideas of primary qualities, those of secondary qualities
(the powers in things of producing different simple ideas in
us through the senses), and those of the powers of things to
cause in other bodies or to receive in themselves such altera-
tions of primary qualities as will produce different ideas in
us from the ideas formerly produced. Indeed, 'most of the
simple ideas that make up our complex ideas of substances,
when truly considered, are only powers, however we are apt
to take them for positive qualities'.[52] For example, the
greater part of our idea of gold is made up of ideas of qualities (such as yellowness, fusibility and solubility in *aqua*

regia) which, as they exist in the gold itself, are only active or passive powers.

Now, in so far as our distinct complex ideas of particular substances are simply combinations of simple ideas received through sensation and reflection, their formation can be explained in terms of Locke's empiricist premisses. For he expressly allowed for the formation of complex ideas by combining simple ideas. But it seems to be doubtful whether his premisses permit of his explaining the formation of the general idea of substance as an occult substratum. Dr. Stillingfleet thought at first that Locke meant that substance is nothing but a combination of qualities. And in his reply Locke distinguished between our complex ideas of particular substances and the general idea of substance. The former are obtained by combining simple ideas, but the latter is not. How, then, is it obtained? By 'abstraction', Locke tells us. But earlier on he has described the process of abstraction as 'separating them (ideas) from all other ideas that accompany them in their real existence'.[53] And in the formation of the general idea of substance it is not a question of fixing the attention on one particular member of a cluster of ideas and omitting or abstracting from the rest, but rather of inferring a substratum. And in this case a novel idea seems to make its appearance which is not obtained by sensation or reflection, or by combining simple ideas, or by abstraction in the sense mentioned above. True, Locke speaks of the general idea of substance as being neither clear nor distinct. But he nevertheless speaks of this 'idea'. And if it is an idea at all, it seems difficult to explain, on Locke's premisses, how it arises. He certainly attributed to the mind an active power. But the difficulty of explaining the origin of the general idea of substance remains, unless Locke is willing to revise or re-state his premisses.

Locke's idea of substance obviously derives from Scholasticism. But it is not, as is sometimes supposed, the same as that of Aquinas. The explicit distinction between substance and accident was for Aquinas, as for Locke, the work of the reflective mind; but for the former it was a distinction made within the total datum of experience, the modified or 'accidentified' thing or substance, whereas for Locke substance lies beyond experience and is an unknown substratum. Again, on Aquinas's view substance is not an unchanging substratum, even though we can distinguish between accidental and

substantial change. Locke, however, speaks as though substance were an unchanging substratum hidden beneath the
changing phenomena. In other words, Aquinas's conception
of substance stands nearer to the point of view of common
sense than does that of Locke.

Locke's distinction between the general idea of substance
and our ideas of particular substances is connected with his
distinction between real and nominal essences. But he does
not discuss this topic before the third book of the *Essay*, and
I leave it aside for the moment to consider his account of
the origin of our idea of causality.

6. It has already been pointed out that in the first draft
of the *Essay* Locke classified relations, together with substances and modes, under the general heading of complex
ideas. But though this classification reappears in the fourth
edition, Locke gives us another as well, in which relations
stand in a class by themselves. This juxtaposition of two
methods of classification is obviously unsatisfactory. However, we are told that relations arise from the act of comparing one thing with another. If I consider Caius as such,
merely by himself, I do not compare him with any other
thing. And the same is true when I say that Caius is white.
'But when I give Caius the name *husband*, I intimate some
other person; and when I give him the name *whiter*, I intimate some other thing: in both cases my thought is led to
something beyond Caius, and there are two things brought
into consideration.'[54] Terms like 'husband', 'father', 'son',
and so on, are obviously relative terms. But there are other
terms which appear at first sight to be absolute but which
'conceal a tacit, though less observable relation'.[55] Such,
for example, is the term 'imperfect'.

Any idea, whether simple or complex, can be compared
with another idea and thus give rise to the idea of a relation.
But all our ideas of relations can in the long run be reduced
to simple ideas. This is one of the points which Locke is
most concerned to make. For if he wishes to show that his
empiricist account of the origin of our ideas is justified, he
has to show that all ideas of relations are ultimately made
up of ideas obtained through sensation or reflection. And he
proceeds to argue that this is true by applying his theory to
certain selected relations, such as causality.

But before we consider Locke's analysis of causality it is
worth while drawing attention to the ambiguous way in

which he speaks about relations. Primarily, indeed, he is concerned to show how the mind acquires its ideas of relations; that is to say, he is primarily concerned with a psychological question rather than with the ontological question, what is the nature of relations. However, as he has described an idea as whatever is the object of the mind when it thinks, it follows that relations, as thought about, are ideas. And some of his pronouncements can hardly be understood as meaning anything else but that relations are purely mental. For example, we are told that 'the nature of relation consists in the referring or comparing two things one to another'.[56] Again, 'relation is a way of comparing or considering two things together, and giving one or both of them some appellation from that comparison; and sometimes giving even the relation itself a name'.[57] Moreover, he states explicitly that a relation is 'not contained in the real existence of things, but (is) something extraneous and superinduced'.[58] And when treating later on of the abuse of words he remarks that we cannot have ideas of relations which disagree with things themselves, because relation is only a way of considering together or comparing two things and so 'an idea of my own making'.[59] At the same time Locke speaks freely about ideas of relations; and he does not make it clear what he means to imply by this. Suppose that I do not consider John simply by himself but 'compare' him with Peter, his son. I can then think of John as father, which is a relative term. Now, as we have seen, Locke says that a relation is the comparing of one thing with another. The relationship in the case in point should be the act of 'comparing' John with Peter. And the idea of the relation should be the idea of the act of comparing. But it would be odd to say that the relationship of fatherhood is the act of comparing one man with another; and it would be still more odd to say that the idea of the relationship of fatherhood is the idea of the act of comparing. Moreover, when in the fourth book of the *Essay* Locke speaks about our knowledge of the existence of God, he clearly implies that all finite things really depend on God as their cause, that is to say, that they have a real relation of dependence on God. The truth of the matter seems to be that he did not work out his theory of relations in any clear and precise way. When speaking of relations in general, he seems to say that they are all mental; but this does not prevent him from speaking about some particular relations as though they were not purely mental. This can be seen, I think, in his treatment of causality.

7. According to Locke, 'that which produces any simple or complex idea we denote by the general name *cause*; and that which is produced, *effect*'.[60] We receive our ideas of cause and effect, therefore, from observing that particular things, qualities or substances, begin to exist. Observing, for instance, that fluidity, a 'simple idea', is produced in wax by the application of a certain degree of heat, 'we call the simple idea of heat, in relation to fluidity in wax, the cause of it, and fluidity the effect'.[61] Similarly, observing that wood, a 'complex idea', is reduced to ashes, another 'complex idea', by the application of fire, we call the fire, in relation to the ashes, *cause* and the ashes *effect*. The notions of cause and effect arise, therefore, from ideas received through sensation or reflection. And 'to have the idea of cause and effect it suffices to consider any simple idea, or substance, as beginning to exist by the operation of some other, without knowing the manner of that operation'.[62] We can discriminate between different kinds of production. Thus when a new substance is produced from pre-existing material we speak of 'generation'. When a new 'simple idea' (quality) is produced in a pre-existent thing we speak of 'alteration'. When anything begins to exist without there being any pre-existent material out of which it is constituted we speak of 'creation'. But our ideas of all these different forms of production are said to be derived from ideas received through sensation and reflection, though Locke does not offer any explanation how this general proposition covers the case of our idea of creation.

In so far as causality is a relation between ideas, it is a mental construction. But it has a real foundation, and this is power; the powers, that is to say, which substances have of affecting other substances and of producing ideas in us. The idea of power is classified by Locke as a simple idea, though 'I confess power includes in it some kind of relation, a relation to action or change'.[63] And powers are divided, as we have already seen, into active and passive. We can ask, therefore, whence we derive our idea of active power and causal efficacy. The answer, according to Locke, is that our clearest idea of active power is derived from reflection or introspection. If we observe a moving ball which hits a ball at rest and sets it in motion, we do not observe any active power in the first ball; for 'it only communicates the motion it had received from another and loses in itself so much as the other received: which gives us but a very obscure idea of an active power moving in body, whilst we observe it only to transfer, but not produce any motion. For it is but a very obscure idea of power which reaches not the production of the action, but the continuation of the passion.'[64] If, however, we turn to introspection, 'we find in ourselves a power to begin or forbear, continue or end several actions of our minds and motions of our bodies, barely by a thought or preference of the mind ordering or, as it were, commanding the doing or not doing such or such a particular action'.[65] It is the exercise of volition, therefore, which gives us our clearest idea of power and causal efficacy.

Locke thus establishes to his own satisfaction the empirical foundations of our ideas of cause and effect and of causal efficacy or the exercise of active power. But he does not give any real analysis of the causal relation. However, he makes it clear, both in his arguments for the existence of God and when writing to Stillingfleet, that he was convinced that the proposition 'everything which has a beginning must have a cause' is an indubitable proposition. It has been made a charge against him that he does not explain how this proposition is established by experience. But, as the fourth book of the *Essay* makes abundantly clear, Locke believed that there is such a thing as intuitive certainty and that the mind can apprehend a necessary connection between ideas. In the case of the proposition in question Locke would doubtless say that we obtain through experience our ideas of a thing beginning to be and of cause, and that then we perceive the necessary connection between the ideas, which is expressed in the statement that everything which begins to be has a cause. Presumably he thought that this account of the matter satisfied the demands of his empiricist theory of the foundations of all our ideas and knowledge. Whether it fits in with his remarks about relations as mental constructions is another question.

8. In connection with relations Locke devotes a chapter to the ideas of identity and diversity. When we see a thing existing in a certain place at a certain instant of time we are sure that it is itself and not another thing which exists at the same time in another place, even though the two things may be alike in other respects. For we are certain that

one and the same thing cannot exist simultaneously in more than one place. Locke here refers to common linguistic usage. If we observe body A existing at time t in place x and if we observe body B existing at time t in place y, we speak of them as two different bodies, however much they may resemble one another. But if A and B both existed at time t in place x, they would be indistinguishable; and we would speak of one and the same body, not of two bodies. I do not mean that Locke thought that this view was 'simply a matter of words': I mean that he adopts the common-sense point of view which finds expression in ordinary linguistic usage. As God is eternal, immutable and omnipresent, there can be, Locke tells us, no doubt about His constant self-identity. But finite things begin to exist in time and space; and the identity of each thing will be determined, as long as it exists, by its relation to the time at which and the place in which it begins to exist. And we can therefore solve the problem of individuation by saying that the principle of individuation is 'existence itself', which determines a being of any sort to a particular time and place, incommunicable to two beings of the same kind'.[66] The last part of this definition is included because two substances of different kinds may occupy the same place at the same time. Presumably Locke is thinking primarily of God's eternity and omnipresence.

But though Locke defines identity in general in relation to the temporal and spatial co-ordinates of a thing's existence, he sees that the matter is rather more complicated than is allowed for by this formula. If two atoms are joined to form one 'mass of matter', we speak of the mass as being the same, as long as the same two atoms are conjoined. But if one atom is taken away and another added, the result is a different mass or body. In organic things, however, we are accustomed to speak of the organism as being the same organic body, even though obvious changes in the matter have taken place. A plant continues to be the same plant 'as long as it partakes of the same life, though that life be communicated to new particles of matter vitally united to the living plant, in a like continued organization conformable to that sort of plant'.[67] The case of animals is similar. The continued identity of an animal is in some ways similar to that of a machine. For we speak of a machine as being the same, even if parts of it have been repaired or renewed, because of the continued organization of all the parts with a view to the attainment of a certain end or purpose. An animal differs from a machine, however, in that in the case of the latter the motion comes from without whereas in the case of the animal the motion comes from within.

The identity of a 'simple' inorganic thing can be defined, therefore, in terms of time and place (though Locke does not mention continuity of the thing's spatio-temporal history as one of the criteria of persisting self-identity). The continued identity of a compound inorganic thing demands the continuous identity (in relation to space and time) of its constituent parts. The continuous identity of an organic body, however, is defined in relation to the organization of parts informed by a common life rather than in relation to the continued identity of the parts themselves. In fact, 'in these two cases, a mass of matter and a living body, identity is not applied to the same thing'.[68] Inorganic and organic bodies are different in kind, and the criteria of identity differ in the two cases, though in both there must be a continuous existence which has some relation to spatio-temporal co-ordinates.

How far can we apply to man the criteria of identity which are applicable to other organic bodies? Locke answers that a man's continued self-identity consists 'in nothing but a participation of the same continued life by constantly fleeting particles of matter in succession vitally united to the same organized body'.[69] He does not explain in exact terms the precise meaning of this statement, but he makes it clear that in his opinion we are accustomed, and justifiably accustomed, to speak of 'the same man' when there is bodily continuity. Whatever psychological changes may take place in a man, we still call him the same man provided that his bodily existence is continuous. If, however, we take identity of soul as the one and only criterion of sameness, strange results follow. For example, if we assume for the sake of argument the hypothesis of reincarnation, we should have to say that X, living in ancient Greece, was the same man as Y, living in mediaeval Europe, simply because the soul was the same. But this way of speaking would be very strange. 'I think nobody, could he be sure that the soul of Heliogabalus were in one of his hogs, would yet say that hog were a man or Heliogabalus.'[70] In other words, Locke appeals here to ordinary linguistic usage. We speak of a man as being the same man when there is bodily continuity. And we have here an empirical criterion of sameness. But, in Locke's opinion, there would be no way of controlling our use of the word 'same' if we said that it is identity of soul that makes a man the same man.

But though we are ordinarily accustomed to speak of a man as the same man when there is bodily continuity, we can still raise the question in what does personal identity consist, meaning by 'person' 'a thinking, intelligent being, that has reason and reflection and can consider itself as itself, the same thinking thing in different times and places'.[71] The answer to this question is consciousness, which Locke declares to be inseparable from thinking and essential to it, 'it being impossible for anyone to perceive without perceiving that he does perceive'.[72] 'As far as this consciousness can be extended backwards to any past action or thought, so far reaches the identity of that person.'[73]

Locke draws the logical conclusion that if it is possible for the same man (that is, a man who is the same man in the sense that there is bodily continuity) to have at time t^1 one distinct and incommunicable consciousness and at time t^2 another distinct and incommunicable consciousness, we could not speak of the man as being the same 'person' at time t^2 as he was at time t^1. This is 'the sense of mankind in the solemnest declaration of their opinions, human laws not punishing the madman for the sober man's actions, nor the sober man for what the madman did, thereby making them two persons; which is somewhat explained by our way of speaking in English, when we say such an one is not himself, or is beside himself; in which phrases it is insinuated as if those who now, or at least first used them, thought that self was changed, the self-same person was no longer in that man'.[74]

9. At the end of the second book of the *Essay* Locke tells us that having given an account of the source and kinds of our ideas he at first proposed to proceed immediately to consider the use which the mind makes of these ideas and the knowledge which we obtain through them. But reflection convinced him that it was necessary to treat of language before going on to discuss knowledge. For ideas and words are clearly closely connected, and our knowledge, as he puts it, consists in propositions. He therefore devoted the third book to the subject of words or language.

God made man a social being by nature. And language was to be 'the great instrument and common tie of society'.[75]

Language consists of words, and words are signs of ideas. 'The use of words is to be sensible marks of ideas; and the ideas they stand for are their proper and immediate signification.'[76] It is true that we take our words to be signs of ideas in other men's minds as well of ideas in our own minds, when, that is to say, we and they are speaking a common language. And we often suppose words to stand for things. None the less a man's words signify primarily and immediately the ideas in his own mind. Words can, of course, be used without meaning. A child can learn and use a word in parrot-fashion, without having the idea which is normally signified by it. But in this case the word is nothing but a non-significant noise.

Although Locke insists tenaciously that words are signs of ideas, he does not give any thorough explanation of the meaning of this statement. However, his general position is clear enough, if we do not pry into it too closely. Ideas, according to Locke's representationist theory, are the immediate objects of thought; and ideas, or some of them rather, stand for things or are signs of things. But ideas are private. And to communicate our ideas to others and to learn others' ideas we stand in need of 'sensible' and public signs. This need is fulfilled by words. But there is this difference between ideas, which are signs of things, and words. Those ideas which signify things or represent things are natural signs. Some of them at least, that is to say, are produced by things, though others are mental constructions. Words, however, are all conventional signs: their signification is fixed by choice or convention. Thus while the idea of man is the same in the minds of a Frenchman and an Englishman, the sign of this idea is *homme* in French and *man* in English. It is clear that Locke assumed that thought in itself is really distinct from the use of words and symbols, and that the possibility of expressing the same thought in different linguistic forms and in different language is a proof of this distinction.

There is, however, a qualification to be added to the statement that words are signs of ideas. 'Besides words which are names of ideas in the mind there are a great many others that are made use of to signify the connection that the mind gives to ideas or propositions one with another.'[77] The mind needs not only signs of the ideas 'before it' but also signs to show or intimate some action of its own in relation to these ideas. For example, 'is' and 'is not' show or intimate or express the mind's acts of affirming and denying. Locke calls words of this kind 'particles', and he includes under this heading not only the copula in propositions but also prepositions and conjunctions. These all mark or express some action of the mind in relation to its ideas.

Although Locke does not give any thorough explanation of his theory of signification, he saw clearly enough that to say that words are signs of ideas and that language, composed of conventional signs, is a means of communicating ideas, constitutes an over-simplification. 'To make words serviceable to the end of communication, it is necessary that they excite in the hearer exactly the same idea they stand for in the mind of the speaker.'[78] But this end is not always attained. For example, a word may stand for a very complex idea; and in this case it is very difficult to ensure that the word always stands for precisely the same idea in common use. 'Hence it comes to pass that men's names of very compound ideas, such as for the most part are moral words, have seldom, in two different men, the same precise signification; since one man's complex idea seldom agrees with another's, and often differs from his own, from that which he had yesterday or will have tomorrow.'[79] Again, as mixed modes are mental constructions, collections of ideas put together by the mind, it is difficult to find any fixed standard of meaning. The meaning of a word such as 'murder' depends simply on choice. And although 'common use regulates the meaning of words pretty well for common conversation',[80] there is no recognized authority which can determine the precise meaning of such words. Hence it is one thing to say that names stand for ideas and another thing to say precisely for what ideas they stand.

This 'imperfection' of language is scarcely avoidable. But there is also such a thing as an avoidable 'abuse' of words. In the first place, men not infrequently coin words which do not stand for any clear and distinct ideas. 'I shall not need here to heap up instances; every man's reading and conversation will sufficiently furnish him; or if he wants to be better stored, the great mint-masters of this kind of terms, I mean the Schoolmen and metaphysicians (under which, I think, the disputing natural and moral philosophers of these latter ages may be comprehended) have wherewithal abundantly to content him.'[81] Secondly, words are often abused in controversy through being used by the same man in different senses. Another abuse consists in taking words for things and supposing that the structure of reality must correspond to one's ways of talking about it. Locke also mentions figurative speech as one abuse of language. He would have done better perhaps to have cited it as a source of or occasion for the abuse of language. Indeed, he feels this himself to some extent. For he remarks that 'eloquence, like the fair sex, has too prevailing beauties in it to suffer itself ever to be spoken against'.[82] But his point is that 'eloquence' and rhetoric are used to move the passions and mislead the judgment, as indeed they not infrequently are; and he is too much of a rationalist to attempt to distinguish clearly between the proper and improper use of emotive and evocative language.

The misuse of words is thus a prolific source of error, and Locke evidently considered this a subject of considerable importance. For at the end of the *Essay* he insists on the need for studying the science of signs. 'The consideration, then, of ideas and words as the great instruments of knowledge makes no despicable part of their contemplation who would take a view of human knowledge in the whole extent of it. And perhaps if they were distinctly weighed and duly considered, they would afford us another sort of logic and critic than what we have been hitherto acquainted with.'[83] But it is only in very recent times that Locke's suggestion has been taken with any great seriousness.

10. As general terms play such a prominent part in discourse, it is necessary to pay special attention to their origin, meaning and use. We must have general terms; for a language made up exclusively of proper names could not be memorized, and, even if it could, it would be useless for purposes of communication. If, for example, a man was unable to refer to cows in general but had to have a proper name for every particular cow which he had seen, the names would have no meaning for another man who was unacquainted with these particular animals. But although it is obviously necessary that there should be general names, the question arises how we come to have them. 'For since all things that exist are only particulars, how come we by general terms or where find we those general natures they are supposed to stand for?'[84]

Locke replies that words become general by being made signs of general ideas, and that general ideas are formed by abstraction. 'Ideas become general by separating from them the circumstances of time and place and any other ideas that may determine them to this or that particular existence. By this way of abstraction they are made capable of representing more individuals than one; each of which having in it a conformity to that abstract idea is (as we call it) of that sort.'[85] A child, let us suppose, is acquainted first of all with one man. It later becomes acquainted with other men. And it frames an idea of the common characteristics, leaving out the characteristics peculiar to this or that individual. It thus comes to have a general idea, which is itself signified by the general term 'man'. And with the growth of experience it can go on to form other wider and more abstract ideas, each of which will be signified by a general term.

It follows that universality and generality are not attributes of things, which are all individual or particular, but of ideas and words: they are 'the inventions and creatures of the understanding, made by it for its own use, and concern only signs, whether words or ideas'.[86] Of course, any idea or any word is also particular; it is this particular idea or this particular word. But what we call general or universal words and ideas are universal in their signification. That is to say, a universal or general idea signifies a sort of thing, like cow or sheep or man; and the general term stands for the idea as signifying a sort of thing. 'That, then, which general words signify is a *sort* of things; and each of them does that by being a sign of an abstract idea in the mind, to which idea, as things existing are found to agree, so they come to be ranked under that name; or, which is all one, be of that sort.'[87]

To say, however, that universality belongs only to words and ideas is not to say that there is no objective foundation for the universal idea. 'I would not here be thought to forget, much less to deny, that nature in the production of things makes several of them alike: there is nothing more obvious, especially in the races of animals and all things propagated by seed.'[88] But it is the mind which observes these likenesses among particular things and uses them as the occasion to form general ideas. And when a general idea has been formed, say the idea of gold, a particular thing is said to be or not to be gold in so far as it conforms or does not conform to this idea.

Locke occasionally speaks in a manner which suggested to Berkeley that the general idea was a composite image consisting of incompatible elements. For instance, he speaks of the general idea of a triangle, which 'must be neither oblique nor rectangle, neither equilateral, equicrural, nor scalenon; but all and none of these at once. . . . It is an idea wherein some parts of several different and inconsistent ideas are put together.'[89] But this statement must be understood in the light of what Locke says elsewhere about 'abstraction'. He does not say that the general idea of a triangle is an image; nor does he say that it is composed of mutually inconsistent or incompatible ideas. He says that it is composed of 'parts' of different and inconsistent ideas. That is to say, the mind omits the notes peculiar to this or that kind of triangle and puts together the common characteristics of different kinds of triangle to form the general idea of triangularity. Abstraction is thus depicted as a process of elimination or leaving out and of putting together what remains, common characteristics. This may, indeed, be unfortunately vague; but there is no need to make Locke talk absolute nonsense by ascribing to him the view that general ideas are composed of mutually incompatible elements.

11. It is important not to understand the word 'abstraction' in the present context as meaning the abstraction of the real essence of a thing. Locke distinguishes two senses of the term 'real essence'. 'The one is of those who, using the word essence for they know not what, suppose a certain number of those essences, according to which all natural things are made, and wherein they do exactly every one of them partake, and so become of this or that species.'[90] This theory is, says Locke, an untenable hypothesis, as is shown by the production of monsters. For the theory presupposes fixed and stable specific essences, and it cannot explain the fact of borderline cases and of variations in type. In other words, it is incompatible with the available empirical data. Further, the hypothesis of stable but unknown specific essences is so useless that it might well be discarded even if it were not contradicted by the empirical data. 'The other and more rational opinion (about real essences) is of those who look on all natural things to have a real but unknown constitution of their insensible parts, from which flow those sensible qualities which serve us to distinguish them one from another, according as we have occasion to rank them into sorts under common denominations.'[91] But though this opinion is 'more rational', there can obviously be no ques-

tion of abstracting unknown essences. Every collection of
simple ideas depends on some 'real constitution' of a thing;
but this real constitution is unknown by us. Hence it cannot
be abstracted.

From real essences Locke distinguishes nominal essences.
We are accustomed to decide whether a given thing is gold
or not by observing whether it possesses those common
characteristics, possession of which is regarded as necessary
and sufficient for a thing to be classed as gold. And the complex idea of these characteristics is the nominal essence of
gold. This is why Locke can say that 'the abstract idea for
which the (general) name stands and the essence of the
species is one and the same',[92] and that 'every distinct
abstract idea is a distinct essence'.[93] It is the nominal essence,
therefore, which is abstracted, by leaving out characteristics
peculiar to individual things as individuals and retaining their
common characteristics.

Locke adds that in the case of simple ideas and modes the
real and nominal essences are the same. 'Thus a figure including a space between three lines is the real as well as
nominal essence of a triangle.'[94] But in the case of substances
they are different. The nominal essence of gold is the abstract idea of the observable characteristics common to the
things which are classed as gold; but its real essence, or substance, is 'the real constitution of its insensible parts, on
which depend all those properties of colour, weight, fusibility, fixedness, etc., which are to be found in it'.[95] And this
real essence, the particular substance of gold, is unknown by
us. Locke's way of speaking is certainly open to criticism. For
in the case of the universal idea of triangularity it is inappropriate to speak about 'real essence' at all, if the latter is
defined as the real but unknown constitution of the insensible parts of a material substance. But his general meaning is
sufficiently clear, namely, that in the case of material substances it makes sense to speak of a real essence distinct
from the nominal essence or abstract idea, whereas in the
case of triangularity it does not.

Chapter Six

LOCKE (3)

Knowledge in general — The degrees of knowledge — The extent and reality of our knowledge — Knowledge of the existence of God — Knowledge of other things — Judgment and probability — Reason and faith.

1. In the draft of the *Essay* Locke remarks that 'it remains now to enquire what kind of knowledge it is we have of or by these ideas, the proper object of knowledge being truth, which lies wholly in affirmation or negation, or propositions either mental or verbal, which is no more but apprehending things to be as really as they are and do exist, or expressing our apprehensions by words fitted to make others apprehend as we do'.[1] But in the published *Essay* he starts the fourth book with the unequivocally representationist statement, 'Seeing the mind in all its thoughts and reasonings hath no other immediate object but its own ideas, which it alone does or can contemplate, it is evident that our knowledge is only conversant about them'.[2] And he goes on to say that knowledge consists exclusively in the perception of the connection and agreement or disagreement and repugnance of any of our ideas. When we see that the three angles of a triangle are equal to two right angles, we perceive a necessary connection between ideas. And therefore we can legitimately be said to know that the three angles of a triangle are equal to two right angles.

But what is meant by 'agreement' and 'disagreement' of ideas? The primary form of agreement or disagreement is what Locke calls 'identity or diversity'. The mind, for example, knows immediately and infallibly that the ideas of white and round (when he has received them through sense-experience, needless to say) are what they are and not the other ideas which we call red and square. A man may, indeed, be in error about the right terms for these ideas; but he cannot possess them without seeing that each agrees with itself and disagrees with other and different ideas. The second form mentioned by Locke is called 'relative'. He is here thinking of the perception of relations between ideas, which may be relations of agreement or of disagreement. Mathematical propositions provide the chief, though not the only, example of relational knowledge. Thirdly, there is agreement or disagreement of coexistence. Thus our knowledge of the truth that a substance remains unconsumed by fire is a knowledge that the power of remaining unconsumed by fire coexists with or always accompanies the other characteristics which together form our complex idea of the substance in question. Finally, there is agreement or disagreement 'of real existence'. Locke gives as an example the statement 'God is'. That is to say, we know that the idea of God 'agrees with' or corresponds to a really existent being.

Two points in this classification of forms of knowledge are immediately evident. In the first place knowledge of identity and knowledge of coexistence are both relational. Locke, indeed, explicitly admits this. 'Identity and coexistence are truly nothing but relations.'[3] But he goes on to claim that they have peculiar features of their own which justify their consideration under separate headings, though he does not explain what these peculiar features are. In the second place knowledge of real existence should evidently cause Locke considerable difficulty. For if an idea is defined as whatever is the object of the mind when it thinks, it is not easy to see how we can ever know that our ideas correspond to real existents, in so far as these latter are not our ideas. However, leaving this point aside for the moment, we can say that knowledge consists for Locke either in perceiving the agreement or disagreement between ideas or in perceiving the agreement or disagreement of ideas with things which are not themselves ideas.

2. Locke proceeds to examine the degrees of our knowledge. And here he shows a decidedly rationalistic turn of mind. For he exalts intuition and demonstration, which is characteristic of, though not confined to, mathematical knowledge, at the expense of what he calls 'sensitive knowledge'. He does not, of course, recant his general empiricist theory

that all our ideas come from experience, from sensation or
reflection. But, presupposing this theory, he then clearly
takes mathematical knowledge as the paradigm of knowledge.
And on this point at least he shows an affinity with
Descartes.

'If we reflect on our own ways of thinking, we shall find
that sometimes the mind perceives the agreement or disagreement of two ideas immediately by themselves, without the
intervention of any other: and this, I think, we may call
intuitive knowledge.'[4] Thus the mind perceives immediately
by intuition that white is not black and that three are more
than two.[5] This is the clearest and most certain kind of
knowledge which the human mind can attain. There is no
room for doubt, and 'it is on this intuition that depends all
the certainty and evidence of all our knowledge'.[6]

The second degree of knowledge is demonstrative knowledge, where the mind does not perceive immediately the
agreement or disagreement of ideas but needs intervening
ideas to be able to do so. Locke is thinking primarily of
mathematical reasoning, where a proposition is proved or
demonstrated. We do not, he says, have immediate intuitive
knowledge that the three angles of a triangle are equal to two
right angles: we need 'intervening ideas' with the aid of
which the agreement in question is proved. Demonstrative
knowledge of this kind lacks, we are told, the facility and
clarity of intuition. At the same time each step in the
reasoning has intuitive certainty. But if Locke had paid
more attention to syllogistic reasoning than he actually did,
he might have felt some doubt about the truth of this last
statement. For there can be a valid syllogistic argument
containing a contingent proposition. And the truth of a
contingent proposition is not known with what Locke calls
intuitive certainty. There is no necessary connection between
the terms; hence we cannot perceive it immediately. In other
words, as commentators have pointed out, Locke's idea of
demonstration inevitably restricts the range of demonstrative knowledge to a very narrow field.

Whatever comes short of intuition and demonstration is
not knowledge 'but faith or opinion, at least in all general
truths'.[7] However, there is sensitive knowledge of particular existence. Some people, Locke remarks, may express doubt
whether there are any existent things corresponding to our
ideas; 'but yet here, I think, we are provided with an evi-

dence that puts us past doubting'.[8] When a man sees the sun by day his perception is different from his thought of the sun during the night; and there is an unmistakable difference between smelling the scent of a rose and recalling the scent of a rose. If he says that all may be a dream, he must none the less admit that there is a great difference between dreaming of being in the fire and actually being in it.

3. There are, therefore, three degrees of knowledge: intuitive, demonstrative and sensitive. But how far is our knowledge capable of extending? If knowledge consists in perceiving the agreement or disagreement between ideas, it follows that 'we can have knowledge no further than we have ideas'.[9] But according to Locke 'the extent of our knowledge comes not only short of the reality of things, but even of the extent of our own ideas'.[10] And it is necessary to examine what he means by this. We can follow him in taking one by one the four forms of knowledge mentioned in the first section and in seeing how far our knowledge extends or can extend in each of these ways of perceiving the agreement or disagreement of our ideas.

In the first place, our knowledge of 'identity and diversity' extends as far as our ideas extend. That is to say, we cannot have an idea without intuitively perceiving that it is itself and that it is different from any other idea.

But this is not the case with regard to our knowledge of 'coexistence'. 'In this our knowledge is very short, though in this consists the greatest and most material part of our knowledge concerning substances.'[11] Our idea of a particular kind of substance is a collection of simple ideas coexisting together. For example, 'our idea of a flame is a body hot, luminous and moving upward; of gold, a body heavy to a certain degree, yellow, malleable and fusible'.[12] But what we perceive is a factual coexistence or togetherness of simple ideas: we do not perceive any necessary connection between them. Our complex ideas of substances are made up of ideas of their secondary qualities, and these depend upon 'the primary qualities of their minute and insensible parts; or if not upon them, upon something yet more remote from our comprehension'.[13] And if we do not know the root from which they spring, we cannot know what qualities necessarily result from or are necessarily incompatible with the insensible constitution of the substance. Hence we cannot know what secondary qualities must always coexist with the complex idea which we have of the substance in question or what qualities are incompatible with this complex idea. 'Our knowledge in all these inquiries reaches very little farther than our experience.'[14] Again, we cannot discern any necessary connection between the powers of a substance to effect sensible changes in other bodies and any of those ideas which together form our notion of the substance in question. 'Experience is that which in this part we must depend on. And it were to be wished that it were more improved.'[15] And if we turn from bodies to spirits, we find ourselves even more in the dark.

The reason which Locke gives for saying that our knowledge of 'coexistence' does not extend very far is of considerable interest. It is clear that he has in his mind an ideal standard of knowledge. To have a 'real knowledge' of the coexistence of the ideas which together form the nominal essence of a thing would mean seeing their necessary connections with one another, in a manner analogous to that in which we perceive necessary connections between ideas in mathematical propositions. But we do not perceive these necessary connections. We see that the complex idea of gold comprises the idea of yellowness as a matter of fact; but we do not perceive a necessary connection between yellowness and the other qualities which together form a complex idea of gold. Hence our knowledge is judged to be deficient; it is simply a knowledge based on experience, on *de facto* connections. We cannot demonstrate propositions in natural science or 'experimental philosophy': 'certainty and demonstration are things we must not, in these matters, pretend to'.[16] We cannot attain 'general, instructive, unquestionable truths'[17] concerning bodies. In all this Locke's attitude seems to be that of a 'rationalist', who takes mathematical knowledge as the ideal standard, rather than that of an 'empiricist'.

At the same time I do not think that this point of view should be over-emphasized. Locke does, indeed, imply that natural science is deficient precisely because it is empirical; but he also attributes its shortcomings simply to contemporary ignorance. 'Though we are not without ideas of these primary qualities of bodies in general, yet not knowing what is the particular bulk, figure and motion of the greatest part of the bodies of the universe, we are ignorant of the several powers, efficacies and ways of operation

whereby the effects which we daily see are produced.'[18] Here
it is a question simply of ignorance. Our senses are not acute
enough to perceive the 'minute particles' of bodies and discover their operations. Our experiments and researches do
not carry us very far, though 'whether they will succeed
again another time, we cannot be certain. This hinders our
certain knowledge of universal truths concerning natural
bodies; and our reason carries us herein very little beyond
particular matter of fact.'[19] Locke does, indeed, strike a
pessimistic note. For he is 'apt to doubt that how far soever
human industry may advance useful and experimental philosophy in physical things, scientifical (knowledge) will still
be out of reach'.[20] And he asserts that though our ideas of
bodies will serve us for ordinary practical purposes, 'we are
not capable of scientifical knowledge; nor shall ever be able to
discover general, instructive and unquestionable truths concerning them. Certainty and demonstration are things we
must not, in these matters, pretend to.'[21] We have here,
as was remarked in the last paragraph, a depreciation of
natural science because it falls short of an ideal knowledge:
we have a clear statement that natural science can never
become 'science'. At the same time, however, Locke's pessimistic remarks about natural science are due in large part
simply to contemporary ignorance and lack of the technical
equipment required for startling advances and discoveries.
Hence, while it is necessary to note the rationalistic attitude which is apparent in the fourth book of the *Essay*, I think
that we should be careful not to over-emphasize it in this
particular context.

As for the third kind of knowledge, relational knowledge, it is difficult to say how far it is capable of extending,
'because the advances that are made in this part of knowledge, depending on our sagacity in finding intermediate
ideas that may show the relations and habitudes of ideas
whose coexistence is not considered, it is a hard matter
to tell when we are at the end of such discoveries'.[22] Locke
is thinking primarily of mathematics. Those who are ignorant of algebra, he says, cannot imagine its potentialities,
and we cannot determine in advance the further resources
and utility of mathematics. But he is not thinking exclusively of mathematics, and he suggests that ethics might be
made a demonstrative science. Locke's ideas about ethics,
however, will be left to the next chapter.

Finally, there is knowledge of the actual existence of things. Locke's position here is easily summarized. 'We have an intuitive knowledge of our own existence; and a demonstrative knowledge of the existence of a God; of the existence of any thing else we have no other but a sensitive knowledge, which extends not beyond the objects present to our senses.'[23] As for knowledge of our own existence, we perceive it so plainly and with such certainty that it neither needs nor is capable of proof. 'If I doubt of all other things, that very doubt makes me perceive my own existence and will not suffer me to doubt of that.'[24] As we have seen in the last chapter, Locke does not mean that I have intuitive certainty of the existence of an immaterial soul in myself. But I perceive clearly that I am a thinking self, though precisely what is intuited Locke does not explain. Our knowledge of God and of things other than God and ourselves will be considered in the following sections of this chapter. Meanwhile, I raise a question which Locke treats under the heading 'the reality of our knowledge'.

We have just seen that according to Locke we can know that things exist. And we can know something about them. But how can we do this if the immediate object of knowledge is an idea? 'It is evident that the mind knows not things immediately, but only by the intervention of the ideas it has of them. Our knowledge therefore is real only so far as there is a conformity between our ideas and the reality of things. But what shall be here the criterion? How shall the mind, when it perceives nothing but its own ideas, know that they agree with things themselves?'[25] The question is clear enough. What is Locke's answer?

We can put mathematical and moral knowledge on one side. Pure mathematics gives us certain and real knowledge, but it is knowledge 'only of our own ideas'.[26] That is to say, pure mathematics is formal: it makes statements about the properties of 'ideas', such as the idea of a triangle or circle, and about the relations between ideas, but not about the world of things. And the truth of mathematical propositions is not affected by the presence or absence of things corresponding to the ideas which the mathematician employs in his reasoning. If he makes a statement about the triangle or the circle, the existence or non-existence of a corresponding triangle or circle in the world is entirely irrelevant to the truth of his statement. If the latter is true, it remains true even though there may be no existent triangle or circle which corresponds to the mathematician's ideas of triangles or circles. For the truth of his statement follows simply from his definitions and axioms. 'In the same manner the truth and certainty of moral discourses abstracts from the lives of men and the existence of those virtues in the world whereof they treat. Nor are Tully's Offices (Cicero's *De officiis*) less true because there is nobody in the world that exactly practises his rules and lives up to that pattern of a virtuous man which he has given us and which existed nowhere, when he writ, but in idea.'[27]

The situation is different, however, with regard to simple ideas. For these are not fabricated by the mind, as is the idea of a perfect circle; they are imposed on the mind. Hence they must be the product of things operating on the mind, and they must have a conformity with things. In view of the fact that colours, for example, bear little resemblance to the powers in objects which produce in us the relevant simple ideas, one might expect Locke to explain more precisely the nature of this 'conformity'. However, he is satisfied with remarking that 'the idea of whiteness, or bitterness, as it is in the mind, exactly answering that power which is in any body to produce it there, has all the real conformity it can, or ought to have, with things without us. And this conformity between our simple ideas and the existence of things is sufficient for real knowledge.'[28] It may be sufficient; but this is not the point at issue. The question is, how do we know, or rather how can we know on Locke's premises, that there is any conformity at all?

Simple ideas, therefore, are said to have a conformity with external objects. What, then, of complex ideas? This question concerns our ideas of substances. For as other complex ideas are 'archetypes of the mind's own making, not intended to be the copies of any thing',[29] the problem of their conformity is not so pressing. They can give us 'real' knowledge as in mathematics, even if nothing corresponds to them outside the mind. But ideas of substances are referred, to use Locke's language, to archetypes outside us; that is to say, they are thought to correspond to external reality. And the question arises, how can we know that they correspond supposing that they do in fact correspond in some way to external reality? This question refers, of course, to nominal essences; for according to Locke we do not know the real essences of things. His answer is that our complex ideas of substances are formed of simple ideas, and that 'whatever simple ideas have been found to coexist in any substance, these we may with confidence join together again, and so make abstract ideas of substances. For whatever have once had an union in nature may be united again.'[30]

Of course, if qualities are simple *ideas*, and if we know immediately only ideas, we can never compare the collections of qualities in our minds with the clusters of qualities outside our minds. And Locke's answer certainly does not clear up this difficulty. But though he talks about 'simple ideas' he also talks about our ideas of qualities and of substances. In other words, he oscillates between a representationist view, according to which ideas are the object of knowledge, and the view that ideas are simply psychic modifications by means of which we know things directly. Or, more accurately, he oscillates, not between two 'views' (since his declared view is that the object of knowledge is ideas), but between two ways of talking, speaking sometimes as though the idea is the *medium quod* of knowledge (his declared view) and sometimes as though it is the *medium quo* of knowledge. And this ambiguity may be partly responsible for his failure to deal seriously with the difficulty which arises out of his representationism.

However, let us assume that we can know the correspondence between our complex ideas of substances and existent sets of compresent qualities. As we have seen, Locke will not allow that any necessary connections are perceived between these qualities. Hence our knowledge, though real, does not extend beyond the actual experience which we have had, and if we express this knowledge in the form of general or universal propositions we cannot legitimately .claim for the latter that they are more than probably true.

4. In the preceding section mention was made of Locke's view that we have, or rather can have, demonstrative knowledge of the existence of God. By this he means that we can deduce the existence of God 'from some part of our intuitive knowledge'.[31] And the intuitively known truth from which he starts is our knowledge of our own existence. More accurately perhaps, the individual's demonstrative knowledge of God's existence is based on his intuitive knowledge of his own existence. But knowledge of one's own existence does not by itself prove God's existence. We need

other intuitively known truths. And the first of these is the proposition that 'bare nothing can no more produce any real being than it can be equal to two right angles'.[32] Intuitive knowledge of my own existence shows me that at least one thing exists. Now, I know that I did not exist from eternity but had a beginning. But that which had a beginning must have been produced by something else; it cannot have produced itself. There must, therefore, says Locke, be something which existed from eternity. He does not make the steps of the argument very clear. But what he evidently means is that for anything at all to exist at any time there must be a being which itself had no beginning; for, if this were not the case, some being would have produced itself or have 'simply happened', and this is inconceivable. That anything which begins to be does so through the efficacy of an already existent extrinsic cause is obviously taken by Locke to be a self-evident proposition. But he does not explain whether he intends to rule out an infinite regress in the temporal order (an infinite regress, that is to say, going back into the past) or an infinite regress in the order of existential dependence here and now, without reference to the past. However, from various remarks which he makes it seems to follow that he is thinking of an infinite regress going back into the past. If this is the case, his line of argument differs from that of Aquinas, for example, who tried to develop a proof of God's existence which would be independent of the question whether or not there is a series of temporal events reaching back indefinitely into the past. In fact, Locke's argument is carelessly constructed and lacks precision. Some would rule it out altogether on the ground that what Locke regards as self-evident truths are not self-evidently true. But even if we are not prepared to do this, it is difficult to say very much about it, because Locke does not state it clearly.

If we assume, however, that there is a being which existed from eternity, the question arises, what is its nature? Here Locke uses the principle that 'what had its being and beginning from another must also have all that which is in and belongs to its being from another too'.[33] As, therefore, man finds in himself powers, and as he also enjoys perception and knowledge, the eternal being on which he depends must also be powerful and intelligent. For a thing which is itself void of knowledge cannot produce a knowing being. And from this Locke concludes that 'there is an eternal, most powerful and most knowing being; which whether anyone will please to call God, it matters not. The thing is evident, and from this idea duly considered will easily be deduced all those other attributes which we ought to ascribe to this eternal being.'[34]

5. A man knows his own existence by intuition and that of God by demonstration. 'The knowledge of the existence of any other thing we can have only by sensation.'[35] For there is no necessary connection between the idea which a man has of anything other than God and the existence of the thing. The fact that we have an idea of a thing does not prove that it exists. We know that it exists only when it is operating upon us. 'It is therefore the actual receiving of ideas from without that gives us notice of the existence of other things and makes us know that something doth exist at that time without us.'[36] The receiving of ideas from without is sensation, and we know the existence of things which affect our sense-organs only while they are doing so. When I open my eyes, it does not depend on my choice what I see; I am acted upon. Further, if I put my hand too near the fire, I feel pain, whereas when I have the mere idea of putting my hand too near the fire I do not suffer pain. Such considerations show us that our confidence in the existence of other things is not ill-grounded. True, our knowledge of the existence of external things extends only as far as the present testimony of our senses; but it is probable that the table which I saw a moment ago is still existing; and it is folly to look for demonstrative knowledge before we are prepared to assent to an existential proposition. 'He that in the ordinary affairs of life would admit of nothing but direct plain demonstration would be sure of nothing in this world but of perishing quickly. The wholesomeness of his meat or drink would not give him reason to venture on it: and I would fain know what it is he could do upon such grounds as are capable of no doubt, no objection.'[37]

6. The mind is said to 'know' when 'it certainly perceives and is undoubtedly satisfied of the agreement or disagreement of any ideas'.[38] We know that X is Y when we clearly perceive a necessary connection between them. But the mind has what Locke calls another 'faculty', namely, judgment, which is 'the putting ideas together or separating them from one another in the mind when their certain agree-

ment or disagreement is not perceived but presumed to be so. . . . And if it so unites or separates them as in reality things are, it is right judgment.'[39] Judgment is therefore concerned with probability and yields 'opinion'.

Probability is defined by Locke as 'the appearance of agreement upon fallible proofs'.[40] That is to say, when we judge that a proposition is probably true, that which moves us to give assent to the proposition as probably true is not its self-evident character (for in this case we would know it to be certainly true) but extrinsic grounds or reasons which are not sufficient to demonstrate its truth. There are two main extrinsic grounds for believing a proposition to be true though it is not self-evidently true. The first of these is 'the conformity of anything with our own knowledge, observation and experience'.[41] For instance, so far as my experience goes, iron sinks in water. If I have often and always seen this happen, the probability that it will happen on future occasions is proportionately greater than if I had only seen it happen once. In fact, when consistent experiences give rise to judgment and this judgment is constantly verified in further experience, probability rises so high that it influences our expectations and actions in practically the same way that the evidence of demonstration influences them. The second ground for believing a proposition to be probably true is testimony. And here again there can be degrees of probability. If, for example, there are a large number of reliable witnesses to some events, and if their testimonies agree, there is a much higher degree of probability than if the witnesses are few and unskilful or if the accounts given disagree with one another.

Locke divides 'the propositions we receive upon inducements of probability'[42] into two classes. The first class consists of propositions concerning 'matters of fact' which fall under observation and can be the object of human testimony. That it froze in England last winter would be an example. The second class consists of propositions concerning matters which cannot be the object of human testimony because they are incapable of empirical investigation. That there are angels would be one example, and that heat consists in 'a violent agitation of the imperceptible minute parts of the burning matter'[43] would be another. In such cases it is from analogy that we draw the grounds of probability. Observing the different stages in the hierarchy of levels of being below

man (animals, plants, inorganic things), we can judge it
probable that between man and God there are finite immaterial spirits. Again, observing that the rubbing of two
bodies together produces heat, we can argue by analogy that
heat probably consists in the violent motion of imperceptible
particles of matter.

It is clear, therefore, that for Locke the propositions of
the natural sciences can enjoy at best only a very high degree
of probability. This view is closely connected, of course,
with his conviction that we know only the nominal essences
of things and not their 'real essences', in the sense explained
in the last chapter. Historical propositions too, which rest
on human testimony, can enjoy only varying degrees of
probability. And Locke reminds his readers that the degree of probability which is enjoyed by a historical statement depends on the value of the relevant testimony and not
on the number of people who may have repeated the statement.

7. It might be expected perhaps that Locke would have
included all statements accepted by faith in the class of
probable propositions. But he did not do so. For he admitted a divine revelation which gives us certainty about
the truth of the doctrines revealed, since the testimony of
God admits of no doubt. 'We may as well doubt of our own
being, as we can whether any revelation from God be true.
So that faith is a settled and sure principle of assent and assurance, and leaves no manner of room for doubt or hesita-
tion.'⁴⁴ This does not mean, of course, that all truths about
God are accepted on faith. For Locke, as we have seen, asserted the demonstrative character of our knowledge of God's
existence. Revealed truths are those which are above,
though not contrary to, reason, and the truth of which we
know on the testimony of God. In other words, Locke
continued the mediaeval distinction between truths about
God which can be discovered by the unaided human reason
and those which cannot be known unless God reveals them.

At the same time Locke had a great dislike of what he
called 'enthusiasm'. He was thinking of the attitude of
those people who are prone to assume that some idea which
comes into their heads constitutes a private divine revelation,
a product of divine inspiration. They do not bother about objective reasons in support of the claim that their ideas are
inspired by God: strong feeling is for them more persuasive

than any reason. 'They are sure because they are sure; and their persuasions are right because they are strong in them.'[45] They say that they 'see' and 'feel'; but what is it they 'see'? That some proposition is evidently true or that it has been revealed by God? The two questions must be distinguished. And if the proposition is not evidently true or if it is not put forward as probably true on the basis of some objective grounds for belief, reasons must be given for thinking that it is in fact revealed by God. But for the people suffering from 'enthusiasm' a proposition 'is a revelation because they firmly believe it, and they believe it because it is a revelation'.[46] Locke insisted, therefore, that even though God can certainly reveal truths which transcend reason, in the sense that reason alone cannot establish them as true, it must be shown by reason that they are in fact revealed before we can be expected to accept them by faith. 'If strength of persuasion be the light which must guide us, I ask how shall anyone distinguish between the delusions of Satan and the inspirations of the Holy Ghost?'[47] After all, 'God, when He makes the prophet, does not unmake the man. He leaves all his faculties in the natural state, to enable him to judge of his inspirations whether they be of divine origin or no.'[48] By disposing of reason to make room for revelation 'enthusiasm' does away with both. In his treatment of enthusiasm Locke's strong common sense is very much in evidence.

Locke did not question, therefore, the possibility of divine revelation. In fact he believed in doctrines such as that of the immortality of the soul and the resurrection of the body on the testimony of God's word. But he insisted that propositions which are contrary to reason cannot have been revealed by God. And it is clear, I think, that when he talks in this way he is thinking very largely of Catholic dogmas such as that of transubstantiation to which he explicitly refers in his chapter on wrong assent or error.[49] The retort might obviously be made that if there is good reason for thinking that a proposition is revealed by God, it cannot be contrary to reason even though it is above reason.[50] But Locke, having made up his mind that certain doctrines were contrary to reason, concluded that they cannot have been revealed and that there cannot be any adequate reason for thinking that they have been revealed. To discuss controversial questions of this kind here would be out of place. But it is worth while drawing attention to the fact that Locke continued the point of view of the Cambridge Platonists or 'latitudinarians'. While rejecting on the one hand what he regarded as the misguided enthusiasm of self-appointed prophets and preachers, he rejected also what would appear to be the logical consequences of a belief in the possibility of divine revelation, namely, that if there are good reasons for thinking that God has revealed truth through a certain mouthpiece no proposition taught by the accredited authority can be contrary to reason. Locke would doubtless reply that the only criterion for deciding whether a doctrine is contrary to reason or simply 'above reason' is reason itself. But he makes his position easier to maintain by admitting, sincerely enough, the possibility of divine revelation without embarking upon the question where this revelation is to be found and through what particular organ or organs it has been made.

Locke's general attitude of moderation and his dislike of extremes, together with his conviction that the reach of certainty is very limited whereas the field of probability, in its various degrees, is very large, led him to espouse, within limits, the cause of toleration. I say 'within limits' because in his *Letter concerning Toleration* he says that toleration should not be extended to atheists, to those whose religion involves allegiance to a foreign power, and to those whose religious faith does not permit them to extend to others the toleration which they claim for themselves. Atheism, in his opinion, necessarily involves lack of moral principles and disregard of the binding character of oaths, covenants and promises. As for the other two classes, he is evidently thinking primarily of Catholics, even if he mentions the Mohammedans. On this matter Locke shared the common attitude of his fellow-countrymen at the time towards Catholics, though it would be interesting to know what he really thought, if he gave any real attention to the matter, of the methods employed in the courts by Lord Chief Justice Scroggs in the trials arising from the 'Popish Plot'. Presumably he sympathized with the ulterior political aims of Shaftesbury and his faction. However, if one takes into consideration the contemporary attitude both in his own country and elsewhere, the remarkable thing is that he advocated toleration at all. He was evidently well aware of this, since he published his writings on the matter anonymously.

Chapter Seven

LOCKE (4)

Locke's ethical theory — The state of nature and the natural moral law — The right of private property — The origins of political society; the social compact — Civil government — The dissolution of government — General remarks — Locke's influence.

1. In the first chapter on Locke's philosophy we saw that in rejecting the theory of innate ideas he denied both that there are innate speculative principles and that there are innate practical or moral principles. Our moral ideas must, therefore, be derived from experience, in the sense that they must, as Locke puts it, 'terminate in simple ideas'; that is to say, at least the elements from which they are composed must be derived from sensation or reflection. But Locke did not think that this empiricist account of the origin of our moral ideas is any bar to our recognizing moral principles which are known with certainty. For once we have obtained our ideas, we can examine and compare them and discern relations of agreement and disagreement. This enables us to enunciate moral rules, and if they express necessary relations of agreement or disagreement between ideas they are certain and knowable as certain. We have to distinguish between the ideas or terms which occur in an ethical proposition and the relation asserted in the proposition. In a moral rule the ideas must be severally derivable, ultimately at least, from experience; but the truth or validity of a moral rule is independent of its observance. If I say, for example, that truth-telling is morally good, the ideas of telling truth and of moral goodness must be ultimately derivable from experience; but the relation asserted between these ideas holds even if most people tell lies.

If we bear in mind this point of view, it is not so surprising as it might otherwise appear that in the third and fourth books of the *Essay* Locke proposes a 'rationalistic' ideal of ethics. He there remarks that 'morality is capable of demonstration, as well as mathematics'.[1] The reason is that ethics is concerned with ideas which are real essences. In natural science we do not know the real, but only the nominal, essences of things. In mathematics, however, this distinction between nominal essence and real essence falls away; and it is the same with ethics. Our idea of justice is derived ultimately from experience, in the sense that the elements of which it is composed are so derived, but there is no entity 'out there' called justice, the real essence of which could be unknown to us. There is, therefore, no reason why ethics should not be made a demonstrative science, 'For certainty being but the perception of the agreement or disagreement of our ideas and demonstration nothing but the perception of such agreement by the intervention of other ideas or mediums; our moral ideas, as well as mathematical, being archetypes themselves and so adequate and complete ideas; all the agreement or disagreement which we shall find in them will produce real knowledge, as well as in mathematical figure.'[2] By saying that our moral ideas are themselves archetypes Locke means, for example, that the idea of justice is itself the standard by which we discriminate between just and unjust actions; justice is not a subsistent entity with which an idea of justice must agree in order to be a true idea. If, therefore, we take the trouble to define our moral terms clearly and precisely, 'moral knowledge may be brought to so great clearness and certainty'[3] as our mathematical knowledge.

These suggestions of Locke may seem to imply that for him ethics is no more than an analysis of ideas in the sense that there is no one set of moral rules which men ought to obey. If we frame this set of ideas, we shall enunciate these rules: if we frame that set of ideas, we shall enunciate those rules. And which set is adopted is a matter of choice. But this was not at all Locke's view of the matter. At least it is certainly not the view which finds expression in the second book of the *Essay* where Locke talks about moral good and evil and about moral rules or laws.

It has already been mentioned that Locke defined good and evil with reference to pleasure and pain. Good is that which is apt to cause or increase pleasure in mind or body, or to diminish pain, while evil is that which is apt to cause or increase any pain or to diminish pleasure.[4] Moral good, however, is the conformity of our voluntary actions to some law, whereby good (that is, 'pleasure') accrues to us according to the will of the law-giver; and moral evil consists in the disagreement of our voluntary actions with some law, whereby evil (that is, 'pain') 'is drawn on us from the will and power of the law-maker'.[5] Locke does not say that moral good and evil are pleasure and pain. Nor is he logically committed to saying this. For he defined good and evil not as pleasure and pain (though he does sometimes carelessly speak in this way), but as that which procures pleasure and that which brings pain. Moral good is the conformity of our voluntary actions to a law backed by sanctions; he does not say that it is the same thing as the reward for conformity.

What sort of a law has Locke in mind? He distinguishes three kinds: the divine law, the civil law and 'the law of opinion or reputation'.[6] By the third type of law he means the approval or disapproval, praise or blame, 'which by a secret and tacit consent establishes itself in the several societies, tribes and clubs of men in the world, whereby several actions come to find credit or disgrace amongst them, according to the judgments, maxims or fashion of that place'.[7] In relation to divine law actions are judged to be duties or sins; in relation to the civil law, innocent or criminal; and in relation to the law of opinion or reputation, virtues or vices. Now, it is obvious that these laws might be at variance with one another. As Locke observes, in a given society men may approve of actions which are contrary to the divine law. And he certainly did not think that the civil law is the ultimate criterion of right and wrong. It follows, therefore, that the divine law is the ultimate criterion, in relation to which voluntary actions are called morally good or morally evil. 'That God has given a rule whereby men should govern themselves, I think there is nobody so brutish as to deny. He has a right to do it, we are his creatures: he has goodness and wisdom to direct our actions to that which is best; and he has power to enforce it by rewards and punishments, of infinite weight and duration in another life: for nobody can take us out of his hands. This is the only true touchstone of moral rectitude.'[8]

Now, if we had to understand Locke as meaning that the

criterion of moral good and evil, of right and wrong actions, is the arbitrary law of God, there would be a flagrant contradiction between what he says in the second book of the *Essay* and what he says in the fourth. For if the divine law were arbitrarily imposed by God, we could know it only by revelation. And in this case the comparison between ethics and mathematics, which we find in the fourth book, would be entirely misplaced. But when speaking of the divine law in the second book Locke explains that 'I mean that law which God has set to the actions of men, whether promulgated to them by the light of nature, or the voice of revelation'.[9] By the light of nature he means reason; and he evidently thought that we can discover something of the law of God by reason alone, even if Christian revelation gives us further light. And when we turn to the fourth book we find him saying that 'the idea of a supreme being infinite in power, goodness and wisdom, whose workmanship we are and on whom we depend, and the idea of ourselves as understanding rational beings, being such as are clear in us, would, I suppose, if duly considered and pursued, afford such foundations of our duty and rules of actions, as might place morality amongst the sciences capable of demonstration; wherein I doubt not but from self-evident principles, by necessary consequences, as incontestable as those in mathematics, the measures of right and wrong might be made out to anyone that will apply himself with the same indifferency and attention to the one as he does to the other of those sciences'.[10] Clearly, Locke thought that by considering the nature of God and that of man and the relation between them we could arrive at self-evident moral principles from which other more particular moral rules could be deduced. And the system of deducible rules would constitute the law of God as known by the light of nature. Whether he thought of the revealed moral law as supplementary or as forming part of the premises, he does not make clear. Nor did he himself make any attempt to demonstrate an ethical system on the lines proposed. The examples he gives of self-evident propositions are not very illuminating: 'where there is no property, there is no injustice' and 'no government allows absolute liberty'.[11] (The second proposition is given as a factual statement, but Locke's explanation shows that he did not intend it to be understood in this way.)

I am not disposed, therefore, to subscribe to the verdict

of those historians who say that Locke gives us two moral
theories which he made no attempt to reconcile. For it
seems to me that he does make some attempt to show how
the lines of thought given in the second and fourth books
of the *Essay* hang together. At the same time it can hardly
be denied that what he has to say is sketchy and muddled
and that it represents a conflation of different elements. Although, as we have seen, he cannot simply be dubbed a
hedonist, even in the second book, there is an element of
hedonistic utilitarianism, partly inspired perhaps by Gassendi. Again, there is an element of authoritarianism, based
on the idea of the rights of the Creator. Finally, Locke's
distinction between the light of nature and revelation recalls
Aquinas's distinction between the natural law, known by
reason, and the divine positive law; and this distinction was
doubtless inspired largely by Hooker, who had taken over a
good deal from mediaeval philosophy.[12] The influence of
Hooker, and of mediaeval theory through Hooker, on Locke's
thought can be seen in the latter's notion of natural rights,
which will be considered presently in connection with his
political theory.

2. In his preface to the *Treatises of Civil Government*[13]
Locke expresses his hope that what he has written is sufficient 'to establish the throne of our great restorer, our present
king William (and) to make good his title in the consent of
the people'. Hume, as will be seen later, thought that Locke's
political theory was unable to fulfil this function. But in
any case it would be a mistake to think that Locke developed
his political theory simply with a view to establishing William's title to the throne; for he was in possession of the
principles of the theory well before 1688. Further, his theory
is of lasting historical importance as a systematic expression of the liberal thought of the day, and his treatises are
much more than a Whig pamphlet.

The first *Treatise of Civil Government* need not detain us.
In it Locke argues against the theory of the divine right of
kings as upheld in Sir Robert Filmer's *Patriarcha* (1680).
The patriarchal theory of the transmission of royal authority
is held up to ridicule. There is no evidence that Adam possessed a divinely granted royal authority. If he had it, there
is no evidence that his heirs had it. If they did, the right of
succession was not determined, and even if there were a
divinely determined order of succession, all knowledge of it

has long since perished. In point of fact Filmer was not such an ass as Locke makes him out to be; for he had already published works of greater merit than the *Patriarcha*. But the work was recently published and had raised discussion, and it is quite understandable that Locke selected it for attack in his first treatise.

In the first *Treatise*[14] Locke asserts that 'Sir Robert Filmer's great position is that "men are not naturally free". This is the foundation on which his absolute monarchy stands.' This theory of the natural subjection of men was flatly rejected by Locke, who maintains in the second *Treatise* that in the state of nature men were naturally free and equal. 'This equality of men by nature the judicious Hooker looks upon as so evident in itself and beyond all question that he makes it the foundation of that obligation to mutual love amongst men on which he builds the duties we owe one another and from whence he derives the great maxims of justice and charity.'[15]

Locke starts, therefore, as did Hobbes, with the idea of the state of nature; and in his view 'all men are naturally in that state and remain so till by their own consents they make themselves members of some politic society'.[16] But his idea of the state of nature is very different from that of Hobbes. Indeed, Hobbes is evidently the chief opponent whom he has in mind in the second *Treatise*, though he does not say so explicitly. There is a radical difference, according to Locke, between the state of nature and the state of war. 'Men living together according to reason, without a common superior on earth with authority to judge between them, is properly the state of nature.'[17] Force, exercised without right, creates a state of war; but this is not to be identified with the state of nature, since it constitutes a violation of the state of nature; that is, of what it ought to be.

Locke can speak of what the state of nature ought to be because he admits a natural moral law which is discoverable by reason. The state of nature is a state of liberty but not of licence. 'The state of nature has a law of nature to govern it, which obliges everyone; and reason, which is that law, teaches all mankind who will but consult it that, being all equal and independent, no one ought to harm another in his life, health, liberty or possessions.'[18] For all men are the creatures of God. And though a man may defend himself against attack and punish aggressors on his private initiative, since, as is supposed, there is no common temporal sovereign or judge, his conscience is bound by the natural moral law which obliges all independently of civil society and its legal enactments. Natural law, therefore, means something quite different for Locke from what it meant for Hobbes. For the latter it meant the law of power and force and fraud, whereas for Locke it meant a universally obligatory moral law promulgated by the human reason as it reflects on God and His rights, on man's relation to God and on the fundamental equality of all men as rational creatures. Hooker has already been mentioned as one of the sources of Locke's theory of the natural moral law. We can also mention the Cambridge Platonists in England and, on the Continent, writers such as Grotius[19] and Pufendorf.

Believing, as he did, in a natural moral law which binds in conscience independently of the State and its legislation, Locke also believed in natural rights. Every man has, for example, the right to preserve himself and to defend his life, and he has a right to his freedom. There are, too, of course, correlative duties. In fact, because a man has a duty to preserve and defend his life, he has a right to do so. And because he is morally obliged to take the means at his disposal to preserve his life, he has not the right either to take it himself or, by subjecting himself to slavery in the fullest sense of the word, to give to another the power of taking it.

3. The natural right to which Locke paid most attention was, however, the right of property. As man has the duty and the right to preserve himself, he has a right to those things which are required for this purpose. God has given to men the earth and all that is in it for their support and well-being. But though God has not divided up the earth and the things on it, reason shows that it is in accordance with God's will that there should be private property, not only with regard to the fruits of the earth and the things on and in it, but also with regard to the earth itself.

What constitutes the primary title to private property? In Locke's view it is labour. In the state of nature a man's labour is his own, and whatever he removes from its original condition by mixing his labour with it becomes his. 'Though the water running in the fountain be everyone's, yet who can doubt but that in the pitcher is his only who drew it out? His labour hath taken it out of the hands of nature, where it was common and belonged equally to all her children, and hath thereby appropriated it to himself.'[20] Suppose that a man picks up apples for his nourishment under a tree in a wood. Nobody will dispute his ownership of them and his right to eat them. But when did they begin to be his? When he had digested them? When he was eating them? When he cooked them? When he brought them home? It is clear that they became his when he picked them up; that is to say, when he 'mixed his labour' with them and so removed them from the state of being common property. And landed property is acquired in the same way. If a man fells the trees in a forest and makes a clearing, ploughs and sows, the land and its produce are his; for they are the fruit of his labour. The land would not bear the corn unless he had prepared it for doing so.

Locke's theory of labour as the primary title to property was eventually to be incorporated in the labour theory of value and to be used in a way that its author never envisaged. But it would be irrelevant to treat of these developments here. It is more to the point if attention is drawn to the frequently asserted view that in stressing so much the right of private property Locke was expressing the mentality of the Whig landowners who were his patrons. No doubt, there is some truth in this assertion. At least it is not unreasonable to think that the attention which Locke devoted to private property was due in part to the influence of the outlook of the section of society in which he moved. At the same time it should be remembered that the doctrine that there is a right of private property independently of the laws of civil societies was not a novel invention on Locke's part. It should also be noted that he did not say that any man is entitled to amass property without limit to the detriment of others. He himself raises the objection that if gathering the fruits of the earth confers a right to them, anyone may amass as much as he likes, and he answers, 'Not so. The same law of nature that doth by this means give us property does also bound that property too.'[21] The fruits of the earth are given for use and enjoyment; and 'as much as anyone can make use of to any advantage of life before it spoils, so much he may by his labour fix a property in: whatever is beyond this is more than his share and belongs to others'.[22] As for land, the doctrine that labour is the title to property sets a limit to property. For 'as much land as man tills, plants, improves, cultivates and can use the product of, so much is his property'.[23] It is clear that Locke presupposes a state of affairs in which there is plenty of land for everybody, as in the America of his day. 'In the beginning all the world was America, and more so than it is now; for no such thing as money was anywhere known.'[24]

It is clear that Locke assumes that there is a natural right to inherit property. In fact he expressly says that 'every man is born with a double right: first, a right of freedom to his own person . . . secondly, a right, before any other man, to inherit with his brethren his father's goods'.[25] The family is a natural society, and fathers have the duty of providing for their offspring. Still, Locke devotes more attention to explaining how property is acquired than to justifying the right of inheritance, a point which he leaves obscure.

4. Although the state of nature is a condition of affairs in which men have no common authority over them, God 'put him (man) under strong obligations of necessity, convenience and inclination to drive him into society'.[26] We cannot say, therefore, that society is unnatural to man. The family, the primary form of human society, is natural to man, and civil or political society is natural in the sense that it fulfils human needs. For although men, considered in the state of nature, are independent of one another, it is difficult for them to preserve their liberties and rights in actual practice. For from the fact that in the state of nature all are bound in conscience to obey a common moral law it does not follow that all actually obey this law. And from the fact that all enjoy equal rights and are morally bound to respect the rights of others it does not follow that all actually respect the rights of others. It is in man's interest, therefore, to form an organized society for the more effectual preservation of their liberties and rights.

Although, therefore, Locke painted a different picture of the state of nature from that painted by Hobbes, he did not look on this state as an ideal condition of affairs. In the first place, 'though the law of nature be plain and intelligible to all rational creatures, yet men being biased by their interest, as well as ignorant for want of studying it, are not apt to allow of it as a law binding to them in the application of it to their particular cases'.[27] It is desirable, therefore, that there should be a written law to define the natural law and decide controversies. In the second place, though a man in the state of nature enjoys the right to punish transgressions, men are only too apt to be over-zealous in their own cause and too remiss in the cause of others. It is desirable, therefore, that there should be an established and commonly recognized judicial system. In the third place, in the state of nature men may often lack the power to punish crimes, even when their sentence is just. 'Thus mankind, notwithstanding all the privileges of the state of nature, being but in an ill condition while they remain in it, are quickly driven into society.'[28]

According to Locke, 'The great and chief end of men's uniting into commonwealths and putting themselves under government is the preservation of their property'.[29] But this assertion is misinterpreted if we take the word 'property' in the ordinary restricted sense. For Locke has already explained that he is using the word in a wider sense. Men join together in society 'for the mutual preservation of their lives, liberties and estates, which I call by the general name, property'.[30]

Now, Locke is concerned to show that political society and government rest on a rational foundation. And the only way he can see of showing this is to maintain that they rest on consent. It is not enough to explain the disadvantages of the state of nature and the advantage of political society, even though this explanation shows that this society is rational in the sense that it fulfils a useful purpose. For the complete freedom of the state of nature is necessarily curtailed to some extent by the institution of political society and government, and this curtailment can be justified only if it proceeds from the consent of those who are incorporated, or, rather, of those who incorporate themselves, into political society and subject themselves to government. A political society arises 'wherever any number of men in the state of nature enter into society to make one people, one body politic, under one supreme government; or else when anyone joins himself to, and incorporates with any government already made. . . .'[31] 'Men being, as has been said, by nature all free, equal and independent, no one can be put out of this estate and subjected to the political power of another without his own consent. The only way whereby anyone divests himself of his natural liberty and puts on the bonds of civil society is by agreeing with other men to join and unite into a community for their comfortable, safe and peaceable living one amongst another, in a secure enjoyment of their properties and a great security against any that are not of it.'[32]

What, then, do men give up when they join together to form a political community? And to what do they give their consent? In the first place, men do not give up their liberty to enter a state of servitude. Each does, indeed, give up his legislative and executive powers in the form in which they belong to him in the state of nature. For he authorizes society, or rather the legislative, to make such laws as are required for the common good, and he relinquishes to society the power to enforce these laws and exact punishment for their infringement. And to this extent the liberty of the state of nature is curtailed. But men relinquish these powers in order to enjoy their liberties more securely. 'For no rational creature can be supposed to change his condition with an intention to be worse.'[33] In the second place, 'whosoever out of a state of nature unite into a community must be understood to give up all the power necessary to the ends for which they unite into society to the majority of the community, unless they expressly agreed in any number greater than the majority'.[34] In Locke's view, therefore, the 'original compact' must be understood as involving the individual's consent to submit to the will of the majority. 'It is necessary the body should move that way whither the greater force carries it, which is the consent of the majority.'[35] Either the unanimous and explicit consent of every individual is required for every measure to be enacted, and this is in most cases impracticable; or the will of the majority must prevail. Locke evidently considered that the right of the majority to represent the community was practically self-evident; but he apparently did not realize that a majority might act tyrannically with regard to the minority. At any rate his main concern was to show that absolute monarchy was contrary to the original social compact, and he doubtless thought that the danger to liberty from majority rule was much less than the danger to liberty which comes from absolute monarchy. And having included consent to majority rule in his 'original compact' he was able to say that 'absolute monarchy, which by some men is counted the only government in the world, is indeed inconsistent with civil society and so can be no form of civil government at all'.[36]

One obvious objection to the theory of the social compact or contract is the difficulty in finding historical instances of it. The question arises, therefore, whether Locke thought of the social compact as an historical event. He himself raises the objection that there are no instances of man in the state of nature meeting together and making an explicit agreement to form a political society. He then proceeds to argue that some instances can in fact be found, such as the beginnings of Rome and Venice and of certain political communities in America. And even if we had no records of any such instances, silence would be no disproof of the hypothesis of a social compact. For 'government is everywhere antecedent to records, and letters seldom come in amongst a people till a long continuation of civil society has, by other more necessary arts, provided for their safety, ease and plenty'.[87] All this suggests that Locke did in fact regard the social compact as an historic event. But he insists at the same time that even if it can be shown that civil society grew out of the family and tribe and that civil government is a development of patriarchal rule, this does not alter the fact that the rational foundation of civil society and government is consent.

A second objection arises, however. Even if it could be shown that political societies originated in a social compact, in the consent of the men who voluntarily created these societies, how would this justify political society as we know it? For it is evident that the citizens of Great Britain, for example, give no explicit consent to being members of their political society and subjects of its government, whatever their remote ancestors may have done. Indeed, Locke himself, who is quite aware of the difficulty, underlines it by maintaining that a father 'cannot, by any compact whatsoever, bind his children or posterity'.[88] A man may lay down conditions in his will so that his son cannot inherit and continue to enjoy his property without being and remaining a member of the same political society as his father. But the latter cannot bind his son to accept the property in question. If his son does not like the conditions, he can renounce his inheritance.

In order to meet the objection Locke has to have recourse to a distinction between explicit and tacit consent. If a man grows up in a certain political society, inherits property in accordance with the laws of the State and enjoys the privileges of a citizen, he must be supposed to have given at least a tacit consent to membership of that society. For it would be utterly unreasonable to enjoy the privilege of a citizen and at the same time to maintain that one was still in the state of nature. In other words, a man who avails himself of the rights and privileges of a citizen of a certain State must be supposed to have voluntarily undertaken, at any rate tacitly, the duties of a citizen of that State. And in answer to the objection that a man who is born as an Englishman or a Frenchman has no choice but to submit himself to the obligations of a citizen, Locke answers that he can in point of fact withdraw from the State, either by going to another State or by retiring to some remote part of the world where he can live in the state of nature.

This answer must be understood, of course, in the light of the circumstances prevailing in Locke's day, when passport regulations, emigration laws, universal military conscription and so on were unknown, and when it was at least physically possible for a man to go off and live in the wilds of America or Africa if he so chose. But all the same, Locke's remarks help to show the artificial and unreal character of the social compact theory. In Locke's account of the origins of political society we find a conflation of two elements; the mediaeval idea, coming from Greek philosophy, of the 'natural' character of political society and the rationalist attempt to find a justification for the limitations of liberty in organized society when a state of nature has been presupposed in which unlimited liberty (except, in Locke's case, for the moral obligation to obey the natural moral law) is enjoyed.

5. Hobbes, as we saw, asserted that there is one covenant by which a number of men hand over to a sovereign the 'rights' which they enjoyed in the state of nature. Thus political society and government are created at the same time by the one consent. It has been argued, however, that Locke's political theory allows for two covenants or compacts or contracts, one whereby political society is formed, the other whereby a government is set up. There is, indeed, no explicit mention of two compacts; but, it has been argued, Locke tacitly assumes that there are two. By the first compact a man becomes a member of a definite political society and obliges himself to accept the decisions of the majority, while by the second compact the majority (or all) of the members of the new-formed society agree either to carry on the government themselves or to set up an oligarchy or a monarchy, hereditary or elective. While, therefore, on the theory of Hobbes the overthrow of the sovereign logically involves

the dissolution of the political society in question, on Locke's theory this is not the case, because political society was formed by a distinct compact and can be dissolved only by agreement of its members.

There is certainly a good deal to be said in favour of this interpretation. But at the same time Locke appears to think of the relation between citizen and government in terms of the idea of trusteeship rather than in terms of a compact. The people set up a government and entrust it with a definite task; and the government is under an obligation to fulfil this trust. 'The first and fundamental positive law of all commonwealths is the establishing of the legislative power.'[39] And 'the community put the legislative power into such hands as they think fit with this trust, that they shall be governed by declared laws, or else their peace, quiet and property will still be at the same uncertainty as it was in the state of nature'.[40]

Locke speaks of the legislature as the 'supreme power' in the commonwealth.[41] And 'all other powers, in any members or parts of the society, (must be) derived from and subordinate to it'.[42] When there is a monarch who possesses supreme executive power he can, in ordinary language, be called the supreme power, especially if acts need his consent to become law and the legislative is not always sitting; but this does not mean that he has in himself all the power of law-making, and it is the whole legislative which is the supreme power in the technical sense. Locke emphasized the desirability of a division of powers in the commonwealth. For example, it is highly undesirable that the persons who make the laws should themselves execute them. For 'they may exempt themselves from obedience to the laws they make, and suit the law, both in its making and execution, to their own private advantage and thereby come to have a distinct interest from the rest of the community'.[43] The executive should, therefore, be distinct from the legislative. And because Locke so emphasized the desirability of a separation of power in the commonwealth it has been argued that he has nothing corresponding to Hobbes's sovereign. This is, of course, true if we attach to the word 'sovereign' the entire meaning which Hobbes attached to it; but, as we have seen, Locke recognizes a supreme power, namely, the legislative. And in so far as it is the supreme power in the commonwealth, to that extent it may perhaps be said to correspond to Hobbes's sovereign.

Though, however, 'there can be but one supreme power, which is the legislative, to which all the rest are and must be subordinate, yet the legislative being only a fiduciary power to act for certain ends, there remains still in the people a supreme power to remove or alter the legislative when they find the legislative act contrary to the trust reposed in them'.[44] Thus the power of the legislative is certainly not absolute: it has a trust to fulfil. And it is, of course, subject to the moral law. Locke accordingly lays down 'the bounds which the trust that is put in them (the members of the legislative) by the society and the law of God and nature have set to the legislative power of every commonwealth in all forms of government'.[45] First, the legislative must govern by promulgated laws which are the same for all and are not varied in particular cases. Secondly, these laws must be designed for no other end than for the good of the people. Thirdly, the legislative must not raise taxes without the consent of the people, given by themselves or their deputies. For the principal purpose for which society is formed is for the presentation and protection of property. Fourthly, the legislative is not entitled to transfer the power of making laws to any person or assembly to which the people has not entrusted this power, nor can it do so validly.

When we speak of the separation of powers, we generally refer to the threefold distinction of the legislative, executive and judicial powers. But Locke's triad is different, consisting of the legislative, the executive and what he calls the 'federative'. This federative power comprises the power to make war and peace, alliances and treaties 'and all the transactions with all persons and communities without the commonwealth'.[46] Locke regarded it as distinct power, though he remarks that it can hardly be separated from the executive in the sense of being entrusted to a different person or to different persons, as this would be apt to cause 'disorder and ruin'.[47] As for the judicial power, Locke seems to have regarded it as part of the executive. In any case the two points on which he insists are that the legislative must be supreme and that every power, including the legislative, has a trust to fulfil.

6. 'Whenever the society is dissolved, it is certain the government of that society cannot remain.'[48] If a conqueror

'mangles societies to pieces'[49] it is obvious that their governments are dissolved. This dissolution by force is called by Locke 'overturning from without'. But there can also take place a dissolution 'from within', and it is to this theme that he devotes most of the last chapter of the second *Treatise*.

The government may be dissolved from within by the legislative being altered. Let us suppose, says Locke, who is evidently thinking of the British constitution, that the legislative power is vested in an assembly of representatives chosen by the people, in an assembly of hereditary nobility, and in a single hereditary person, the prince, who possesses the supreme executive power and also the right to convoke and dissolve the two assemblies. If the prince substitutes his arbitrary will for the laws, or if he hinders the legislative (that is, the assemblies, particularly the representative assembly) from coming together at the proper time or from acting freely; or if he arbitrarily changes the method of election without the people's consent and contrary to the interest of the people; in all such cases the legislative is altered. Again, if the holder of supreme executive power abandons or neglects his charge so that the laws cannot be enforced, government is effectually dissolved. Further, governments are dissolved when the prince or the legislative act in a manner contrary to their trust, as when either of them invades the property of citizens or tries to obtain arbitrary dominion over their lives, liberties or property.

When government is 'dissolved' in any of these ways, rebellion is justified. To say that this doctrine encourages frequent rebellion is no sound argument. For if the citizens are subjected to the arbitrary caprice of tyrannical power, they will be ready to seize the opportunity to rebel however much the sacred character of the rulers may have been extolled. Moreover, rebellions do not occur in point of fact 'upon every little mismanagement in public affairs'.[50] And though we speak of 'rebellion' and 'rebels' when speaking of subjects and their acts, we might more properly speak of the rulers as rebels when they turn themselves into tyrants and act in a manner contrary to the will and interest of the people. True, there can be unjustified insurrections and rebellions, and these are crimes, but the possibility of misuse does not take away the right to rebel. And if it is asked who is to judge when circumstances render rebellion legitimate, 'I reply, the people shall be judge'.[51] For it is only they, under God, who can decide whether the trustee has abused his trust or not.

7. Locke's political theory is obviously open to criticism on several grounds. Together with other political theories which are more than the enunciation of very general principles, so general that they can be called 'perennial', it shares the defect of being too closely related to contemporary historical circumstances. This is, of course, inevitable in the case of a theory which enters more or less into detail. And there is nothing surprising in the fact that Locke's *Treatise on Civil Government* reflects to some extent the contemporary historical circumstances and its author's private political convictions as a Whig and as an opponent of the Stuarts. For unless the political philosopher wishes to confine himself to enunciating propositions such as 'government should be carried on with a view to the common good', he cannot help taking as the material for his reflection the political data of his time. In political theories we see a certain outlook and spirit and movement of political life attaining reflective expression; and in varying degrees political theories are inevitably dated. This is obviously true of Plato's political theory. It is also true of the Marxist political theory. And it is only natural that it should be true of Locke's theory as well.

It may be said that what is practically speaking inevitable, cannot properly be called a 'defect'. But if a political philosopher puts forward his theory as *the* theory, it would be idle, I think, to cavil at the use of this word. In any case Locke's political theory suffers from other defects as well. Attention has already been drawn to the artificiality of the social compact theory. And we may also note Locke's failure to give any thorough analysis of the concept of the common good. He tends to assume without more ado that the preservation of private property and the promotion of the common good are to all intents and purposes synonymous terms. It may be said that this criticism is made from the point of view of one who looks back on a development of economic, social and political life which Locke could not have foreseen, a development which necessitated a revision of the liberalism of his time. And this is partly true. But it does not follow that even within the framework of his own historical circumstances Locke could not have given a more adequate account of the function of political society and of government. There is something wanting from his account which was present both in Greek and in mediaeval political thought, even if in a rudimentary form.

To say, however, that Locke's political theory is open to criticism is not to say that it does not possess some lasting value. And to say that the principles which can be considered of perennial validity are principles which transcend limitation and restriction to a particular epoch or set of circumstances precisely because of their generality is not the same thing as to say that these principles are worthless. A principle is not rendered worthless because it has to be applied in different ways at different times. Locke's principle that the government, in the wide sense of the State organization and not merely in the narrow sense in which the term 'the government' is generally used today, has a trust to fulfil and that it exists to promote the common good is as true now as it was when he enunciated it. It was not, of course, a novelty. Aquinas would have said the same. But the point is that the principle needs constant reiteration. To be operative, it has to be applied in different ways at different times; and Locke tried to show how, in his opinion, it should be applied in the circumstances of his time, which were not those of the Middle Ages.

The responsibility of government to the people and its function of promoting the common good would be generally admitted. But I should wish to add, as a position of lasting validity, a position which Locke himself constantly adopted but which has been called in question. I refer to the doctrine that there are natural rights and that there is a natural moral law which obliges in conscience both governors and governed. This doctrine is not bound up inextricably with the theories of the state of nature and of the social compact; and it is a lasting safeguard against tyranny when it is sincerely accepted.

Quite apart, however, from its intrinsic merits and demerits, Locke's political theory is of great historical importance. Despite some criticism it obtained general acceptance in his own country in the eighteenth century. And even when writers such as Hume attacked the theory of the social compact Locke's general notions about government were none the less accepted. Later on, of course, different lines of thought made their appearance, with Benthamism on the one hand and the theories of Burke on the other. But much of what Locke had said remained common property. Meanwhile his political theory became known on the Continent, in Holland, of course, where he had lived in exile, and also in France, where he influenced writers of the Enlightenment such as Montesquieu. Further, there can be no doubt of his great influence in America, even if it is difficult to assess the precise degree of his influence on individual leaders of the revolution such as Jefferson. In fine, the widespread and lasting effects of Locke's *Treatise of Civil Government* is a standing disproof of the notion that philosophers are ineffectual. It is doubtless true that Locke himself brought to articulate expression an already existing movement of thought; but this articulate expression was itself a powerful influence in the consolidation and dissemination of the movement of thought and drift of political life which it expressed.

8. According to d'Alembert, the French Encyclopaedist, Locke created metaphysics in much the same way that Newton created physics. By metaphysics in this connection d'Alembert meant the theory of knowledge as conceived by Locke, as, that is to say, the determination of the extent, powers and limitations of the human understanding. And the impetus given by Locke to the development of the theory of knowledge and to a treatment of metaphysics in function of an analysis of the human understanding was, indeed, one of the principal ways in which he exercised a powerful influence on philosophical thought. But his influence was also powerful in ethics, through hedonistic elements in his ethical theory, and, as we saw in the last section, in political theory. It may be added that economic liberalism of the *laissez-faire* type, such as is found in the writings of the French 'physiocrats' (for instance, François Quesnay, 1694–1774) and in Adam Smith's *Wealth of Nations* (1776), has at least a remote connection with Locke's economic and political theories.

The influence of Locke's empiricism is best seen in the philosophies of Berkeley and Hume, which will be considered later. In the course of this development of thought his empiricist principle was applied in ways which he had not himself envisaged. But there is nothing surprising in this. Locke was a moderate and balanced thinker. He could appeal, therefore, to a man like Samuel Clarke, who evidently had a considerable respect for him. But it is only natural that different aspects of Locke's thought should have been developed by others in a way which he himself would have considered to be exaggerated. For example, his remarks about reason as the judge of revelation exercised an influence on the deists, who will be considered later, and we find Bolingbroke extolling Locke as the one leading philosopher for whom he had any respect. Again, Locke's observations in the *Essay* about the association of ideas bore fruit later on in the associationist psychology of David Hartley (1705–57) and Joseph Priestley (1733–1804). Both these men emphasized the connection between physical and psychical events, and the latter at any rate adopted a materialist position. Locke himself was not, of course, a materialist; nor did he regard thoughts and ideas as being simply transformed sensations. At the same time he made statements which could be used as a basis for sensationalism. He said, for example, that for all we know God might give the power of thinking to a purely material thing. And these elements of sensationalism influenced, for instance, Peter Browne (d. 1735), bishop of Cork, and the French philosopher, Condillac (1715–80). Indeed, the elements of sensationalism in Locke's philosophy exercised a considerable influence, direct or indirect, on the thinkers of the French Enlightenment, such as the Encyclopaedists.

In brief, Locke was one of the outstanding figures of the period of the Enlightenment in general, representing in himself and in his writings the spirit of free inquiry, of 'rationalism' and of dislike of all authoritarianism which was characteristic of the age. It must be added, however, that he possessed qualities of moderation, of piety and of a serious sense of responsibility which were sometimes lacking in the continental thinkers who came under his influence.

But if Locke was one of the master-thinkers of his age, Newton was another. And d'Alembert was not unjustified in mentioning them together. Hence, although this work is certainly not intended to be a history of physical science, something at least must be said about the great mathematician and physicist who exercised such a profound influence on men's thought.

Robert Boyle – Sir Isaac Newton.

1. Locke's circle of friends included Robert Boyle (1627–91). As a chemist and physicist, Boyle was interested in particular analyses of sensible data rather than in framing wide and far-reaching hypotheses about Nature in general; and in his conception of scientific method he laid stress on experimental research. He thus carried on the work of men such as Gilbert and Harvey. In the emphasis which he laid on experiment he shows an affinity, of course, with Francis Bacon; but in his earlier years he purposely avoided serious study of the works of those whom he subsequently acknowledged as his chief predecessors, namely, Bacon, Descartes and Gassendi, in order to escape premature indoctrination with theories and hypotheses. And he is rightly regarded as one of the leading promoters of experimental science and as a man who contributed to making clear by his own work the inadequacy of theorizing which is unaccompanied by controlled experimental verification or confirmation. Thus his experiments on air and the vacuum by means of an air-pump, an account of which was given in his *New Experiments Physico-Mechanical* (1660), disposed of Hobbes's *a priori* theorizing and dealt a fatal blow to opponents of the experimental method. Again, in his *Sceptical Chymist* (1661) he criticized with effect not only the doctrine of four elements but also the current theory of salt, sulphur and mercury as the three constituent principles of material things. (A chemical element, according to his definition, is a substance which cannot be decomposed into simpler constituents, though he was unable himself to supply a list of these elements.) In 1662 he achieved the generalization

which is known as Boyle's Law, namely, the statement that the pressure and volume of a gas are inversely proportional. He himself believed in alchemy, but his own insistence on and use of the experimental method constituted a most effective means of putting an end to alchemy.

To say that Boyle insisted on and used the experimental method in physics and chemistry is not, of course, to say that he was merely an 'experimenter' and that he eschewed all hypotheses. Had he done this, he would scarcely have achieved eminence as a scientist. What he objected to was not the formation of hypotheses as such but the hasty assertion of theories without the controlling use of the experimental method and the confident assertion of the truth of theories and hypotheses which enjoy only varying degrees of probability. It is preferable to accumulate a little knowledge which is securely based on experiment than to construct sweeping philosophical systems which cannot be verified. But this does not mean that hypotheses should not be formed. For the scientist endeavours to interpret and explain the facts which he has ascertained. At the same time, even when it is possible to show that a given explanatory hypothesis is more probable than any other hypothesis which purports to explain the same facts, there is no guarantee that it will not be superseded in the future. Boyle, it may be noted, embraced the hypothesis of ether; that is to say, of a subtle ethereal substance diffused throughout space. The hypothesis of ether had been postulated to avoid the notion of a vacuum and to explain the propagation of motion without any apparent medium. But there were also phenomena such as magnetism of which no satisfactory explanation had been given in terms of the mechanical conception of the world. Boyle accordingly suggested that the ether might be composed of two kinds of particles or corpuscles, by the aid of one of which we might explain phenomena such as magnetism. He was thus able to avoid Henry More's theory of a spirit of Nature or soul of the world, which the Cambridge Platonist offered as an explanation of phenomena such as magnetism and gravity.[1] In other words, Boyle suggested a more naturalistic and 'scientific' hypothesis. But he was well aware that his own hypothesis was no more than probable and that it might have to be discarded. He did not claim for his own scientific theories a final truth which he would not allow to the theories of others. He was acutely conscious of the limitations of human knowledge in general and of the hypothetical and provisional character of scientific explanation in particular.

Further, to say that Boyle insisted on the experimental method in science is not to say that he was blind to the rôle of mathematics in physics. Although he was not himself a great mathematician, he was in full sympathy with Galileo and Descartes in their views about the mathematical structure of Nature, considered as a system of bodies in motion; and he even looked on mathematical principles as transcendent truths which are the foundation and instrument of all our knowledge. And, with a qualification which will be mentioned shortly, he accepted the mechanical interpretation of Nature. He postulated a theory of atoms, endowed with primary qualities of size and shape, and he argued that the natural phenomena of the material world can be explained mechanically if we also postulate motion. Motion is not an inherent quality of matter and does not pertain to its essence; hence it has to be postulated in addition to matter. It is, so to speak, super-added by God, and the laws of motion are determined by God. Boyle would not accept Descartes' metaphysical proof of the conservation of the same sum-total of motion or energy, namely, the proof from the divine immutability. This metaphysical argument does not constitute a proof, and we do not know that the sum-total of motion must always remain constant. However, given matter and motion, the system of Nature is a cosmic mechanism, though we must reject the view of Hobbes that motion must necessarily be communicated to a body by another contiguous body. For if we accept this view, we involve ourselves in an infinite regress and we rule out the causal activity of a spiritual God.

But though Boyle shared to a large extent the Cartesian interpretation of the mechanical system of Nature, he considered that this interpretation was exaggerated and stood in need of a qualification. He saw, indeed, and explicitly stated that an explanation of events in terms of final causality is not an answer to the question how these events occur, and any slick substitution of a teleological explanation for an answer to a question about efficient causality was as foreign to his mind as it was to that of Descartes. At the same time he insisted on the validity of the notion of final causality and on the possibility of teleological explanation, even if it is not the business of the physicist or of the chemist as such to concern himself with such matters. Descartes, it is true, had not denied that there are final causes when he excluded teleological explanations from physics or experimental philosophy. And Boyle's insistence on the relevance of final causality to metaphysics should not be described as a counterblast to Descartes. But what he has to say on the subject shows his dissatisfaction with the mechanical interpretation of the world, as maintained by Descartes and Hobbes, when it is taken as an adequate interpretation. It may be adequate for certain purposes or within a restricted field; but as a general philosophy of the world it is inadequate. Boyle was convinced that no satisfactory interpretation or general account of creation can be given without reference to an intelligent Author and Disposer of things, who adapts means to ends.

Boyle was strongly opposed to the materialism of Hobbes. But he was also opposed to what he regarded as the tendency of Galileo and Descartes to depreciate man's importance in the world and to relegate him to the condition of a spectator. He evidently considered it paradoxical that those who had contributed so much to the rise of a new natural philosophy and of a new outlook on the world should tend to push out of the picture, as it were, the very being who had evolved this new philosophy. If one may be permitted to employ a later way of speaking, he thought it odd that the subject should be eager to depreciate its own importance in favour of the object, when the new conceptions of the object were themselves due to the subject.

An expression of Boyle's point of view can be seen in his insistence that though our perception of secondary qualities can be explained mechanically, this is no sufficient ground for saying that secondary qualities are unreal. To say this is to forget man's factual presence in the world. For, given this factual presence, secondary qualities are as real as the primary.

However, though Boyle insisted on the importance of man's position within the cosmos, his interpretation of man's nature was sufficiently Cartesian in character to compel him to draw attention to the great difficulty encountered in solving the problem of interaction. For he thought of the spiritual soul as residing in some mysterious way in the conarion, shut away, as it were, within the brain where it awaits messages from the organs of sense. Further, he inferred from the soul's situation that the mind's power is necessarily very limited and restricted. And this inference has a close connection with Boyle's views about the hypothetical and provisional character of our theories and about the need for experimental verification, though the latter can never prove the absolute truth of an hypothesis.

One conclusion which Boyle drew from the restricted reach of our minds is that we ought to attach all the more value to the Christian religion, which enlarges our knowledge. He was in fact a deeply religious man. He regarded his experimental work in science as a service of God, and he founded the series of Boyle lectures with a view to answers being provided to difficulties about Christianity which might arise out of the scientific and philosophical developments of the time. In his writings he insisted that consideration of the cosmic system in general and of the faculties and operations of the human soul in particular affords sure evidence of the existence of a supremely powerful, wise and good Creator, who has also revealed Himself in the Scriptures. This does not mean that Boyle postulated God simply as the originator of the universe and of motion. He spoke frequently of the divine conservation of the world and of God's 'concurrence' with all its operations. He may not have attempted any systematic harmonization of this doctrine with his view of Nature as a mechanical system; but it was perhaps necessary to do so if he held, as he did, that the laws of Nature have no intrinsic necessity. Further, he insisted that God is by no means bound to His ordinary and general concurrence; that is, to maintaining the system of Nature precisely as we know it in normal experience. Miracles are possible and have occurred.

In Boyle, therefore, we see an interesting combination of an insistence on the experimental method in science and on the hypothetical character of scientific theories with a Cartesian view of the relation of soul to body and with theological convictions which came, indirectly, from mediaeval and Renaissance Scholasticism. His theory of the divine concurrence and his theory that God sees all that He knows intuitively in Himself illustrate the last-mentioned element in his thought.

2. Another of Locke's friends was Sir Isaac Newton (1642-1727), who has already been mentioned in the third volume of this *History*.[2] It is scarcely necessary to add that

we have here a greater name than that of Boyle. For it was Newton's genius which achieved the completion of the world-view prepared by men such as Copernicus, Galileo and Kepler,[3] and his name dominated science up to recent times. We are still accustomed to speak of modern physics up to the coming of the quantum mechanics as the Newtonian physics.

Born at Woolsthorpe in Lincolnshire, Newton went to Trinity College, Cambridge, in June 1661 and took his degree in January 1665. After spending the intervening period at Woolsthorpe, where he gave his attention to the problem of gravitation and also discovered the integral calculus and the binomial theorem, he was elected a Fellow of Trinity in 1667, and in 1669 he became Lucasian professor of mathematics. In 1687 he published his *Philosophiae naturalis principia mathematica*, commonly known as Newton's *Principia*, the cost of printing being defrayed by his friend, the astronomer Halley. He twice represented the University of Cambridge in Parliament, from 1689 to 1690 and from 1701 to 1705. In 1703 he was elected president of the Royal Society, of which he had become a member in 1672. He was knighted by Queen Anne in 1705. The second and third editions of the *Principia* appeared in 1713 and 1726. Newton was buried in Westminster Abbey.

Newton's genius as a mathematical physicist and his power of co-ordination, unification and simplification are, of course, unquestioned. For example, using Kepler's laws he was able to show that the motion of the planets round the sun can be explained if it is supposed that the sun exerts a force on each planet which varies in inverse proportion to the square of the distance of that planet from the sun. He then asked whether, if we suppose that the earth's attraction extends to the moon, the moon's retention in its orbit can be explained in a manner consonant with this basis. And eventually he was able to enunciate a universal law of gravitation, determining the mutual attraction of masses. Any body of mass M and any other body of mass m attract one another along the line between them with a force F, this force being equivalent to GMm/d^2, when d is the distance between the bodies and G is a universal constant. Newton was thus able to bring under a single mathematical law such major phenomena as the motions of the planets, the comets, the moon and the sea. He was able to show that the move-

ments of terrestrial bodies follow the same laws of motion
as celestial ones; and he thus completed the destruction of
the Aristotelian theory that terrestrial and celestial bodies
obey essentially different laws.

In general, Newton suggested that all the phenomena of
motion in Nature might also be derived mathematically
from mechanical principles. For instance, in his work *Opticks* (1704) he maintained that, given the relevant theorems relating to the refraction and composition of light, the
phenomena of colours could be explained in mathematical-
mechanical terms. In other words, he expressed the hope
that in the long run all natural phenomena might prove to
be explicable in terms of mathematical mechanics. And his
own outstanding successes in the solution of particular problems obviously tended to confer authority on his general
view. His achievement thus gave a powerful impetus to the
mechanical interpretation of the world. At the same time it
must be noted that his theory was generally regarded as
weakening the extreme mechanism of Descartes, because his
'gravitational force' did not seem to be reducible to the mere
motion of material particles. Some eighteenth-century apolo-
gists used the existence of gravity, as something inexplicable
on a purely mechanistic theory, as an argument for the existence of God.

It is to be noted that for Newton natural philosophy
studies the phenomena of motions. Its object is 'from the
phenomena of motions to investigate the forces of nature,
and then from these forces to demonstrate the other phenomena'.[4] What are these 'forces of nature'? They are defined as the causes of changes in motion. But we have to be
careful not to misunderstand the meaning of the word
'cause' in this context. Needless to say, Newton is not referring to the efficient, metaphysical cause of phenomena,
namely, God. Nor is he referring to the hypothetical, physical causes which are postulated either to explain those phenomena that have not been successfully reduced to the
operation of mechanical laws or to explain the factual conformity of actual motions to these laws. He is referring to
the mechanical laws themselves. These descriptive laws are
not, of course, physical agents; they do not exercise efficient
causality. They are 'mechanical principles'.

The passage quoted from the *Principia mathematica* indicates Newton's conception of scientific method. It com-

prises two main elements, the inductive discovery of mechanical laws from a study of the phenomena of motions and the deductive explanation of phenomena in the light of these laws. In other words, the method consists of analysis and of synthesis or composition. Analysis consists in making experiments and observations and in deriving general conclusions from them by induction. Synthesis consists in assuming the established laws or principles or 'causes' and in explaining phenomena by deducing consequences from these laws. Mathematics is the mind's tool or instrument in the whole process. It is needed from the start, in the sense that the motions to be studied must be measured and reduced to mathematical formulation. And the scope of the method and of natural philosophy is thereby restricted. But mathematics is regarded by Newton as an instrument or tool which the mind is forced to use rather than, as with Galileo, an infallible key to reality.

This is, indeed, a point of some importance. That Newton attributed to mathematics an indispensable role in natural philosophy is indicated by the very title of his great work, the *Mathematical Principles of Natural Philosophy*. The great instrument in the demonstrations of natural philosophy is mathematics. And this may suggest that for Newton mathematical physics, proceeding in a purely deductive manner, gives us the key to reality, and that he stands closer to Galileo and Descartes than to English scientists such as Gilbert, Harvey and Boyle. This, however, would be a misconception. It is doubtless right to stress the importance which Newton attached to mathematics; but one must also emphasize the empiricist aspect of his thought. Galileo and Descartes believed that the structure of the cosmos is mathematical in the sense that by the use of the mathematical method we can discover its secrets. But Newton was unwilling to make any such presupposition. We cannot legitimately assume in advance that mathematics gives us the key to reality. If we start with abstract mathematical principles and deduce conclusions, we do not know that these conclusions provide information about the world until we have verified them. We start with phenomena and discover laws or 'causes' by induction. We can then derive consequences from these laws. But the results of our deductions stand in need of experimental verification, so far as this is possible. The use of mathematics is necessary, but it is not by itself a guarantee of scientific knowledge about the world.

True, Newton himself makes certain assumptions. Thus in the third book of the *Principia mathematica* he lays down some rules for philosophizing or rules of reasoning in natural philosophy. The first of these is the principle of simplicity, which states that we ought not to admit more causes of natural things than such as are both true and sufficient to explain their appearances. The second rule states that to the same natural effects we must, as far as possible, assign the same causes. And the third states that those qualities of bodies which admit of neither intension nor remission of degrees, and which are found to belong to all bodies within the reach of experiment, are to be accounted the universal qualities of all bodies whatsoever. The question arises, therefore, whether Newton regarded the first two rules, which state the simplicity and uniformity of nature, as *a priori* truths or as methodological assumptions suggested by experience. Newton does not provide us with any clear answer to this question. He does, indeed, speak of the analogy of nature, which tends to simplicity and uniformity. But he seems to have thought that Nature observes simplicity and uniformity because it has been so created by God, and this may suggest that the first two rules have for him a metaphysical basis. The fourth rule, however, suggests that the first two should be regarded as methodological postulates or assumptions. It states that in experimental philosophy we ought to look on propositions which are the result of induction from phenomena as being accurately or very nearly true, in spite of any contrary hypotheses which may be imagined, until such time as other phenomena occur which may make the propositions either more accurate or liable to exceptions. And this seems to imply that experimental verification is the ultimate criterion in natural philosophy and that the first two rules are, even if Newton does not say so, methodological postulates.

Now, Newton says of this fourth rule that we ought to follow it 'that the argument of induction may not be evaded by hypotheses'. And in the *Opticks* he states roundly that 'hypotheses are not to be regarded in experimental philosophy'.[5] Again, in the *Principia mathematica* he states that he has been unable to discover the cause of the properties of gravity from phenomena, adding 'and I frame no hypotheses'.[6] And these statements obviously stand in need of some comment.

When Newton rejected hypotheses in natural philosophy, he was thinking primarily, of course, of unverifiable speculations. Thus when he says that the fourth rule should be followed in order that arguments from induction may not be evaded by hypotheses, he was thinking of theories for which no experimental evidence is offered. Propositions which have been arrived at by induction should be accepted until experiment shows that they are not accurate, and unverifiable contrary theories should be disregarded. When he says that he has been unable to discover the causes of the properties of gravity inductively and that he frames no hypotheses, he means that he is concerned only with the descriptive laws which state how gravity acts and not with the nature or essence of gravity. This is made clear by a statement in the *Principia mathematica*. 'Whatever is not deduced from the phenomena is to be called a hypothesis; and hypotheses, whether metaphysical or physical, whether of occult qualities or mechanical, have no place in experimental philosophy. In this philosophy particular propositions are inferred from the phenomena, and afterwards rendered general by induction. Thus it was that the impenetrability, the mobility, and the impulsive force of bodies, and the laws of motion and of gravitation, were discovered.'[7]

Of course, if we understand the word 'hypothesis' in the sense in which it is used in physical science today, we shall have to say that Newton's exclusion of hypotheses constitutes an exaggeration. Further, it is clear that Newton himself framed hypotheses. For example, his atomistic theory, namely, that there are extended, hard, impenetrable, indestructible, mobile particles, endowed with the *vis inertiae*, was an hypothesis. So was his theory of an ethereal medium. Neither of these hypotheses was gratuitous. The theory of the ether was postulated primarily to account for the propagation of light. And the theory of particles was not unverifiable in principle. Newton himself suggested that we might be able to perceive the largest of these particles or atoms if we possessed more powerful microscopes. But the theories were none the less hypotheses.

We must, however, allow for the fact that Newton made a distinction between experimental laws and speculative hypotheses which were, as he recognized, merely plausibly or possibly true. And from the start he refused to look on the latter as *a priori* assumptions which constituted an integral part of the scientific explanation of natural phenomena. As, however, he found it difficult to make people grasp this distinction, he came to make pronouncements about the necessity of excluding from physics or experimental philosophy all 'hypotheses', whether metaphysical or physical. The occult qualities of the Aristotelians, he tells us, constitute a hindrance to progress in science, and to say that a specific type of thing is endowed with a specific occult quality in virtue of which it acts and produces its observable effects is to say nothing at all. 'But to derive two or three general principles of motion from phenomena and afterwards to tell us how the properties and actions of all corporeal things follow from those manifest principles would be a very great step in philosophy, though the causes of those principles were not yet discovered.'[8] Newton may have spoken sometimes in an exaggerated way, and he may not have done justice to the part which has been played by speculative hypotheses in the development of science. But his fundamental intention is clear enough, to rule out useless and unverifiable hypotheses and to warn people against questioning the results of inductively ascertained principles or laws in the name of 'hypotheses' in the sense of unverified speculative assumptions. We are to admit no objections against inductively ascertained 'conclusions' apart from those objections which are based on experiments or on truths which are certain. This is what he means by saying that hypotheses are not to be regarded in experimental philosophy.

The tendency of Newton's thought, therefore, was to continue the purification of physical science from metaphysics and to exclude from science the search for 'causes', whether ultimate efficient causes or what the Scholastics called 'formal causes', namely, natures or essences. Science for him consisted in laws, formulated mathematically when possible, which are inferred from phenomena, which state how things act and which are empirically verified by consequences derived from them. But to say this is not to say that he eschewed all speculation in actual practice. Mention has already been made of his theory of ether, which he postulated to account for the propagation of light. He also believed that it served the purpose of providing for the conservation and increase, when needed, of the decaying motion in the world. He evidently thought that the conservation of energy could not be explained without introducing this additional factor which contains active principles. The ether is not, as Descartes imagined, a kind of dense, pervasive fluid; it is somewhat like air, though much rarer, and Newton sometimes spoke of it as 'spirit'. But he did not really attempt to describe its nature in any precise manner. He does not appear to have felt any doubt about the existence of an ethereal medium; but he recognized that his speculations about its character were only tentative hypotheses, and his general policy of abstaining from descriptions of unobserved entities prevented him from making dogmatic pronouncements about its precise nature.

Newton's theories of absolute space and time provide further examples of speculative hypotheses. Absolute time, as distinct from relative, apparent and common time, is said to flow equably without regard to anything external, and 'by another name (it) is called duration'.[9] Absolute space, as distinct from relative space, 'remains always similar and immovable'.[10] Newton did, indeed, make some attempt to justify his postulating absolute space and time, not, of course, by suggesting that they are observable entities, but by arguing that they are presuppositions of experimentally measurable motion. In so far, however, as he tends to speak of them as entities in which things move, he certainly transcends the sphere of that experimental philosophy from which hypotheses are banished. Further, there are internal difficulties in Newton's conception of the triad, absolute motion, absolute space and absolute time. For instance, relative motion is a change in a body's distance from some other particular body or the translation of a body from one relative place into another. Absolute motion, therefore, will be the translation of a body from one absolute place into another. And this seems to demand absolute space in order to provide absolute, and not relative, points of reference. But it is difficult to see how absolute, infinite and homogeneous space can provide any such points of reference.

So far we have a mechanical description of the world, with the introduction of certain hypotheses, such as that of ether, to account for phenomena when these apparently cannot be explained in purely mechanical terms. Newton defined bodies as masses, meaning that in addition to its geometrical properties each possesses a *vis inertiae* or force of inertia, measurable by the acceleration which a given external force imparts to the body. We have, therefore, the conception of masses moving in absolute space and time according to the mechanical laws of motion. And in this world of the scientist there are only primary qualities. In things, colours, for instance, are 'nothing but a disposition to reflect this or that sort of rays more copiously than the rest, (while) in the rays they are nothing but their dispositions to propagate this or that motion into the sensorium, and in the sensorium they are sensations of those motions under the forms of colours'.[11] If we prescind, therefore, from man and his sensations we are left with a system of masses, possessing the primary qualities, moving in absolute space and time and pervaded by the ethereal medium.

Yet this picture conveys a very inadequate idea of Newton's total outlook on the world. For he was a religious man and a firm believer in God. He wrote a number of theological treatises, and though these are somewhat unorthodox, particularly on the subject of the Trinity, he certainly looked on himself as a good Christian. Further, even though a distinction can be made between his scientific and his religious beliefs, he did not think that science is in no way relevant to religion. He was convinced that the cosmic order provides evidence for the existence of God, and that it appears 'from phenomena that there is a being, incorporeal, living, intelligent, omnipresent'.[12] Indeed, he seems to have thought that the motion of the planets round the sun was an argument for God's existence. Moreover, God exercises the function of maintaining the stars at their proper distances from one another, so that they do not collide, and of 'reforming' irregularities in the universe. In Newton's opinion, therefore, God does not simply conserve His creation in a general sense of the word, but He also actively intervenes to keep the machine going.

Furthermore, Newton gave a theological interpretation to his theory of absolute space and time. In the *General Scholium* to the second edition of the *Principia mathematica* he speaks of God as constituting duration and space by existing always and everywhere. Indeed, infinite space is described as the divine *sensorium* or 'sensory' in which God perceives and comprehends all things. Things move and are known 'within His boundless uniform sensorium'.[13] This may appear at first sight to lead to pantheism, but Newton did not maintain that God is to be identified with absolute space and time. Rather does He constitute absolute space and time through His omnipresence and eternity; and He is said to know things in infinite space as it were in His sensorium, because through His omnipresence everything is immediately present to Him.

It is clear that Newton was a philosopher as well as a mathematician and physicist. But it is not so clear how his metaphysics fits in with his views of the nature and function of physical science. In the *Opticks* he does, indeed, say that 'the main business of natural philosophy is to argue from phenomena without feigning hypotheses, and to deduce causes from effects, till we come to the very first cause, which certainly is not mechanical'.[14] And he goes on to argue that reflection on phenomena shows us that there is a spiritual, intelligent Being, who sees all things in infinite space, as it were in His sensory. Thus he obviously thought that his philosophical theology followed from his scientific ideas. But it can hardly be maintained, I think, that there is a perfect harmony between his metaphysics and his more 'positivistic' pronouncements about the nature of science. Nor does Newton seem to have made it very clear which functions are fulfilled by the ether and which by God. Further, Newton's philosophical theology labours under an obvious disadvantage from the point of view of the theist, as Berkeley saw and noted. If, for example, we argue to God's existence from 'irregularities' in Nature and from the need of putting the machine right from time to time, so to speak, such arguments will be deprived of all cogency if the supposed irregularities turn out to be empirically explicable and if phenomena which once appeared to be incapable of mechanical explanation are eventually found to fit without difficulty into a mechanical account of Nature. Again, the concepts of absolute space and time provide weak foundations for a proof of God's existence. It was not without reason that Berkeley feared that Newton's way of arguing to the existence of God would bring philosophical theism into disrepute. In any case, of course, arguments based on physical hypotheses can have no greater validity than the hypotheses themselves. There cannot be a certain *a posteriori* proof of God's existence unless it is based on propositions the truth of which is certain independently of scientific developments, so that it remains unaffected by progress in science.

It is not, however, Newton's philosophical theology which constitutes the chief reason why he should be mentioned in any history of modern philosophy. Nor is it even his philosophy of science, in the sense of his account of scientific method and of the nature of natural or experimental philosophy, an account which was not elaborated in altogether clear, consistent and precise terms. The chief reason is his great importance as one of the outstanding makers of the modern mind, of the scientific conception of the world. He carried on the work which had been developed by men such as Galileo and Descartes, and by giving to the mechanical interpretation of the material cosmos a comprehensive scientific foundation he exercised a vast influence on succeeding generations. It is not necessary to accept the views of those who rejected Newton's theological ideas and who regarded the world as a self-sustaining mechanism in order to recognize his importance. Within the scientific sphere he gave a powerful impetus to the development of empirical science, as distinct from *a priori* theorizing, and by developing the scientific interpretation of the world he helped to provide subsequent philosophical thought with one of the most important data for its reflections.

Chapter Nine

RELIGIOUS PROBLEMS

Samuel Clarke — The deists — Bishop Butler.

1. Among Newton's fervent admirers was Samuel Clarke (1675–1729). In 1697 he published a Latin translation of Jacques Rohault's *Traité de physique*, with notes designed to facilitate the transition to Newton's system. Becoming an Anglican clergyman, he published a number of theological and exegetical works, and he delivered two series of Boyle lectures, the first in 1704 on the being and attributes of God, the second in 1705 on the evidences of natural and revealed religion. In 1706 he wrote against Henry Dodwell's view that the soul is naturally mortal but that God confers immortality on it through His grace with a view to punishment or reward in the next life. He also published a translation of Newton's *Opticks*. In the years 1715 and 1716 he was engaged in controversy with Leibniz about the principles of religion and natural philosophy. At the time of his death he was rector of St. James's, Westminster, a benefice which had been conferred upon him by Queen Anne in 1709.

In his Boyle lectures,[1] which were directed against 'Mr. Hobbes, Spinoza, the author of the *Oracles of Reason* and other deniers of natural and revealed religion', Clarke develops at length an *a posteriori* argument for God's existence. He declares his intention of urging 'such propositions only as cannot be denied without departing from that reason which all atheists pretend to be the foundation of their unbelief'.[2] He then proceeds to enunciate and prove a number of propositions, designed to exhibit in a logical and systematic way the rational character of belief in God.

The propositions are as follows. First, 'it is absolutely and undeniably certain that something has existed from all eternity'.[3] For there are things which exist now; and they cannot have arisen out of nothing. If anything now exists, something existed from eternity. Secondly, 'there has existed from eternity some one unchangeable and independent being'.[4] There are dependent beings, and so there must be a non-dependent being. Otherwise there is no adequate cause for the existence of any dependent thing. Thirdly, 'that unchangeable and independent being, which has existed from eternity, without any external cause of its existence, must be self-existing, that is, necessarily-existing'.[5] Clarke then argues that this necessary being must be simple and infinite, and that it cannot be the world or any material thing. For a necessary being is necessarily all that it is and is thus unchangeable. But though we can know what this being is not, we cannot comprehend its substance. Hence the fourth proposition states that 'what the substance or essence of that being, which is self-existent or necessarily-existing, is, we have no idea, neither is it at all possible for us to comprehend it'.[6] We do not comprehend the essence or substance of anything; much less of God. Nevertheless, says the fifth proposition, 'though the substance or essence of the self-existent being is itself absolutely incomprehensible to us, yet many of the essential attributes of His nature are strictly demonstrable, as well as His existence. Thus, in the first place, the self-existent being must of necessity be eternal.'[7] The sixth proposition[8] states that the self-existent being must be infinite and omnipresent, the seventh[9] that this being must be one and one only, the eighth[10] that God must be intelligent, the ninth[11] that He must be endowed with liberty, the tenth[12] that He must be infinitely powerful, the eleventh[13] that the supreme cause must be infinitely wise, and the twelfth that the supreme cause must be a being 'of infinite goodness, justice and truth and all other moral perfections such as become the supreme governor and judge of the world'.[14]

In the course of his reflections and arguments Clarke passes some more or less conventional criticism on the Scholastics; for example, that they used meaningless terms. Apart, however, from the fact that he lays himself open to the same type of criticism by using technical terms, it is obvious to any reader who knows anything of the Scholastic tradition that Clarke makes copious use of it. This is not to say, however, that there is nothing in Clarke except what comes from the Scholastics. For example, when he tries to defend his sixth proposition (that the self-existent being is necessarily infinite and omnipresent) against the objection that ubiquity or omnipresence does not necessarily pertain to the notion of a self-existent being, he argues that space and duration (that is, absolute and infinite space and duration) are properties of God.[15] 'Space is a property of the self-existent substance, but not of any other substance. All other substances are *in* space and are penetrated by it, but the self-existent substance is not in space, nor penetrated by it, but is itself (if I may so speak) the substratum of space, the ground of the existence of space and duration itself. Which space and duration being evidently necessary and yet themselves not substances but properties, show evidently that the substance without which these properties could not subsist is itself much more (if that were possible) necessary.'[16] In answer to further objections Clarke admits that to say that 'the self-existent substance is the substratum of space, or space a property of the self-existent substance, are not perhaps very proper expressions'.[17] But he goes on to indicate that he regards infinite space and duration as being in some sense realities which are independent of finite things. They are not, however, substances. Clarke does not prove God's existence in the first place from space and duration. As we have seen, he proves the existence of a self-existent substance before he arrives at his sixth proposition. But, having proved God's existence, he argues that infinite space and duration must be properties of God. There seems, however, to be an important ambiguity in his account of the matter, which he does not clarify. For to say that space and duration are properties of God and to say that God in some sense grounds space and time are not the same thing. It may be said that for Clarke infinite space and infinite duration are the divine omnipresence and eternity. But if this is the case, an explanation is needed of how we can know them without already knowing God.

Clarke's views on this matter bear such a marked resemblance to Newton's that it has sometimes been maintained that he took them from the latter's writings. But historians have rightly pointed out that Clarke had first expounded his ideas some nine years before Newton published the *General Scholium* to the second edition of the *Principia*. But even though Clarke did not borrow his ideas from Newton, it is perfectly understandable that in his correspondence with Leibniz he undertook to defend Newton's theory against the criticism passed by the latter, who evidently considered it to be absurd. He also takes the opportunity of developing his own ideas. Thus 'space is not a being, an eternal and infinite being, but a property or consequence of a being infinite and eternal. Infinite space is immensity; but immensity is not God; and therefore infinite space is not God'.[18] Leibniz objected that absolute or pure space is imaginary, a construction of the imagination; but Clarke answered that 'extra-mundane space (if the material world be finite in its dimensions) is not imaginary but real'.[19] The precise relation of this space to God is, however, left obscure. To say that it is not God but a property of God is not very illuminating, and confusion is simply increased if it is also spoken of as a 'consequence' of God. According to Clarke, 'if no creatures existed, yet the ubiquity of God and the continuance of His existence would make space and time to be exactly the same as they are now'.[20] Leibniz, however, contended that 'if there were no creatures, space and time would be only in the ideas of God'.[21]

Leaving aside Clarke's rather obscure theory about space and time, we can say in general that in his eyes the existence of God is or ought to be plain to anyone who gives careful consideration to the implications of the existence of any one finite thing. So also does he consider that anyone can discern without difficulty the objective distinctions between right and wrong. 'There are certain necessary and eternal differences of things, and certain consequent fitnesses or unfitnesses of the application of different things or different relations one to another; not depending on any positive constitutions, but founded unchangeably in the nature and reason of things, and unavoidably arising from the differences of the things themselves.'[22] For example, man's relation to God makes it unchangeably fitting that he should honour, worship and obey his Creator. 'In like manner, in men's dealing and conversing one with another it is undeniably more fit, absolutely and in the nature of the thing itself, that all men should endeavour to promote the universal good and welfare of all than that all men should be continually contriving the ruin and destruction of all.'[23]

Clarke insists against Hobbes that these relations of fitness and unfitness are independent of any social compact or covenant, and that they give rise to obligations quite apart from any legal enactment and from the application of sanctions, present or future. In fact, moral principles are so 'plain and self-evident that nothing but the extremest stupidity of mind, corruption of manners or perverseness of spirit can possibly make any man entertain the least doubt concerning them'.[24] These 'eternal moral obligations are indeed of themselves incumbent on all rational beings, even antecedent to the consideration of their being the positive will and command of God'.[25] But their fulfilment is in fact positively willed by God, and He rewards and punishes men according to their fulfilment or infringement of the moral law. We can thus speak of a 'secondary and additional obligation', but 'the original obligation of all . . . is the eternal reason of things'.[26] There is, in other words, a natural moral law, the main principles of which at least are discerned by the minds of all who are neither idiots nor thoroughly corrupted. And 'that state which Mr. Hobbes calls the state of nature is not in any sense a natural state but a state of the greatest, most unnatural and most intolerable corruption that can be imagined'.[27]

Though, however, the fundamental principles of the moral law are self-evident to the unclouded and unperverted mind, and though more particular rules can be deduced from these, the actual condition of man is such that instruction in moral truth is necessary to him. This means in the end that revelation is morally necessary; and the true divine revelation is the Christian religion. Christianity comprises not only truths which reason can, in principle, find out for itself but also truths which transcend reason, though they are not contrary to it. But 'every one of these doctrines has a natural tendency and a direct and powerful influence to reform men's lives and correct their manners. This is the great end and ultimate design of all true religion.'[28] And the truth of the Christian religion is confirmed by miracle and prophecy.

2. Like the Cambridge Platonists or Latitudinarians, Clarke was a 'rationalist' in the sense that he appealed to reason and maintained that Christianity has a rational foundation. He was not the man to appeal to faith without any reference to the rational grounds for believing. And we can even find in his writings a tendency to rationalize Christianity and to play down the concept of 'mystery'. At the same time

he distinguished himself sharply from the deists. In the second series of his Boyle lectures he divides the so-called deists into four sorts or groups. The first group consists of those who acknowledge that God created the world but who deny that He plays any part in governing it. The second group consists of those who believe that all natural events depend on the divine activity but who at the same time assert that God takes no notice of man's moral behaviour, on the ground that moral distinctions depend simply on human positive law. The third group consists of those who think indeed that God expects moral behaviour from His rational creatures but who do not believe in the immortality of the soul. The fourth group consists of those who believe that there is a future life in which God rewards and punishes but who accept only those truths which can be discovered by reason alone. And 'these, I say, are the only true Deists'.[29] In Clarke's opinion these 'only true Deists' are to be found exclusively among those philosophers who lived without any knowledge of divine revelation but who recognized and lived up to the principles and obligations of natural religion and natural morality. In other words, he recognizes as 'true' deists those pagan philosophers, if any, who fulfilled the necessary qualifications, and not the contemporary deists.

Clarke's observations about the deists are highly polemical in tone; but his classification, even if over-schematized, is useful in that it draws attention both to common ground and to differences. The word 'deism' was first used in the sixteenth century, and it is employed for a number of writers belonging, for the most part, to the last part of the seventeenth and the early part of the eighteenth century, who rejected the idea of supernatural revelation and of revealed mysteries. Locke himself did not reject the idea of revelation, but, as we have seen, he insisted that reason is the judge of revelation, and his book on the *Reasonableness of Christianity* (1695) acted as a powerful impetus in the direction of the rationalization of the Christian religion. The deists applied his ideas in a more radical manner and tended to reduce Christianity to a purely natural religion, discarding the idea of a unique revelation and trying to find the rational essence at the heart of the different historical religions. They had in common a belief in God, which differentiated them from the atheists, together with a disbelief in any unique revelation and supernatural scheme of salvation, which differentiated them from the orthodox Christians. In other words, they were rationalists who believed in God. At the same time they differed very much among themselves, and there is no such thing as a school of deism. Some were hostile to Christianity while others were not hostile, though they tended to reduce the Christian religion to a natural religion. Some believed in the immortality of the soul, others did not. Some spoke as though God created the world and then left it to proceed on its way according to natural laws. These were obviously strongly influenced by the new mechanical conception of the cosmic system. Others had some belief at least in divine providence. Finally, some tended to identify God and nature, while others believed in a personal God. But in the course of time the word 'theist' was used to designate the latter as distinct from the naturalistic pantheists and from those who denied all divine providential government. In fine, eighteenth-century deism meant the desupernaturalizing of religion and the refusal to accept any religious propositions on authority. For the deists reason, and reason alone, was the judge of truth in religion as elsewhere. They were therefore also called 'free-thinkers', the word indicating that for them the activity of reason should be restricted by no tradition and by no authority, whether of the Scriptures or of the Church.

This appeal to reason as the one and only arbiter of religious truth is represented by such books as *Christianity Not Mysterious* (1696) by John Toland (1670–1722) and *Christianity as Old as the Creation; or, the Gospel a Republication of the Religion of Nature* (1730) by Matthew Tindal (c. 1656–1733). The last-named work was regarded as a kind of deistic Bible and elicited a number of replies, such as the *Defence of Revealed Religion* (1732) by John Conybeare. Butler's *Analogy of Religion* was also directed in large measure against Tindal's work. Other deistic writings of the same kind are *The Religion of Nature Delineated* (1722) by William Wollaston (1659–1724) and *The True Gospel of Jesus Christ* (1739) by Thomas Chubb (1679–1747). The rights of 'free-thinking' were proclaimed by Anthony Collins (1676–1729) in his work *A Discourse of Free-thinking, occasioned by the Rise and Growth of a Sect called Free-thinkers* (1713).

Some of the deists, such as Tindal, were doubtless concerned simply with expounding what they considered to be the common essence of true, natural religion. And the essence of Christianity consisted for them principally in its ethical teaching. They had no sympathy with the dogmatic disputes of different Christian bodies, but they were not radically hostile to Christianity. Other deists, however, were more radical thinkers. John Toland, who was for a short time a convert to Catholicism before he returned to Protestantism, ended as a pantheist, this phase of his thought being represented by his *Pantheisticon* (1720). He blamed Spinoza for not seeing that motion is an essential attribute of body, but he approximated to the former's position, with the qualification that he was much more of a materialist than was Spinoza. For Toland the mind was simply a function or epiphenomenon of the brain. Again, Anthony Collins put forward a frankly deterministic theory in his *Inquiry concerning Human Liberty* (1715). And Thomas Woolston (1669–1733), under cover of allegorizing the Bible, called in question the historicity of Christ's miracles and of the Resurrection. *The Trial of the Witnesses of the Resurrection of Jesus* (1729) by Thomas Sherlock was an answer to Woolston's *Discourses* so far as they concerned the Resurrection.

Notable among the deists by reason of his prominence in political life was Henry St. John, Viscount Bolingbroke (1678–1751). Bolingbroke acknowledged Locke as his master, but his way of interpreting Locke's empiricism was hardly consonant with the latter's spirit. For he tended to develop it in a positivistic direction. Plato and 'Platonists', including St. Augustine, Malebranche, Berkeley, the Cambridge Platonists and Samuel Clarke, were anathema to him. Metaphysics was in his eyes a creature of the imagination. This did not prevent him, indeed, from maintaining that the existence of an omnipotent and all-wise Creator can be proved by means of reflection on the cosmic system. But he stressed the divine transcendence and rejected the 'Platonist' idea of 'participation'. It is nonsense to speak of God loving man: such talk merely ministers to man's desire to exaggerate his importance. This means, of course, that Bolingbroke had to eviscerate Christianity of its characteristic elements and reduce it to what he regarded as natural religion. He did not explicitly deny that Christ was the Messiah or that He performed miracles: indeed he affirms both propositions. But the work of St. Paul and his successors was the object of bitter attack. The purpose of Christ's coming and of His activity was simply to confirm the truth of natural religion. The theology of redemption and salvation is a worthless accretion. In spite of all his esteem for Locke, Bolingbroke was entirely lacking in Locke's genuine Christian piety, and his outlook was contaminated by a cynicism which was conspicuously absent from the mind of the father of British empiricism. In Bolingbroke's opinion the masses should be left to adhere to the dominant and prevailing religion and not be disturbed by free-thinkers. Free-thought should be a prerogative of the aristocratic and educated.

The English deists were by no means profound philosophers; but the movement exercised a certain considerable influence. In France, for example, Voltaire was an admirer of Bolingbroke, and Diderot was, for a time at least, a deist. The American statesman, Benjamin Franklin, who had once written from an irreligious point of view against Wollaston's *Religion of Nature Delineated*, also confessed himself a deist. But there was, of course, a considerable difference between the French and the American deists. The former were inclined to bitter scoffing and attack against orthodox Christianity, whereas the latter were more akin to the English deists in their positive concern for natural religion and morality.

3. The most eminent among the opponents of the deists was Joseph Butler (1692–1752), bishop of Durham. In 1736 appeared his chief work, *The Analogy of Religion, Natural and Revealed, to the Constitution and Course of Nature*.[30] In the preface or 'advertisement' to this book Butler remarks that 'it is come, I know not how, to be taken for granted by many persons that Christianity is not so much as a subject of inquiry, but that it is now at length discovered to be fictitious. And accordingly they treat it as if, in the present age, this were an agreed point among all people of discernment, and nothing remained but to set it up as a principal subject of mirth and ridicule, as it were by way of reprisal for its having so long interrupted the pleasures of the world.'[31] At the time at which Butler was writing religion was at a very low ebb in England, and his chief concern was to show that belief in Christianity is not unreasonable. So far as he was concerned with the deists in particular, he looked on them as symptomatic of the general decline of religion. But that he was concerned with them is clear from the fact that

he presupposes the existence of God and does not undertake to prove it.

The purpose of *The Analogy of Religion* is not to prove that there is a future life, that God rewards and punishes after death, and that Christianity is true. The scope of the work is more limited, being that of showing that the acceptance of such truths is not unreasonable, unless the deists are prepared to say that all their beliefs about the system and course of nature are unreasonable. Our knowledge of nature is probable. True, probability can vary much in degree; but the knowledge which we possess of nature is based on experience and, even when it attains a very high degree of probability, it is still only probable. And there is much that we do not understand. Yet in spite of the limitations of our knowledge the deists do not question the reasonableness and legitimacy of our beliefs about nature simply because much is obscure to us. We can argue by analogy, therefore, that if in the sphere of religious truth we encounter difficulties similar to those encountered in our knowledge of nature, which is admittedly God's creation, these difficulties are no reason for rejecting religious doctrines out of hand. In other words, the deists advance difficulties against certain truths of natural religion, such as the immortality of the soul, and against the truths of revealed religion; but the existence of such difficulties does not constitute a disproof of the propositions in question if the former are analogous to or have their counterpart in our knowledge of the constitution and course of nature, the author of which is admitted by the deists themselves to be God. In his introduction Butler cites Origen to the effect that a man who believes the Scriptures to be the work of Him who is the Author of nature may well expect to find the same sort of difficulties in them as are found in nature. 'And in a like way of reflection it may be added that he who denies the Scriptures to have been from God upon account of these difficulties may, for the very same reason, deny the world to have been formed by Him.'[32]

Butler does not, of course, confine himself to arguing that difficulties in the sphere of religious truth do not constitute a disproof of religious propositions when they are analogous to difficulties encountered in our knowledge of nature. He argues further that natural facts provide a ground for inferring the probable truth of natural and revealed religion. And since it is a question of propositions which are of vital concern to us in the practical order, and not simply of propositions the truth or falsehood of which is a matter of indifference to us, we ought to act according to the balance of probability. For example, there is no natural fact which forces us to say that immortality is impossible; and, further, analogies drawn from our present life make it positively probable that there is a future life. We see caterpillars turning eventually into butterflies, birds breaking their shells and entering upon a fuller life, human beings developing from an embryonic to a mature state; and 'therefore that we are to exist hereafter in a state as different (suppose) from our present as this is from our former, is but according to the analogy of nature'.[33] True, we see the dissolution of the body, but while death deprives us of any 'sensible proof' that a man's powers survive, it does not mean that he does not survive, and the unity of consciousness in this life suggests that he can do so. Again, even in this life our actions meet with natural consequences, happiness and unhappiness depending upon our behaviour. The analogy of nature suggests, therefore, that our actions here meet with reward and punishment in the future life. As for Christianity, it is not true to say that it is merely a 'republication' of natural religion. For it teaches us much that we could not have known otherwise. And if our natural knowledge is deficient and limited, as it is, there is no *a priori* reason why we should not acquire fresh light through revelation. Further, 'analogy of nature shows that we are not to expect any benefits without making use of the appointed means for obtaining or enjoying them. Now reason shows us nothing of the particular immediate means of obtaining either temporal or spiritual benefits. This therefore we must learn either from experience or revelation. And experience the present case does not admit of.'[34] It is folly, therefore, to treat Christian revelation and teaching as light and trivial matters. For we cannot obtain the end and reward proposed by God without using the means appointed by Him, means which are known through revelation.

If Butler's arguments are interpreted as proofs of the truths of natural and revealed religion, they seem to be often extremely weak. But he was aware of this himself. He says, for instance, that 'it is most readily acknowledged that the foregoing treatise is by no means satisfactory; very far indeed from it'.[35] And he considers the objection that 'it is a poor thing to solve difficulties in revelation by saying that there are the same in natural religion, when what is wanting is to clear both of them of these their common, as well as other their respective, difficulties. . . .'[36] At the same time he points out that he has been concerned with a particular line of objection brought against religion, namely, that there are difficulties and doubtful points in it, and that if it were true, it would be free from these. But this objection presupposes that there are no difficulties and doubts in natural non-religious knowledge; and this is not the case. Yet in their temporal concerns people do not hesitate to act upon evidence of the same kind that is available in religious matters. 'And as the force of this answer lies merely in the parallel which there is between the evidence for religion and for our temporal conduct, the answer is equally just and conclusive whether the parallel be made out by showing the evidence of the former to be higher or the evidence of the latter to be lower.'[37] The object of the treatise is not to clear up all difficulties and justify divine providence but to show what we ought to do. It may be said that we ought not to act without evidence. But for the truth of Christianity we have historical evidence, especially miracles and prophecies.

The *Analogy of Religion* is obviously very deficient if it is considered as a philosophy of religion. But it was not intended to be this, and it should not be judged as such. It is also deficient if considered as a book of systematic apologetics, though it is interesting to observe that Butler outlines the notion of a cumulative argument for Christianity amounting to a proof. 'But the truth of our religion, like the truths of common matters, is to be judged by all the evidence taken together. And unless the whole series of things which may be alleged in this argument, and every particular thing in it, can reasonably be supposed to have been by accident (for here the stress of the argument for Christianity lies) then is the truth of it proved.'[38] This is a valuable line of thought in apologetics. Still, the work was not intended to be a work of systematic apologetics in the modern sense. It was meant to be an answer to the deists' line of objection against revealed religion, an answer based on the analogy of nature in the sense described above. It must be admitted, I think, that some of Butler's analogies are not convincing. There are, for example, obvious objections against arguing from the fact that temporal happiness and unhappiness depend upon our conduct in this life to the probability that happiness and unhappiness in the next life also depend on our behaviour in *this* life. At the same time the great strength of the work seems to lie in Butler's awareness of the role of probability in our interpretation of Nature and in our conduct in temporal concerns, and in his argument that in this case we ought to act according to the balance of probability also in religious affairs, without demanding that all difficulties and obscurities should first be cleared up. This line of argument may be an *argumentum ad hominem*, namely, against the deists; but it is an effective line of argument in this connection. For the contemporary deists were not, like Lord Herbert of Cherbury, upholders of the theory of innate ideas, but stood rather in the empiricist tradition. And Butler places himself on the same ground, though how this may affect our knowledge of the existence of God he does not explain.

Butler's ethical theory will be considered in the next chapter. But it is not inappropriate to say something here of his views on personal identity, which are given in the first dissertation appended to *The Analogy of Religion*.

In the first place, says Butler, personal identity cannot be defined. Yet to say this is not to say that we are not aware of personal identity or that we have no notion of it. We cannot define similarity or equality, but we know what they are. And we know what they are by viewing, for example, the similarity of two triangles or the equality between twice two and four. In other words, we come to have the notions of similarity and equality by acquaintance with instances. And so it is with personal identity. 'Upon comparing the consciousness of oneself or one's own existence in any two moments there immediately arises to the mind the idea of personal identity.'[39]

Butler does not intend to say that consciousness makes personal identity. Indeed, he criticizes Locke for defining personal identity in terms of consciousness. 'One should really think it self-evident that consciousness of personal identity presupposes, and therefore cannot constitute, personal identity, any more than knowledge in any other case can constitute truth, which it presupposes.'[40] Butler admits that to be endowed with consciousness is inseparable from our idea of a person or intelligent being. But it does not follow that present consciousness of past actions or feelings is necessary to our being the same persons who performed those actions or had those feelings. True, the successive consciousnesses which we have of our own existence are distinct. But 'the person of whose existence the consciousness is felt now, and was felt an hour or a year ago, is discerned to be, not two persons, but one and the same person; and therefore is one and the same'.[41] To attempt to prove the truth of what we perceive in this way is futile; for we could only do so by means of the perceptions themselves. In the same way we cannot prove the ability of our faculties to know truth; for to do so we should have to rely on these very faculties. Butler evidently thinks that the fault lies, not with the person who cannot demonstrate what is evident, but with him who demands a demonstration of what cannot be demonstrated and what does not need to be demonstrated. The reason why he discusses the problem of personal identity is its connection with the problem of immortality. And though he can hardly be said to have treated the question very thoroughly, he certainly makes a good point against Locke.

Chapter Ten

PROBLEMS OF ETHICS

*Shaftesbury — Mandeville — Hutcheson — Butler — Hart-
ley — Tucker — Paley — General remarks.*

1. In the seventeenth century Hobbes had defended an interpretation of man as essentially egoistic and an authoritarian conception of morality, in the sense that according to
him the obligatory character of moral laws, as we normally
conceive them, depends on the will either of God or of the
political sovereign. And as it is the latter who interprets the
law of God, we can say that for Hobbes the source of obligation in social morality is the authority of the sovereign.

Locke, as we have seen, was in important respects strongly
opposed to Hobbes. He did not share the latter's pessimistic
views about human nature when considered in abstraction
from the constraining influence of society and government;
nor did he think that the obligatory character of moral laws
depends on the authority and will of the political sovereign.
But in some of his pronouncements on ethics he certainly
implied that moral obligation depends on the divine will.
Indeed, he sometimes implied that moral distinctions depend on this will. Thus he did not hesitate to state that
moral good and evil are the agreement or disagreement of
our voluntary actions with a law whereby good or evil is
'drawn on us' by the will and power of the law-maker, this
law-maker being God. Again, he asserted that if a Christian
is asked why a man ought to keep his word, he will answer
that God, who has the power of eternal life and death, requires it of us. To be sure, this authoritarian element represents only one part or aspect of Locke's reflections on morality. But it is none the less an element.

In the first half of the eighteenth century, however, there was a group of moralists who opposed not only Hobbes's interpretation of man as essentially egoistic but also all authoritarian conceptions of the moral law and of moral obligation. As against Hobbes's idea of man they insisted on man's social nature; and as against ethical authoritarianism they insisted on man's possession of a moral sense by which he discerns moral values and moral distinctions independently of the expressed will of God, and still more of the law of the State. They tended, therefore, to set ethics on its own feet, so to speak; and for this reason alone they are of considerable importance in the history of British moral theory. They also gave a social interpretation of morality, in terms of a social rather than of a private end. And in eighteenth-century moral philosophy we can see the beginnings of the utilitarianism which is associated above all with the name of J. S. Mill in the nineteenth century. At the same time we should not allow an interest in the development of utilitarianism to lead us to overlook the peculiar characteristics of moralists of the eighteenth century such as Shaftesbury and Hutcheson.

The first philosopher of the group to be considered here was a pupil of Locke. Anthony Ashley (1671–1713), third earl of Shaftesbury and grandson of Locke's patron, was associated with Locke for three years (1686–9). But though he retained respect for his tutor, he was never a disciple of Locke, in the sense of accepting all the latter's ideas. Shaftesbury was an admirer of what he regarded as the Greek ideal of balance and harmony, and in his opinion Locke would have rendered better service to moral and political philosophy if he had possessed a profounder knowledge and appreciation of Greek thought. For one thing, he would then have been in a position to see more clearly the truth of Aristotle's view that man is by nature a social being. As it was, his dislike of Scholastic Aristotelianism prevented him from appreciating the historic Aristotle and the truths presented in the *Ethics* and *Politics*. The human end, which sets a standard for the distinctions between good and evil, right and wrong, is a social end, and in virtue of his nature man has a natural feeling for these distinctions. To say this is not incompatible with Locke's rejection of innate ideas. The salient question is not about the time at which moral ideas enter the mind but rather whether man's nature is such that in due course moral ideas or ideas of moral values inevitably arise in him. They do not arise because they are innate in the sense in which Locke understood and rejected innate ideas, but because man is what he is, a social being with a moral end which is social in character. Moral ideas are 'connatural' rather than innate.

Shaftesbury had no intention of denying that the individual naturally seeks his own good. 'We know that every creature has a private good and interest of his own, which nature has compelled him to seek.'[1] But man is part of a system, and 'to deserve the name of *good* or *virtuous* a creature must have all his inclinations and affections, his dispositions of mind and temper, suitable and agreeing with the good of his kind or of that system in which he is included and of which he constitutes a part'.[2] A man's individual or private good consists in the harmony or balance of his appetites, passions and affections under the control of reason. But because man is part of a system, that is, because he is by nature a social being, his affections cannot be perfectly harmonized and balanced unless they are in harmony with respect to society. We are not forced to choose between self-love and altruism, between concern for one's own good and concern for the public good as though they are of necessity mutually exclusive. True, 'if there be found in any creature a more than ordinary self-concernment or regard to private good, which is inconsistent with the interest of the species or public, this must in every respect be esteemed an ill and vicious affection. And this is what we commonly call *selfishness*.'[3] But if a man's regard for his private good is not only consistent with the public good but contributes to it, it is in no way blameworthy. For example, though concern for one's own preservation is to be esteemed vicious if it renders one incapable of any generous or benevolent action, a well-ordered concern for their own preservation on the part of individuals contributes to the common good. Thus Shaftesbury does not answer Hobbes by condemning all 'egoism': he maintains that in the moral man the self-regarding impulses and the altruistic or benevolent impulses are harmonized. Benevolence is an integral part of morality, and it is rooted in man's nature as part of a system; but it is not the entire content of morality.

Shaftesbury conceives, therefore, the good of man as something objective, in the sense that it is that which satisfies man as man and in the sense that its nature can be determined by reflection on human nature. 'There is that in which the nature of man is satisfied, and which alone must be his good.'[4] 'Thus is philosophy established. For everyone, of necessity, must reason concerning his own happiness, what his good is and what his ill. The question is only, who reasons best.'[5] This good is not pleasure. To say without qualification or discrimination that pleasure is our good 'has as little meaning as to say, "We choose what we think eligible" and "We are pleased with what delights or pleases us". The question is whether we are rightly pleased and choose as we should do.'[6] Shaftesbury does not describe the nature of the good very precisely. On the one hand he speaks of it as virtue. Thus he writes of 'that quality to which we give the name of goodness or virtue'.[7] The emphasis is placed on the affections or passions. 'Since it is therefore by affection merely that a creature is esteemed good or ill, natural or unnatural, our business will be to examine which are the good and natural, and which the ill and unnatural affections.'[8] When a man's affections and passions are in a proper state of harmony and balance, with regard both to himself and to society, 'this is rectitude, integrity or virtue'.[9] Here the emphasis is laid on character rather than on actions or on any extrinsic end to be achieved by action. On the other hand, Shaftesbury speaks about the affections as directed towards the good, and of the good as 'interest'. 'It has already been shown that in the passions and affections of particular creatures, there is a constant relation to the interest of a species or common nature.'[10] And this may seem to imply that the good is something other than virtue or moral integrity. Shaftesbury had a low opinion of academic, pedantic philosophy, and it is perhaps not surprising that he did not express his ethical ideas in unambiguous terms. But we can say at any rate that the emphasis is consistently laid on virtue and character. For example, a man is not to be esteemed good merely because he happens to do something which is advantageous to mankind; for he may perform such actions under the impulse of a purely selfish affection or through unworthy motives. In actual fact, a man will contribute to his own interest or good or happiness and to the public or common interest or good or happiness in proportion as he is virtuous. Virtue and interest thus go together; and to show that this is so is one of Shaftesbury's main concerns. He can thus say that 'virtue is the good, and vice the ill of everyone'.[11]

Every man, Shaftesbury considered, is capable, to some degree at least, of perceiving moral values, of discriminating between virtue and vice. For all men possess conscience or the moral sense, a faculty which is analogous to that whereby men perceive differences between harmonies and discords, proportion and lack of proportion. 'Is there a natural beauty of figures? And is there not as natural a one of actions? . . . No sooner are actions viewed, no sooner the human affections and passions discerned (and they are most of them as soon discerned as felt) than straight an inward eye distinguishes and sees the fair and shapely, the amiable and admirable, apart from the deformed, the foul, the odious or the despicable. How is it possible therefore not to own that as these distinctions have their foundation in nature, the discernment itself is natural and from nature alone?'[12] It may be that there are wicked and depraved persons who lack any real antipathy towards what is wrong and any real love for what is right for its own sake; but even the wickedest man has some moral sense, to the extent at least that he can distinguish to some degree between meritorious conduct and conduct which is deserving of punishment.[13] The sense of right and wrong is natural to man, though custom and education may lead people to have false ideas of what is right and what is wrong. In other words, there is in all men a fundamental moral sense or conscience, though it may be darkened or perverted through bad customs, through erroneous religious ideas, and so on.

We find, therefore, in Shaftesbury the assimilation of the moral to the aesthetic 'sense' or faculty. The mind 'feels the soft and harsh, the agreeable and disagreeable, in the affections, and finds a foul and a fair, a harmonious and a dissonant, as really and truly here as in any musical numbers or in the outward forms or representations of sensible things. Nor can it withhold its admiration and ecstasy, its aversion and scorn, any more in what relates to the one than to the other of these subjects.'[14] This does not mean that there are innate ideas of moral values. We know, for example, the affections and actions of pity and gratitude by experience. But then 'there arises another kind of affection towards those very affections themselves, which have been already felt and are now become the subject of a new liking or dislike'.[15]

The moral sense is innate, but moral concepts are not innate.

A point on which Shaftesbury insists is that virtue should be sought for its own sake. Rewards and punishments can, indeed, be profitably used for educational purposes. But the object of this education is to produce a disinterested love of virtue. It is only when a man comes to love it 'for its own sake, as good and amiable in itself'[16] that he can properly be called virtuous. To make virtue dependent on the will of God or to define it in relation to divine rewards is to begin at the wrong end. 'For how can Supreme Goodness be intelligible to those who know not what goodness itself is? Or how can virtue be understood to deserve reward, when as yet its merit and excellence is unknown? We begin surely at the wrong end, when we would prove merit by favour and order by a Deity.'[17] Ethics, in other words, possesses a certain independence: we ought not to start with the ideas of God, of divine providence and of eternal reward and punishment and base moral concepts on these ideas. At the same time virtue is not complete unless it comprises piety towards God; and piety reacts on the virtuous affections, giving them firmness and constancy. 'And thus the perfection and height of virtue must be owing to the belief of a God.'[18]

Given this point of view, it is scarcely necessary to add that Shaftesbury does not define obligation in terms of obedience to divine will and authority. One might perhaps expect him to say that the moral sense or conscience discerns obligations and to leave the matter there. But in considering obligation he tries to show that concern for one's own interest and concern for the public interest or common good are inseparable, and that virtue, to which benevolence is essential, is to the advantage of the individual. To indulge in selfishness is to be miserable, whereas to be completely virtuous is to be supremely happy. This answer to the problem of obligation is influenced by the way in which he states the question. 'It remains to inquire, what obligation there is to virtue; or what reason to embrace it.'[19] The reason which he gives is that virtue is necessary for happiness, and that vice spells misery. Probably one can see here the influence of Greek ethical thought.

Shaftesbury's ethical writings had a considerable effect on the minds of other philosophers, both in Great Britain and abroad. Hutcheson, whose moral philosophy will be considered presently, owed a great deal to him, and through Hutcheson Shaftesbury influenced later thinkers such as Hume and Adam Smith. He was also appreciated by Voltaire and Diderot in France, and by German literary figures such as Herder. But the next section will be devoted to one of Shaftesbury's critics.

2. Bernard de Mandeville (1670–1733) subjected Shaftesbury's ethical theory to criticism in his work *The Fable of the Bees or Private Vices Public Benefits* (1714; 2nd edition, 1723), which was a development of *The Grumbling Hive or Knaves turned Honest* (1705). Shaftesbury, says Mandeville, called every action which is performed with regard to the public good a virtuous action, and he stigmatizes as vice all selfishness which excludes regard for the common good. This view supposes that it is a man's good qualities which make him sociable and that he is naturally gifted with altruistic inclinations. But daily experience teaches us the contrary. We have no empirical evidence that man is naturally an altruistic being. Nor have we any cogent evidence that society benefits only by what Shaftesbury called virtuous actions. On the contrary, it is vice (that is, self-regarding affections and actions) which benefits society. A society which was endowed with all the 'virtues' would be a static and stagnant society. It is when individuals, seeking their own enjoyment and comfort, contrive or promote new inventions and when, by luxurious living, they circulate capital, that society progresses and flourishes. In this sense private vices are public benefits. Further, Shaftesbury's notion that there are objective standards of morality and objective moral values is incompatible with the empirical evidence. We cannot make objectively grounded distinctions between virtue and vice and between higher and lower pleasures. Exalted notions of social virtues are the result partly of a selfish desire for self-preservation on the part of those who combine together in society to secure this end, partly of an equally selfish desire to assert man's superiority over the brutes, and partly of the activity of politicians playing on man's vanity and pride.

Mandeville's ideas, which were criticized by Berkeley in *Alciphron*, naturally give the impression of being the fruit of a thorough-going moral cynicism. He continued Hobbes's egoistic interpretation of human nature, but at the same time, whereas Hobbes considered that man can and in some sense ought to be constrained by external power to pursue social morality, Mandeville maintained that society is best served by the flourishing of private vices. And this view, so described, necessarily appears to be the expression of moral cynicism. But we have to bear in mind what Mandeville meant by 'vices'. The search for 'luxury', that is, for material amenities which are more than what is necessary, was stigmatized by him as 'vicious'. And seeing the impetus given by this search to the development of material civilization, he asserted that private vice can be a public benefit. But it is obviously by no means everyone who would be willing to call this search for luxury 'vicious'; and to do so is in part an expression of a certain puritanical rigorism rather than of moral cynicism. However, the view that altruistic and disinterested conduct is secured by the ability of statesmen to play on human vanity and pride can legitimately be called cynical; and it was this sort of notion which appeared fashionable to some of his contemporaries and monstrous and hateful to others. Mandeville can certainly not be reckoned a great moral philosopher; but his general idea that private egoism and the public good are not at all inconsistent is of some importance. It is an idea which is implicit in the *laissez-faire* type of political and economic theory.

3. Shaftesbury was neither a systematic nor a particularly clear and precise thinker. His ideas were, however, to a certain extent systematized and developed by Francis Hutcheson (1694–1746), who was for some time professor of moral philosophy at Glasgow. I say 'to some extent' because Shaftesbury was by no means the only influence on Hutcheson's mind and on the formation of his ideas. In the first edition of his first work, *An Inquiry into the Original of our Ideas of Beauty and Virtue* (1725), Hutcheson explicitly set out to explain and defend the principles of Shaftesbury as against those of Mandeville. But his *Essay on the Nature and Conduct of the Passions and Affections, with Illustrations on the Moral Sense* (1728) shows evidence of Butler's influence. Further modifications are observable in his *System of Moral Philosophy*, which was edited by William Leechman and appeared posthumously in 1755, though Hutcheson had completed it by 1737. Finally, the *Philosophiae moralis institutio compendiaria libris tribus ethices et jurisprudentiae naturalis principia continens* (1742) shows the influence, in a minor degree, of Marcus Aurelius, the greater part of

whose *Meditations* had been translated by Hutcheson about the time that he was writing his Latin work. It is not possible, however, to note all the successive modifications, changes and developments in his moral philosophy in the brief account which is all that can be given in the present section.

Hutcheson takes up again the subject of the moral sense. He is aware, of course, that the word 'sense' is ordinarily used with reference to vision, touch, and so on. But in his opinion the extended use of the word is justified. For the mind can be passively affected not only by objects of sense in the ordinary meaning of the term but also by objects in the aesthetic and moral orders. He makes a distinction, therefore, between the external and internal senses. By external sense the mind receives, in Locke's terminology, simple ideas of single qualities of objects. 'Those ideas which are raised in the mind upon the presence of external objects and their acting upon our bodies are called sensations.'[20] By internal sense we perceive relations which give rise to a feeling or feelings which are different from the seeing or hearing or touching of separate related objects. And internal sense in general is divided into the sense of beauty and the moral sense. The object of the former is 'uniformity amidst variety',[21] a term which Hutcheson substituted for Shaftesbury's 'harmony'. By the moral sense 'we perceive pleasure, in the contemplation of such (good) actions in others, and are determined to love the agent (and much more do we perceive pleasure in being conscious of having done such actions ourselves) without any view of further natural advantage from them'.[22]

In his account of our reception of simple ideas Hutcheson is obviously dependent to a great extent on Locke. The idea of the moral sense comes, of course, from Shaftesbury, not from Locke. To postulate a moral sense would hardly fit in well with the latter's pronouncements on ethics. But the passivity of external sense, which is found in Locke's theory of our reception of simple ideas, is reflected in Hutcheson's account of the passivity of the moral sense. Moreover, Hutcheson is sufficiently influenced by Locke's empiricism to emphasize the difference between the theory of the moral sense and the theory of innate ideas. In exercising the moral sense we do not contemplate innate ideas, nor do we draw ideas out of ourselves. The sense itself is natural and inborn;

but by it we perceive moral qualities as by the external sense we perceive sensible qualities.

What precisely is it that we perceive by the moral sense? Hutcheson does not seem to be very clear on this point. Sometimes he speaks of perceiving the moral qualities of actions; but his considered view seems to be rather that we perceive qualities of character. Of course, the whole matter is complicated, at least in the *Inquiry*, by the hedonistic colouring of his way of describing the activity of the moral sense. Thus in the passage quoted above he speaks of perceiving *pleasure* in the contemplation of good actions, whether in ourselves or in others. But in the *System of Moral Philosophy* he describes the moral sense as 'the faculty of perceiving moral excellence and its supreme objects'.[23] The 'primary objects of the moral sense are the affections of the will'.[24] Which affections? Primarily those which Hutcheson calls the 'kind affections', namely, affections of benevolence. We have, he tells us, a distinct perception of beauty or excellence in the kind affections of rational agents. In the *Inquiry* he speaks of the perception of excellence 'in every appearance or evidence of benevolence',[25] and a similar emphasis on benevolence is clear in his later writings. But there is an obvious difficulty in claiming that the primary object of the moral sense consists in affections, as far as other people at least are concerned. For it may be asked how we can be said to perceive affections other than our own. According to Hutcheson, 'the object of the moral sense is not any external motion or action, but the inward affections and dispositions which by reasoning we infer from the actions observed'.[26] Perhaps we can conclude that the primary object of the moral sense is benevolence as manifested in action. The moral sense tends to become a capacity for a particular type of approbation of a particular type of action (or, rather, of affection or disposition in the agent) rather than a perception of 'pleasure'. The hedonistic element in Hutcheson's theory tends to retreat into the background, as far as the actual activity of the moral sense is concerned, though it by no means disappears.

Given the emphasis which Hutcheson lays on benevolence, what is the place of self-love? We experience a great number of particular self-regarding desires, and they cannot all be satisfied; for the satisfaction of one desire frequently interferes with or prevents the satisfaction of another. But we

can reduce them to harmony, in accordance with the principle of calm self-love. In Hutcheson's opinion this calm
self-love is morally indifferent. That is to say, actions which
spring from self-love are not bad unless they injure others
and are incompatible with benevolence; but at the same time
they are not morally good. It is only benevolent actions which
are morally good. Or, more precisely, it is only the kind or
benevolent affections (which are the primary object of the
moral sense and which, in the case of persons other than the
subject of the moral sense, are inferred from their actions)
that are morally good. Thus Hutcheson tends to make virtue
synonymous with benevolence. In the *Essay on the Passions*
calm, universal benevolence, as the desire of universal happiness, becomes the dominating principle in morality.

By concentrating on the idea of the beauty of virtue and
the ugliness or deformity of vice, Shaftesbury had already
given to morality a strongly aesthetic colouring. And Hutcheson continued this tendency to speak of the activity of the
moral sense in aesthetic terms. But it is not, I think, true to
say simply that he reduces ethics to aesthetics. He does,
indeed, speak about a moral sense of beauty; but what he
means is a sense of moral beauty. The aesthetic sense and
the moral sense are different functions or faculties of internal
sense in general; and though they have some characteristics
in common, they are distinguishable from one another. The
object of the feeling for beauty or of the aesthetic sense may
be a single object, considered with reference to the proportion
and disposition of its parts and qualities. We then have what
Hutcheson calls 'absolute beauty'. Or it may be a relation or
set of relations between different objects. And then we have
'relative beauty'. In a case of relative beauty it is not required that each object, taken separately, should be beautiful.
For example, a painting of a family group can be beautiful,
exhibiting 'uniformity in variety', even though we would not
say of any individual person depicted in the group that he or
she is beautiful. The primary object of the moral sense is, as
we have seen, benevolent affections, giving rise to a feeling
of approbation. Therefore, even though Hutcheson, like
Shaftesbury, tends to assimilate ethics to aesthetics, the
moral sense has an assignable object of its own; and he can
speak of two internal senses.[27]

It must be added, however, that Hutcheson is very uncertain about the number of the internal senses or about the

divisions of internal sense. In the *Essay on the Passions* he gives a fivefold division of sense in general. Besides external sense and the internal sense of beauty (the aesthetic sense) there are public sense or benevolence, the moral sense, and the sense of honour, which makes approbation or gratitude on the part of others for any good action that we have done a necessary source of pleasure. In the *System of Moral Philosophy* we find various subdivisions of the sense of beauty or aesthetic sense, and we also read of the sense of sympathy, the moral sense or faculty of perceiving moral excellence, the sense of honour and the sense of decency or decorum. In the Latin *Compendiaria* Hutcheson adds the senses of the ridiculous and of veracity. Obviously, once we begin to distinguish senses and faculties according to distinguishable objects and aspects of objects, there is hardly any limit to the number of senses and faculties which we can postulate.

In Hutcheson's ethical theory, in which virtue as a quasi-aesthetic excellence of character is the chief theme, we would hardly expect to find much attention devoted to the subject of obligation, especially when he practically reduces liberty to spontaneity. But he offers a criterion for judging between different possible courses of action. 'In comparing the moral quality of actions in order to regulate our elections among various actions proposed, or to find which of them has the greatest moral excellence, we are led by our moral sense of virtue to judge thus: that in equal degrees of happiness, expected to proceed from the action, the virtue is in proportion to the number of persons to whom the happiness shall extend . . . so that that action is best which procures the greatest happiness for the greatest numbers, and that worst which in like manner occasions misery.'[28] Here we have a clear anticipation of utilitarianism. Indeed, Hutcheson is one of the sources of the utilitarian moral philosophy.

Now, the idea of a moral sense, considered as the perception of pleasure in contemplating good actions, suggests feeling rather than a rational process of judging. But the sentence quoted in the last paragraph, which is taken from the same early work in which Hutcheson speaks of the moral sense in hedonistic terms, describes this sense as passing a judgment about the consequences of actions. And in later writings he attempts to bring together these two points of view in a systematic manner. Thus in the *System of Moral Philosophy* he distinguishes between the material and formal goodness of actions. An action is materially good when it tends towards the interest of the system; that is, towards the common interest or happiness, whatever the affections or motives of the agent may be. An action is formally good when it proceeds from good affections in a just proportion. Both the material and formal goodness are objects of the moral sense. Hutcheson borrows Butler's word 'conscience' and distinguishes between antecedent and subsequent conscience. Antecedent conscience is the faculty of moral decision or judgment and prefers that which appears most conducive to the virtue and happiness of mankind. Subsequent conscience has as its object past actions in relation to the motives or affections from which they sprang.

In the *Inquiry* obligation is described as 'a determination, without regard to our own interest, to approve actions and to perform them, which determination shall also make us displeased with ourselves and uneasy upon having acted contrary to it'.[29] And Hutcheson explains that 'no mortal can secure to himself a perfect serenity, satisfaction and self-approbation but by a serious inquiry into the tendency of his actions and a perpetual study of universal good according to the justest notions of it'.[30] But such remarks scarcely touch the problem of obligation. From his description of the moral sense it would appear that it is the moral beauty of virtue rather than the obligatory character of certain actions which is immediately revealed to us. Perhaps he would say that the fitness of actions contributing to the greater good of the greatest possible number is immediately evident to anyone who enjoys the use of an unclouded moral sense. But in the *System of Moral Philosophy* and in the Latin *Compendiaria* 'right reason' makes its appearance as the source of law, as possessing authority and jurisdiction. The affections are Nature's voice, and Nature's voice echoes the voice of God. But this voice needs interpretation and right reason, as one of the functions of conscience or the moral faculty, issues commands. It is called by Hutcheson, using a Stoic phrase, τὸ ἡγεμονικόν. Here the moral sense, become the moral faculty, takes on a rationalistic colouring.

There are so many different elements in Hutcheson's ethical theory that it does not seem possible to harmonize them all. But one of the chief features of his reflections on morals, a feature which they have in common with those of Shaftesbury, is the assimilation of morals to aesthetics. And when we bear in mind the fact that both men speak of the aesthetic and moral 'senses', it may seem that intuitionalism should have the last word in their theories. But both writers were concerned to refute Hobbes's theory of man as essentially egoistic. And with Hutcheson especially benevolence is brought so much to the fore that it tends to usurp the whole field of morality. The ideas of benevolence and altruism naturally foster concentration on the idea of the common good and on promoting the greater good or happiness of the greatest possible number. There is, therefore, an easy passage to a utilitarian interpretation of ethics. But utilitarianism, with its regard for the consequences of actions, involves judgment and reasoning, so that the moral sense must be something more than a 'sense'. And if one wishes, as Hutcheson did, to link up morality with metaphysics and theology, the decisions of the moral faculty or conscience become a reflection of the voice of God, not in the sense that morality depends on the divine choice, but in the sense that the moral faculty's approval of moral excellence reflects or mirrors God's approval of this excellence. This line of thought, however, which was doubtless influenced to some extent by Hutcheson's reading of Butler, is not the line of thought which we immediately associate with the former's name. In the history of moral theory Hutcheson is remembered as a champion of the moral sense theory and as a precursor of utilitarianism.

4. Both Shaftesbury and Hutcheson endeavoured to redress the balance which had been upset by Hobbes's egoistic interpretation of man's nature. For both men, as we have seen, insisted on the social character of man and on the naturalness of altruism. But whereas Shaftesbury, by finding the essence of virtue in a harmony of the self-regarding with the altruistic affections, had included self-love within the sphere of complete virtue, Hutcheson tended to identify virtue with benevolence. And though he did not condemn 'calm self-love', he regarded it as morally indifferent. On this point Bishop Butler[31] took his stand with Shaftesbury rather than with Hutcheson.

In his *Dissertation of the Nature of Virtue*, which was published in 1736[32] as an appendix to *The Analogy of Religion*, Butler remarks that 'it may be proper to observe that benevolence and the want of it, singly considered, are in no sort the whole of virtue and vice'.[33] And though he does not mention Hutcheson by name, he is probably thinking of him when he says that 'some of great and distinguished merit have, I think, expressed themselves in a manner which may occasion some danger to careless readers of imagining the whole of virtue to consist in singly aiming, according to the best of their judgment, at promoting the happiness of mankind in the present state, and the whole of vice in doing what they foresee, or might foresee, is likely to produce an overbalance of unhappiness in it'.[34] This is a terrible mistake, Butler observes. For it might appear on occasion that grave acts of injustice or of persecution would increase human happiness in the future. It is certainly our duty to contribute, 'within the bounds of veracity and justice',[35] to the common happiness. But to measure the morality of actions simply according to their apparent capacity or lack of it for promoting the greater happiness of the greatest possible number is to open the door to all sorts of injustice perpetrated in the name of mankind's future happiness. We cannot know with certainty what the consequences of our actions will be. Further, the object of the moral sense is action; and though intention forms part of the action considered as a total action, it is not the whole of it. We may intend good and not bad consequences; but it does not necessarily follow that the consequences will actually be what we wish or expect them to be.

Virtue, therefore, cannot be reduced simply to benevolence. Benevolence is, indeed, natural to man; but so is self-love. The term 'self-love' is, however, ambiguous, and some distinctions must be made. Everyone has a general desire for his own happiness, and this 'proceeds from or is self-love'.[36] It 'belongs to man as a reasonable creature reflecting upon his own interest or happiness'.[37] Self-love in this general sense pertains to man's nature, and though it is distinct from benevolence, it does not exclude the latter. For desire for our own happiness is a general desire, whereas benevolence is a particular affection. 'There is no peculiar contrariety between self-love and benevolence; no greater competition between these than between any other particular affection and self-love.'[38] The fact of the matter is that happiness, the object of self-love, is not identifiable with self-love. 'Happiness or satisfaction consists only in the enjoyment of those objects which are by nature suited to our several particular appetites, passions and affections.'[39] Benevolence is one particular, natural human affection. And there is no reason why its exercise should not contribute to our happiness. Indeed, if happiness consists in the gratification of our natural appetites, passions and affections, and if benevolence or love of the neighbour is one of these affections, its gratification does contribute to our happiness. Benevolence, therefore, cannot be inconsistent with self-love, which is the desire of happiness. There can, however, be a clash between the gratification of a particular appetite or passion or affection, say the desire of riches, and benevolence; and we all know what the word 'selfish' means. When people say that self-love and benevolence or altruism are incompatible, this is often due to a confusion of selfishness with self-love. But this is an unfortunate way of speaking. For it disregards the fact that what we call selfishness may very well be incompatible with true self-love. 'Nothing is more common than to see men give themselves up to a passion or an affection to their known prejudice and ruin, and in direct contradiction to manifest and real interest and the loudest calls of self-love.'[40]

Butler sometimes contrasts 'reasonable self-love' or 'cool self-love' with 'immoderate self-love'.[41] He also contrasts reasonable self-love with 'supposed self-love' or 'supposed interest'; and this way of talking is possibly preferable. For he is contrasting the desire of those ends the attainment of which do in fact confer happiness with the desire of those ends which are mistakenly thought to confer happiness. The particular enjoyments which make up 'the sum total of our happiness' are sometimes 'supposed to arise from riches, honours and the gratification of sensual appetites'.[42] But it is a mistake to think that these enjoyments are the sole components of human happiness. And the people who think in this way have a wrong notion of what true self-love demands.

It may be objected, of course, that happiness is something subjective, and that each individual is the best judge of what constitutes his happiness. But Butler can meet this objection, provided that he can show that 'happiness' has some definite and objective meaning which is independent of different persons' various ideas of happiness. And this he tries to do by giving a definite objective content to the concept of nature, that is to say, human nature. In the first place he mentions two possible meanings of the word 'nature' in order to exclude them. 'By nature is often meant no more than some principle in man, without regard either to the kind or degree of it.'[43] But when we say that nature is the rule of morality, it is obvious that we are not using the word 'nature' in this sense, namely, to indicate any appetite or passion or affection without regard to its character or intensity. Secondly, 'nature is frequently spoken of as consisting in those passions which are strongest and most influence the actions'.[44] But this meaning of nature must also be excluded. Otherwise we should have to say that a man in whose conduct sensual passion, for instance, was the dominating factor was a virtuous man, acting according to nature. We must look, therefore, for a third sense of the term. According to Butler, the 'principles', as he calls them, of man form a hierarchy, in which one principle is superior and possesses authority. 'There is a superior principle of reflection or conscience in every man, which distinguishes between the internal principles of his heart, as well as his external actions: which passes judgment upon himself and them; pronounces determinately some actions to be in themselves just, right, good; others to be in themselves evil, wrong, unjust. . . .'[45] In so far as conscience rules, therefore, a man acts according to his nature, while in so far as some principle other than conscience dictates his actions, these actions can be called disproportionate to his nature. And to act in accordance with nature is to attain happiness.

But what does Butler mean by conscience? The last quotation shows, of course, that in his view conscience passes judgment on goodness and badness of character, whether in oneself or others, and on the goodness and badness, rightness and wrongness of actions. But this does not tell us what is the precise nature and status of conscience. In the *Dissertation of the Nature of Virtue* he speaks of conscience as 'this moral approving and disapproving faculty'.[46] And in the next section he speaks again of this 'moral faculty, whether called conscience, moral reason, moral sense, or divine reason; whether considered as a sentiment of the understanding or as a perception of the heart, or, which seems the truth, as including both'.[47] Furthermore, Butler sometimes seems at first sight to imply that conscience and self-love are the same.

To take the last point first. Butler maintained that self-love is a superior principle in man. 'If passion prevails over self-love, the consequent action is unnatural; but if self-love prevails over passion, the action is natural: it is manifest that self-love is in human nature a superior principle to passion. This may be contradicted without violating that nature; but the former cannot. So that, if we will act conformably to the economy of man's nature, reasonable self-love must govern.'[48] But he did not maintain that self-love and conscience are identical. They generally coincide, in Butler's opinion; but to say this is to imply that they are not precisely the same thing. 'It is manifest that, in the common course of life, there is seldom any inconsistency between our duty and what is called interest: it is much seldomer that there is an inconsistency between duty and what is really our present interest; meaning by interest, happiness and satisfaction.'[49] 'Self-love, then, though confined to the interest of the present world, does in general perfectly coincide with virtue; and leads us to one and the same course of life.'[50] Again, 'conscience and self-love, if we understand our true happiness, always lead us in the same way. Duty and interest are perfectly coincident; for the most part in this world, but entirely and in every instance if we take in the future and the whole; this being implied in the notion of a good and perfect administration of things.'[51] Conscience may dictate a course of action which is not, or does not appear to be, in accordance with our temporal interest; but in the long run, if we take into account the future life, conscience always dictates that which is to our true interest, that which contributes to our complete happiness. But it does not follow from this that conscience is the same thing as self-love; for it is conscience which tells us that we should do what contributes to our complete happiness as human beings. Nor does it necessarily follow that we should do what conscience dictates from the conscious motive of serving our true interest. For to say that conscience dictates what is to our interest or that duty and interest coincide and to say that we should do our duty with the motive of securing our interest are not one and the same statement.

In his *Dissertation of the Nature of Virtue* Butler says that the object of the faculty of conscience is 'actions, comprehending under that name active or practical principles: those principles from which men would act, if occasions and circumstances gave them power; and which, when fixed and habitual in any person, we call his character'.[52] 'Acting, conduct, behaviour, abstracted from all regard to what is, in fact and event, the consequence of it, is itself the natural object of the moral discernment; as speculative truth and falsehood is of speculative reason. Intention of such and such consequences, indeed, is always included; for it is part of the action itself.'[53] Secondly, our perception of the goodness or badness of actions involves a 'discernment of them as of good or ill desert'.[54] Thirdly, the perception of vice and 'ill desert' arises from a comparison of actions with the capacities of the agents. We do not judge the action of a madman, for example, in the same way that we judge the actions of sane men.

Conscience, therefore, is concerned with actions without regard to the consequences which occur in point of fact, though not without regard to the agent's intention. For his intention is part of his action when considered as the object of the moral sense or faculty. Actions, therefore, must have objective moral qualities to be discerned. And this was, indeed, Butler's view. The goodness or badness of actions arises simply 'from their being what they are; namely, what becomes such creatures as we are, what the state of the case requires, or the contrary'.[55] Now, this view may give rise to a misunderstanding. For Butler might be interpreted as meaning that we reason from an analysis of human nature to the goodness or badness, rightness or wrongness, of particular actions. This is not, however, quite what he means. We can, indeed, reason in this way. But to do so is more characteristic of the moral philosopher than of the ordinary moral agent. In Butler's opinion, we can generally discern the rightness or wrongness of actions by inspecting the given situation, without referring to general rules or performing any work of deduction. 'The inquiries which have been made by men of leisure after some general rule, the conformity to or disagreement from which should denominate our actions good or evil, are in many respects of great service. Yet let any plain honest man, before he engages in any course of action, ask himself, Is this I am going about right, or is it wrong? Is it good, or is it evil? I do not in the least doubt, but that this question would be answered agreeably to truth and virtue, by almost any fair man in almost any circumstance.'[56]

What, then, of obligation? Butler does not express himself very clearly on this matter. But his dominant view is that conscience, when it recognizes this action as right and that action as wrong, pronounces authoritatively that the former ought and that the latter ought not to be performed. In the Preface to the *Sermons* he says that 'the natural authority

of the principle of reflection is an obligation the most near
and intimate, the most certain and known'.[57] Similarly,
'Take in then that authority and obligation, which is a constituent part of this reflex approbation and it will undeniably follow, though a man should doubt of everything else,
yet, that he would still remain under the nearest and most
certain obligation to the practice of virtue; an obligation
implied in the very idea of virtue, in the very idea of reflex
approbation.'[58] He seems to imply that virtue carries with it
its own claim on us, and that to approve morally is to declare
obligatory, in the sense that if, when faced with an actual
choice, I recognize one line of action as good, the other as
evil, I inevitably assert that I ought to follow the first line of
action and avoid the second. Assuming that there is a law of
our nature, he asks, what obligation are we under to follow
it! And he replies that 'the question carries its own answer
along with it. Your obligation to obey this law is its being the
law of your nature. That your conscience approves of and
attests to such a course of action is itself alone an obligation.
Conscience does not only offer itself to show us the way we
should walk in, but it likewise carries its own authority with
it. . . .'[59] He does not say that the fact that an action is to
our interest constitutes by itself obligation, but rather, as we
have seen, that duty and interest are coincident, in the sense
at least that God will see to it that doing what we recognize
to be our duty will lead in the long run to our complete happiness and satisfaction.

Doubtless, Butler paid insufficient attention to varieties
and differences in moral outlook and convictions. He admits,
indeed, that there may be doubt about particular points;
but he insists that 'in general there is in reality a universally
acknowledged standard of it (of virtue). It is that which all
ages and all countries have made profession of in public; it
is that which every man you meet puts on the show of: it is
that which the primary and fundamental laws of all civil constitutions over the face of the earth make it their business
and endeavour to enforce the practice of upon mankind:
namely, justice, veracity, and regard to common good.'[60]
But though he does not adequately discuss the difficulties
arising from the strong element of *de facto* relativism in the
moral codes of humanity, the important point to notice in
his ethical theory seems to me to be his assertion of an ethics
which is neither purely authoritarian on the one hand nor

purely utilitarian on the other. Conscience promulgates, as it were, the moral law, which does not depend on the arbitrary choice of God, and still less on the law of the State. At the same time, he neither identifies morality with benevolence nor makes self-love the unique supreme principle in morality. The moral law has reference to human nature and is founded on it; but conscience ought to be followed even when duty does not coincide with interest as far as this life is concerned. That duty and interest coincide infallibly in the long run is due to divine providence. But this does not mean that we should act simply with a view to obtaining reward and avoiding punishment. The supreme authority is conscience. 'Had it strength, as it has right; had it power, as it has manifest authority, it would absolutely govern the world.'[61] Butler's ethical theory is inadequate on any count; for there are topics of importance which are scarcely discussed. One could wish, for example, for a more exact analysis of the terms good and evil, right and wrong, and a discussion of the precise relations between the terms. Again, further analysis of obligation and a clear explanation of what is actually said about this subject would be desirable. Yet Butler's ethical theory is a remarkable piece of work, even as it stands, and it certainly provides valuable material for any more thoroughly worked-out and elaborate moral philosophy.

5. In connection with the influence of Locke mention was made of David Hartley (1705–57). Abandoning his original intention of becoming an Anglican clergyman, he devoted himself to the study of medicine and subsequently practised as a doctor. In 1749 he published his *Observations on Man*. In the first part of this work he deals with the connection between body and mind, while in the second part he treats of matters relating to morality, especially under its psychological aspect. His general position is based on that of Locke. Sensation is the prior element in cognition, and antecedently to sensation the mind is empty or blank. Hence the need of showing how man's ideas in all their diversity and complexity are formed from the data of the senses. And here Hartley makes use of Locke's notion of the association of ideas, though in his preface to the *Observations on Man* he acknowledges his debt to the *Dissertation concerning the Fundamental Principles of Virtue and Morality* which had been written by John Gay (1699–1745), a clergyman, and

which had been prefixed by Bishop Law to his translation of the Latin work on the *Origin of Evil* (1731) by Archbishop King. But while Hartley's psychological theories were prompted by Gay's dissertation, his physical theory about the connection between body and mind was influenced by Newton's speculations about nervous action in the *Principia*. We can say, therefore, that Hartley's reflections were influenced by Locke, Newton and Gay. In turn, he himself gave an impulse to the study of the connections between body and mind and to the associationist psychology.

Hartley, while agreeing with Locke that the mind is originally devoid of content, disagreed with him about the status of reflection. The latter is not a distinct source of ideas: the only source is sensation. And sensation is the result of vibrations in the particles of the nerves, which are transmitted by means of the ether, the idea of which was suggested by Newton's hypothesis of an ether to account for the action of forces at a distance. Some vibrations are moderate, and these produce pleasure; others are violent, and these produce pain. Memory is explained by postulating faint vibrations or 'vibratiuncles', tendencies which are imprinted by vibrations on the medullary substance of the brain. Indeed, there are always vibrations in the brain, though what they are depends on a man's past experience and, of course, on present external influences. We can thus account for the cause of memories and ideas even when there is no obvious cause in present sensation. The building-up of man's complex mental life is to be explained in terms of association, which Hartley reduced to the influence of 'contiguous' elements, where 'contiguous' includes successive contiguity. When different sensations are frequently associated with one another, each of them becomes associated with the ideas produced by the others; and the ideas which correspond to associated sensations enter into a mutual association.

The principle of association was employed by Hartley in explaining the genesis of man's moral ideas and feelings. But it is important to note his insistence that the product of association can be a new idea, in the sense that it is more than the mere summation of its component elements. He also insisted that that which is prior in the order of nature is less perfect than that which is posterior. In other words, Hartley did not attempt to reduce the moral life to non-moral elements by saying that it is no more than the latter.

Rather did he attempt to explain, by employing the idea of association, how the higher and new emergent is produced from lower elements, and ultimately from one original source, namely, sensation. Thus he tried to show that the moral sense and altruistic affections are not original characteristics of human nature, but that they emerge, through the operation of association, from self-regarding affections and the tendency to secure private happiness.

Hartley, in accordance with the demands of his physiological and psychological theories, embraced, if reluctantly, the determinist position. But though some critics maintained that his theories amounted to a materialistic sensationalism, he himself thought otherwise, and he tried to trace the evolution of the higher out of the lower pleasures, from the pleasures of sense and of self-interest, through the pleasures of sympathy and benevolence, up to the supreme pleasure of the pure love of God and of perfect self-denial.

6. While considering the ethical theory of Hutcheson, we noticed the element of utilitarianism which it contains. Clearer anticipations of later utilitarianism can be seen in the theories of Tucker and Paley (to omit Hume, who will be treated separately and more at length).

Abraham Tucker (1705–74), author of *The Light of Nature Pursued*, of which three volumes appeared during his lifetime, believed that the moral-sense theory was an ethical variant of the theory of innate ideas which Locke had successfully demolished. And, like Hartley, though he does not mention his debt to the latter, he tried to account for the 'moral sense' and for our ethical convictions with the aid of the principle of association, which he named 'translation'.

In the Introduction to *The Light of Nature Pursued* Tucker informs his readers that he has examined human nature and has found that satisfaction, each man's own private satisfaction, is the ultimate spring of all his actions. But he also tells his readers that he has aimed at establishing the rule of universal charity or benevolence, directed towards all men without exception, and that the fundamental rule of conduct is to labour for the common good or happiness; that is, to increase the common stock of satisfaction. He has, therefore, to show how such altruistic conduct is possible if every man is impelled by nature to seek his own satisfaction. This he does by arguing that through 'translation' that which was at first a means came to be regarded as an end. For example, the 'pleasure of benefiting' prompts us to do services to others because we like doing them. In time benevolence or service of others becomes an end in itself, in the sense that no thought is given to the securing of one's own satisfaction. By analogous processes virtue comes to be desired for its own sake and general rules of conduct are formed.

But Tucker found some difficulty in explaining the more complete acts of self-sacrifice. A man may be kind to others because he likes behaving in a kindly way and finds no satisfaction in unkindness. And he may very well come to behave in a kindly manner without adverting to his own satisfaction. But, as Tucker remarks, it is one thing to practise benevolence and take measures to increase the public happiness while one is not conscious of the tendency of such behaviour to increase one's own happiness, and it is another thing to discern clearly that the measures which one takes for the common good extinguish one's own capacity for satisfaction. The man who sacrifices his life for his country may be aware that his act is contrary to his own happiness, in the sense that it extinguishes the capacity for further enjoyment. How can such acts be explained and justified?

The problem is solved, to Tucker's satisfaction at least, by passing beyond human nature considered in itself as something empirically given and by introducing the concepts of God and of the other world. He supposes that there is a 'bank of the universe', a common stock of happiness which is administered by God. Men have really no merits, and God parcels out the common stock of happiness or pleasure in equal shares. By working to increase the public happiness I therefore inevitably increase my own; for God will certainly give me my share in due time, in the next world if not in this. If my sacrifice of myself is for the common good, I shall not be the loser in the long run. Indeed, I shall increase my ultimate satisfaction.

This ingenious argument is obviously not the most important feature of Tucker's ethical theory from the historical point of view. More important are his quantitative estimate of pleasure (pleasures differ in degree, but not in kind), his insistence on private satisfaction as the ultimate motive of conduct, his assessment of moral rules in terms of conduciveness to the general happiness or pleasure, and his attempt to show how man's fundamental egoism can be reconciled with benevolence and altruistic conduct. Here we find the elements of later utilitarianism. The difficulties common to Tucker's version and to the utilitarianism of Bentham and the Mills can best be discussed in connection with the latter.

7. William Paley (1743–1805) became fellow and tutor of Christ's College, Cambridge, where he had studied as an undergraduate. He subsequently occupied various ecclesiastical positions, though he was never given high office, because, it is said, of his latitudinarian views.

Paley is best known for his writings in defence of the credibility of natural religion and of Christianity, especially for his *View of the Evidences of Christianity* (1794) and his *Natural Theology, or Evidences of the Existence and Attributes of the Deity collected from the Appearances of Nature* (1802). In the last-named work he presented his development of the argument from design. He does not base his argument upon the phenomena of the heavens. 'My opinion of Astronomy has always been that it is *not* the best medium through which to prove the agency of an intelligent Creator; but that, this being proved, it shows, beyond all other sciences, the magnificence of his operations.'[62] He takes his stand instead on anatomy, as he puts it; that is, on evidence of design in the animal organism, particularly in the human organism. And he argues that the data are inexplicable without reference to a designing mind. 'Were there no example in the world of contrivance except that of the *eye*, it would be alone sufficient to support the conclusion which we draw from it as to the necessity of an intelligent Creator.'[63] It is not infrequently said that Paley's argument from design has been deprived of all force by the evolutionary hypothesis. If this means that the evolutionary hypothesis is incompatible with any teleological argument for the existence of God, it is a disputable opinion. But if it is meant that Paley's argument as he states it is insufficient and, in particular, that the evolutionary hypothesis and its supporting data need to be considered in any restatement of the argument, most people would, I suppose, agree. Paley was not a particularly original writer. For example, his famous analogy of the watch at the beginning of the work was not his invention. And he probably took too much for granted. But he showed very considerable skill and ability in his arrangement of his matter and in the development of his argument. And it is, in my opinion, an exaggeration to suggest, as is sometimes done, that his line of thought is worthless.

However, we are concerned here rather with Paley's work on *The Principles of Moral and Political Philosophy* (1785), a revision and enlargement of lectures delivered at Cambridge. Here again he is not particularly original; but he did not pretend to be. And in his Preface he makes a frank acknowledgement of his debt to Abraham Tucker.

Moral philosophy is defined by Paley as 'that science which teaches men their duty and the reasons of it'.[64] He does not think that we can build a moral theory on the hypothesis of a moral sense, considered as a kind of instinct. 'Upon the whole it seems to me either that there exist no such instincts as compose what is called the moral sense, or that they are not now to be distinguished from prejudices and habits; on which account they cannot be depended upon in moral reasoning.'[65] We cannot draw conclusions about the rightness or wrongness of actions without considering their 'tendency'; that is to say, without considering their end. This end is happiness. But what is meant by happiness? 'In strictness, any condition may be denominated happy, in which the amount or aggregate of pleasure exceeds that of pain; and the degree of happiness depends upon the quantity of this excess. And the greatest quantity of it ordinarily attainable in human life is what we mean by happiness, when we inquire or pronounce what human happiness consists in.'[66]

In determining what happiness is in the concrete, Paley accepts Tucker's view that 'pleasures differ in nothing but in continuance and intensity'.[67] It is impossible, he says, to lay down a universal ideal of happiness valid for all, because men differ so much from one another. But there is a presumption in favour of those conditions of life in which men generally appear to be most cheerful and contented. These include the exercise of the social affections, the exercise of our mental or bodily faculties in the pursuit of some 'engaging end' (an end which provides continuing interest and hope), prudent habits and good health.

Virtue is defined in a frankly utilitarian spirit. It is 'the doing good to mankind, in obedience to the will of God, and for the sake of everlasting happiness'.[68] The good of mankind is the subject-matter of virtue; the will of God provides the rule; and everlasting happiness provides the motive. For the most part we act, not as a result of deliberate reflection, but according to pre-established habits. Hence arises the importance of forming virtuous habits of conduct.

Given this definition of virtue, one would expect a utilitarian interpretation of moral obligation. And this is in fact what we find. Answering the question what we mean when we say that a man is obliged to do something, Paley answers that 'a man is said to be obliged when he is urged by a violent motive resulting from the command of another'.[69] 'We can be obliged to nothing but what we ourselves are to gain or lose something by: for nothing else can be a "violent motive" to us.'[70] If the further question be asked, why I am obliged to do something, the answer that I am urged to do so by a 'violent motive' is quite sufficient. Paley admits that when he first turned his mind to moral philosophy there seemed to him to be something mysterious in the subject, especially with regard to obligation. But he came to the conclusion that moral obligation is like all other obligations. 'Obligation is nothing more than an inducement of sufficient strength, and resulting, in some way, from the command of another.'[71] If it be asked what is the difference between an act of prudence and an act of duty, the answer is that the only difference is this. 'In the one case we consider what we shall gain or lose in the present world; in the other case we consider also what we shall gain or lose in the world to come.'[72] Paley can say, therefore, that 'private happiness is our motive, and the will of God our rule'.[73] He does not mean that God's will is purely arbitrary, in the sense that actions are commanded which have no relation to our happiness. God wills the happiness of men and thus wills the acts which conduce to this happiness. But by attaching eternal sanctions of reward and punishment to human conduct God imposes moral obligation by providing an inducement or violent motive which transcends the motive of prudence, in so far as prudence is concerned simply with this world.

Hume, Paley notes, in the fourth appendix to his Enquiry concerning the Principles of Morals, takes exception to attempts to link ethics closely with theology. But if there are eternal sanctions, Paley insists, they must be taken into consideration by the Christian moralist. What is peculiar to Christian morality is not so much the content of morality, so to speak, as the additional motive, provided by a knowledge of eternal sanctions, which operates as an inducement to perform or not to perform some action.

'So then actions are to be estimated by their tendency. Whatever is expedient, is right. It is the utility of any moral rule alone which constitutes the obligation of it.'[74] And in estimating the consequences of actions we should ask what the consequences would be if the same sort of action were universally permitted. The statement that whatever is expedient is right must be understood of long-term expediency or utility, taking into account collateral and remote effects, as well as those which are direct and immediate. Thus while the particular consequence of forgery is the loss of a particular sum to a particular man, the general consequence would be the destruction of the value of all currency. And moral rules can be established by estimating the consequences of actions in this general sense.

Paley is, indeed, consistently utilitarian. But it is noticeable that in treating of particular moral rules and duties and of the rightness or wrongness of particular types of actions he tends to forget his original insistence on the motive of private happiness and to take public benefit as a criterion. Moreover, by insisting on the need for developing and preserving good habits he evades to some extent the very great difficulties which arise out of the idea of calculation of consequences as a criterion of good and evil, right and wrong. But Paley is inclined to slur over or make short work of serious difficulties against his position. And he takes far too much for granted. It is not at all evident, for example, that when a man says that he is morally obliged he means that he is urged by a violent motive resulting from the command of another. It may be added that in Paley's opinion all moral systems come more or less to the same conclusions. Thus those who say that I am obliged to do X because X is agreeable to the fitness of things must mean by fitness, fitness to produce happiness. In other words, Paley assumes that all moral philosophers are implicitly asserting utilitarianism.

Paley was also, of course, a utilitarian in his political theory. From the historical point of view 'government, at first, was either patriarchal or military: that of a parent over his family, or of a commander over his fellow-warriors'.[75] But if we ask for the ground of the subject's obligation to obey the sovereign, the only true answer is 'the will of God as collected from expediency'.[76] Paley explains what he means by this. It is the will of God that human happiness should be promoted. Civil society conduces to this end. Civil societies cannot be maintained unless the interest of the whole society is binding on every member. Hence it is the will of God that the established government should be obeyed as long as it 'cannot be resisted or changed without public inconveniency'.[77] Thus Paley rejects the contract-theory and substitutes the concept of public benefit or 'public expediency' as the ground (and also, of course, as indicating the limit) of political obligation. Hume had already maintained the same view.

8. In this chapter Shaftesbury and Hutcheson have been depicted as concerned to refute Hobbes's view of man by showing that the benevolent or altruistic impulses are as natural to the human being as the egoistic impulses, or that benevolence is as natural as self-love. And Mandeville was depicted as a critic and adversary of Shaftesbury and so, by implication, as a defender of Hobbes's point of view. But in one sense at least Mandeville was a critic of Hobbes. For while the latter considered that it is ultimately only through fear and constraint that human beings are led to act altruistically and with a view to the good of society, Mandeville maintained that egoism of itself serves the common good and that private 'vices' are public benefits. He thus adopted a point of view different from that of Hobbes, who regarded the natural egoism of the individual as something to be overcome through the constraints imposed by society. However, it obviously remains true that the principal opponents of Hobbes were Shaftesbury and Hutcheson.

Hobbes had, or course, other critics and opponents. An earlier chapter was devoted to the Cambridge Platonists, and in the last chapter something was said about Samuel Clarke. The Cambridge Platonists and Clarke were rationalists, in the sense that they believed that the human reason apprehends eternal and immutable moral principles. And in upholding this view they were opposed to Hobbes. But Shaftesbury and Hutcheson, who were also opposed to Hobbes, did not follow them in their rationalism. Instead, they had recourse to the theory of the moral sense. I do not mean to imply that there was no common ground at all between the rationalists and the defenders of the moral-sense theory. For in both types of ethical theory there was, for example, an element of intuitionalism. But there were also important differences. For the rationalist the mind apprehends eternal and immutable moral principles, which he can use as a guide to conduct. For the adherent of the moral-sense theory a man apprehends immediately moral qualities in concrete instances rather than abstract principles.

This means that the defender of the moral-sense theory is probably more likely than the rationalist to pay attention to the way in which the ordinary man's mind works when he makes moral decisions and judgments. In other words, we would perhaps expect to find him paying more attention to what we may call the psychology of ethics. And in point of fact we find in Butler in particular a considerable psychological acumen. Further, the moral-sense theory in general reflects an apprehension of the part played by 'feeling', by immediacy, in the moral life. The analogy drawn between moral discrimination and aesthetic appreciation helps to bring out this fact.

But if we examine the ordinary moral consciousness, it will be seen that 'feeling' or immediacy is only one element. There are also, for example, moral judgment or decision and an authoritative imperative to take into account. Bishop Butler tried to do justice to this side of the matter in his analysis of conscience. And by doing so he transformed to a great extent the original moral-sense theory and helped to show the differences between moral discrimination and aesthetic appreciation.

There is another point about Butler's moral theory which should be noticed. Shaftesbury and Hutcheson had laid emphasis on 'moral excellence', on virtue as a state of character, on 'affections'. The primary object of the moral sense was for Hutcheson, as we saw, the kind or benevolent affections. But conscience and moral decision are concerned primarily with actions. So with Butler we can see a tendency to shift the emphasis from affections to actions, not, of course, actions considered merely as external actions but actions as informed by motives, as proceeding from human beings. And the more the emphasis is laid on actions, the more the assimilation of ethics to aesthetics retreats into the background.

Now, in the ethical theories of Shaftesbury and Hutcheson there were several latent potentialities. In the first place the idea of universal benevolence, when coupled with the idea of producing happiness, naturally leads to a utilitarian theory. And we have seen that there was an anticipation of utilitarianism in one aspect of Hutcheson's philosophy. This element was developed by other moralists whom we have considered. Thus, on the psychological side, Hartley and Tucker, using Locke's principle of association, tried to show how altruism and benevolence are possible, even if man seeks by nature his own satisfaction. Further, with Tucker, and still more with Paley, we find a theological utilitarianism. But when Paley emphasized, as a motive for acting altruistically, the thought of divine reward, he was adopting, of course, a point of view very different from that of Shaftesbury and Hutcheson.

In the second place we find in both Shaftesbury and Hutcheson, with their emphasis on virtue and character, a point of departure for an ethics based on the idea of the self-perfection of man or on the harmonious and complete development of human nature rather than on the principles of hedonistic utilitarianism. And in so far as Butler adumbrated the idea of a hierarchy of principles in man under the dominating authority of conscience, he helped to develop this idea. Further, Shaftesbury's idea of the correspondence between man, the microcosm, and the whole of which he forms a part was developed to some extent by Hutcheson, who linked up the idea with the idea of God. Here we have the introduction of metaphysical considerations and materials, as it were, for the development of an idealistic ethic. But it was the utilitarian element in the thinkers with whom we have dealt in this chapter[78] that was most influential. The impetus to a development of idealistic ethics in the nineteenth century came from another source.

There was thus a considerable number of divergent elements and potentialities in the moral theories of the philosophers who have been mentioned in this chapter. But the overall picture is of the growth of moral philosophy as a separate subject of study, separated for the most part from theology and standing on its own feet, even though men such as Hutcheson and Butler tried, very naturally and properly, to link up their ethics with their theological beliefs. This interest in moral philosophy has remained one of the characteristic features of British thought.

APPENDIX

A Short Bibliography

For general remarks and for General Works see the Bibliography at the end of A HISTORY OF PHILOSOPHY, *Volume 4, Modern Philosophy: Descartes to Leibniz.*

Chapters One–Two: Hobbes

Texts

Hobbes: Opera philosophica quae latine scripsit. Edited by W. Molesworth. 5 vols. London, 1839–45.

The English Works of Thomas Hobbes. Edited by W. Molesworth, 11 vols. London, 1839–45.

The Metaphysical System of Hobbes. Selections edited by M. W. Calkins. Chicago, 1905.

Hobbes: Selections. Edited by F. J. E. Woodbridge. New York, 1930.

The Elements of Law, Natural and Politic (together with *A Short Treatise on First Principles* and parts of the *Tractatus opticus*), edited by F. Tönnies. Cambridge, 1928 (2nd edition).

De Cive or the *The Citizen.* Edited by S. P. Lamprecht. New York, 1949.

Leviathan. Edited with an introduction by M. Oakeshott. Oxford, 1946.

Leviathan. With an introduction by A. D. Lindsay. London (E.L.).

Of Liberty and Necessity, edited with an introduction and notes by Cay von Brockdorff. Kiel, 1938.

Studies

Battelli, G. *Le dottrine politiche dell' Hobbes e dello Spinoza.* Florence, 1904.

Bowle, J. *Hobbes and His Critics: A Study of Seventeenth-Century Constitutionalism.* London, 1951.

Brandt, F. *Thomas Hobbes' Mechanical Conception of Nature.* London, 1928.

Brockdorff, Cay von. *Hobbes als Philosoph, Pädagoge und Soziologe.* Kiel, 1929.

   Die Urform der Computatio sive Logica des Hobbes. Kiel, 1934.

Gooch, G. P. *Hobbes.* London, 1940.

Gough, J. W. *The Social Contract: A Critical Study of Its Development.* Oxford, 1936 (revised edition, 1956).

Hönigswald, R. *Hobbes und die Staatsphilosophie.* Munich, 1924.

Laird, J. *Hobbes.* London, 1934.

Landry, B. *Hobbes.* Paris, 1930.

Levi, A. *La filosofia di Tommaso Hobbes.* Milan, 1929.

Lyon, G. *La philosophie de Hobbes.* Paris, 1893.

Polin, R. *Politique et philosophie chez Thomas Hobbes.* Paris, 1953.

Robertson, G. C. *Hobbes.* Edinburgh and London, 1886.

Rossi, M. M. *Alle fonti del deismo e del materialismo moderno.* 1, *Le origini del deismo.* 2, *L'evoluzione del pensiero di Hobbes.* Florence, 1942.

Stephen, L. *Hobbes.* London, 1904.

Strauss, L. *The Political Philosophy of Hobbes.* Translated by E. M. Sinclair. Oxford, 1936.

Taylor, A. E. *Thomas Hobbes.* London, 1908.

Tönnies, F. *Thomas Hobbes: Leben und Lehre.* Stuttgart, 1925 (3rd edition).

Vialatoux, J. *La cité de Hobbes. Théorie de l'État totalitaire. Essai sur la conception naturaliste de la civilisation.* Paris, 1935.

Chapter Three: Herbert of Cherbury and the Cambridge Platonists

1. Lord Herbert of Cherbury

Texts

The Autobiography of Edward, Lord Herbert of Cherbury, with introduction and notes by S. L. Lee. London, 1886.

Tractatus de veritate. London, 1633.

De veritate. Translated with an introduction by M. H. Carré. Bristol, 1937.

De causis errorum. London, 1645.
De religione gentilium. Amsterdam, 1663 and 1670; London, 1705.
De religione laici. Translated with a critical discussion of Lord Herbert's life and philosophy and a comprehensive bibliography of his works by H. R. Hutcheson. New Haven (U.S.A.) and London, 1944.
A Dialogue between a Tutor and His Pupil. London, 1768.

Studies
De Rémusat, C. *Lord Herbert of Cherbury, sa vie et ses œuvres.* Paris, 1853.
Güttler, C. *Edward, Lord Herbert of Cherbury.* Munich, 1897.
Köttich, R. G. *Die Lehre von den angeborenen Ideen seit Herbert von Cherbury.* Berlin, 1917.

2. Cudworth

Texts
The True Intellectual System of the Universe. London, 1743 (2 vols.), 1846 (3 vols). There is an edition (London, 1845) by J. Harrison with a translation from the Latin of Mosheim's notes.
Treatise concerning Eternal and Immutable Morality. London, 1731.
A Treatise of Free Will. Edited by J. Allen. London, 1838.

Studies
Aspelin, G. *Cudworth's Interpretation of Greek Philosophy.* Bonn, 1935.
Beyer, J. *Cudworth.* Bonn, 1935.
Lowrey, C. E. *The Philosophy of Ralph Cudworth.* New York, 1884.
Passmore, J. A. *Cudworth, an Interpretation.* Cambridge, 1950.
Scott, W. R. *An Introduction to Cudworth's Treatise.* London, 1891.

3. Henry More

Texts
Opera omnia. 3 vols. London, 1679.
Enchiridion metaphysicum. London, 1671.
Enchiridion ethicum. London, 1667.

The Philosophical Writings of Henry More. Selected by F. I. Mackinnon. New York, 1925.

Study

Reimann, H. *Henry Mores Bedeutung für die Gegenwart. Sein Kampf für Wirken und Freiheit des Geistes.* Basel, 1941.

4. *Cumberland*

Text

De legibus naturae disquisitio philosophica. London, 1672. English translation by J. Maxwell. London, 1727.

Studies

Payne, S. *Account of the Life and Writings of Richard Cumberland.* London, 1720.

Spaulding, F. E. *Richard Cumberland als Begründer der englischen Ethik.* Leipzig, 1894.

5. *Other Works*

Text

The Cambridge Platonists. Selections from Whichcote, Smith and Culverwel, edited by E. T. Campagnac. London, 1901.

Studies

Cassirer, E. *The Platonic Renaissance in England.* Translated by J. P. Pettegrove. Edinburgh and London, 1953.

De Pauley, W. C. *The Candle of the Lord: Studies in the Cambridge Platonists.* New York, 1937.

De Sola Pinto, V. *Peter Sterry; Platonist and Puritan, 1613–1672. A Biographical and Critical Study with Passages selected from His Writings.* Cambridge, 1934.

Mackinnon, F. I. *The Philosophy of John Norris.* New York, 1910.

Muirhead, J. H. *The Platonic Tradition in Anglo-Saxon Philosophy.* London, 1920.

Powicke, F. J. *The Cambridge Platonists: A Study.* London, 1926.

Tulloch, J. *Rational Theology and Christian Philosophy in England in the Seventeenth Century:* II, *The Cambridge Platonists.* Edinburgh and London, 1872.

Chapters Four–Seven: Locke

Texts

The Works of John Locke. 9 vols. London, 1853.

The Philosophical Works of John Locke (On the Conduct of the Understanding, An Essay concerning Human Understanding, the controversy with Stillingfleet, An Examination of Malebranche's Opinion, Elements of Natural Philosophy and Some Thoughts concerning Reading). Edited by J. A. St. John. 2 vols. London, 1854, 1908.

Locke: Selections. Edited by S. P. Lamprecht. New York, 1928.

An Essay concerning Human Understanding. Edited with introduction and notes by A. C. Fraser. 2 vols. Oxford, 1894.

An Essay concerning Human Understanding. Abridged and edited by A. S. Pringle-Pattison. Oxford, 1924.

An Essay concerning Human Understanding. Abridged and edited by R. Wilburn. London (E.L.).

An Early Draft of Locke's Essay, together with Excerpts from His Journal. Edited by R. L. Aaron and J. Gibb. Oxford, 1936.

An Essay concerning the Understanding, Knowledge, Opinion and Assent. Edited by B. Rand. Cambridge (U.S.A.), 1931. (These two last-mentioned works are early drafts of Locke's Essay. According to Professor von Leyden, 'the text of the draft edited by Rand can only be considered authentic in a small degree. . . .' See Notes concerning Papers of John Locke in the Lovelace Collection by W. von Leyden in The Philosophical Quarterly, January 1952, pp. 63–9. The Lovelace Collection is now housed in the Bodleian Library.)

Two Treatises of Government (containing also Filmer's Patriarcha, edited by T. I. Cook). New York, 1947.

Two Treatises of Civil Government. With an introduction by W. S. Carpenter. London (E.L.).

Second Treatise of Civil Government and Letter on Toleration. Edited by J. W. Gough. Oxford, 1948.

John Locke: Essays on the Law of Nature. Latin text with translation, introduction and notes by W. von Leyden. Oxford, 1954.

Original Letters of Locke, Sidney and Shaftesbury. Edited by T. Forster. London, 1847 (2nd edition).

The Correspondence of John Locke and Edward Clarke. Edited by B. Rand. Cambridge (U.S.A.), 1927. (See the remarks of Professor von Leyden in the article referred to above in the passage in parentheses.)

Lettres inédites de John Locke à ses amis N. Thoynard, Ph. van Limborch et E. Clarke. Edited by H. Ollion. The Hague, 1912.

(R. Filmer's *Patriarcha and other Political Works*, edited by P. Laslett, were published at Oxford in 1949.)

Studies

Aaron, R. I. *John Locke.* Oxford, 1955 (2nd edition). (This study can be highly recommended.)
    Great Thinkers: X, Locke (in *Philosophy* for 1937).

Alexander, S. *Locke.* London, 1908.

Aspelin, G. *John Locke.* Lund, 1950.

Bastide, C. *John Locke.* Paris, 1907.

Bianchi, G. F. *Locke.* Brescia, 1943.

Carlini, A. *La filosofia di G. Locke.* 2 vols. Florence, 1920. *Locke.* Milan, 1949.

Christophersen, H. O. *A Bibliographical Introduction to the Study of John Locke.* Oslo, 1930.

Cousin, V. *La philosophie de Locke.* Paris, 1873 (6th edition).

Fowler, T. *Locke.* London, 1892 (2nd edition).

Fox Bourne, H. R. *The Life of John Locke.* 2 vols. London, 1876.

Fraser, A. C. *Locke.* London, 1890.

Gibson, J. *Locke's Theory of Knowledge and Its Historical Relations.* Cambridge, 1917.

Gough, J. W. *John Locke's Political Philosophy.* Oxford, 1950.
    The Social Contract (see Hobbes).

Hefelbower, S. G. *The Relation of John Locke to English Deism.* Chicago, 1918.

Hertling, G. V. *Locke und die Schule von Cambridge.* Freiburg i. B., 1892.

Hofstadter, A. *Locke and Scepticism.* New York, 1936.

Kendall, W. *John Locke and the Doctrine of Majority-Rule.* Illinois, 1941.

King, Lord. *The Life and Letters of John Locke.* 2 vols. London, 1858 (3rd edition). (This work includes some extracts from Locke's journals and an abstract of the *Essay.*)

Klemmt, A. *John Locke: Theoretische Philosophie.* Meisenheim, 1952.

Krakowski, E. *Les sources médiévales de la philosophie de Locke.* Paris, 1915.

Lamprecht, S. P. *The Moral and Political Philosophy of John Locke.* New York, 1918.

MacLean, K. *John Locke and English Literature of the Eighteenth Century.* New Haven (U.S.A.), 1936.

Marion, H. *John Locke, sa vie et son œuvre.* Paris, 1893 (2nd edition).

O'Connor, D. J. *John Locke.* Penguin Books, 1952.

Ollion, H. *La philosophie générale de Locke.* Paris, 1909.

Petzäll, A. *Ethics and Epistemology in John Locke's Essay concerning Human Understanding.* Göteborg, 1937.

Tellkamp, A. *Das Verhältnis John Lockes zur Scholastik.* Münster, 1927.

Thompson, S. M. *A Study of Locke's Theory of Ideas.* Monmouth (U.S.A.), 1934.

Tinivella, G. *Giovanni Locke e i pensieri sull'educazione.* Milan, 1938.

Yolton, J. W. *John Locke and the Way of Ideas.* Oxford, 1956.

Chapter Eight: Boyle and Newton

1. Boyle

Text

The Works of the Honourable Robert Boyle. Edited by T. Birch. 6 vols. London, 1772 (2nd edition).

Studies

Farrington, F. *A Life of the Honourable Robert Boyle.* Cork, 1917.

Fisher, M. S. *Robert Boyle, Devout Naturalist: A Study in Science and Religion in the Seventeenth Century.* Philadelphia, 1945.

Masson, F. *Robert Boyle.* Edinburgh, 1914.

Meier, J. *Robert Boyles Naturphilosophie.* Munich, 1907.

Mendelssohn, S. *Robert Boyle als Philosoph.* Würzburg, 1902.

More, L. T. *The Life and Works of the Hon. Robert Boyle.* Oxford, 1945.

2. *Newton*

Texts

Opera quae existunt omnia. Edited by S. Horsley. 5 vols. London, 1779–85.

Philosophiae naturalis principia mathematica. Edited by R. Cotes. London, 1713, and reprints.

Mathematical Principles of Natural Philosophy and System of the World. Translated by A. Motte, revised and annotated by F. Cajori. Cambridge, 1934.

Opticks. London, 1730 (4th edition); reprint New York, 1952.

Sir Isaac Newton: Theological Manuscripts. Selected and edited by H. McLachlan. Boston, 1950.

Newton's Philosophy of Nature. Selections from his writings edited by H. S. Thayer. New York, 1953.

Studies

Andrade, E. N. da C. *Sir Isaac Newton.* London, 1954.

Bloch, L. *La Philosophie de Newton.* Paris, 1908.

Clarke, G. N. *Science and Social Welfare in the Age of Newton.* Oxford, 1949 (2nd edition).

De Morgan, A. *Essays on the Life and Work of Newton.* Edited by F. E. B. Jourdain. London, 1914.

Dessauer, F. *Weltfahrt der Erkenntnis. Leben und Werk Isaak Newtons.* Zürich, 1945.

McLachlan, H. *The Religious Opinions of Milton, Locke and Newton.* Manchester, 1941.

More, L. T. *Isaac Newton, A Biography.* New York, 1934.

Randall, J. H., Jr. *Newton's Natural Philosophy: Its Problems and Consequences* (in *Philosophical Essays in Honor of Edgar Arthur Singer, Jr.* Edited by F. P. Clark and M. C. Nahm. Philadelphia, 1942, pp. 335–57).

Rosenberger, I. *Newton und seine physikalischen Prinzipien.* Leipzig, 1893.

Steinmann, H. G. *Ueber den Einfluss Newtons auf die Erkenntnistheorie seiner Zeit.* Bonn, 1913.

Sullivan, J. W. N. *Isaac Newton, 1642–1727.* London, 1938.

Volkmann, P. *Ueber Newtons Philosophia Naturalis*. Königsberg, 1898.
Whittaker, E. T. *Aristotle, Newton, Einstein*. London, 1942.

3. *General Works*

Burtt, E. A. *The Metaphysical Foundations of Modern Physical Science. A Historical and Critical Essay*. London, 1925; revised edition, 1932.
Cassirer, E. *Das Erkenntnisproblem in der Philosophie und Wissenschaft der neueren Zeit*. 3 vols. Berlin, 1906–20; later edition, 1922–3.
Dampier, W. C. *A History of Science and its Relations with Philosophy and Religion*. Cambridge, 1949 (4th edition).
Mach, E. *The Science of Mechanics*. Translated by T. J. MacCormack. La Salle (Illinois), 1942 (5th edition).
Strong, E. W. *Procedures and Metaphysics: A Study in the Philosophy of Mathematical Physical Science in the Sixteenth and Seventeenth Centuries*. Berkeley, U.S.A., 1936.

Chapter Nine: Religious Problems

1. *Clarke*

Texts
Works. With a preface by B. Hoadley. 4 vols. London, 1738–42.
Œuvres philosophiques. Translated by C. Jourdain. Paris, 1843.
A Demonstration of the Being and Attributes of God. London, 1705.
A Discourse concerning the Unchangeable Obligations of Natural Religion. London, 1706.
One hundred and Twenty Three Sermons. Edited by J. Clarke. 2 vols. Dublin, 1734.
A Collection of Papers which passed between the late learned Mr. Leibniz and Dr. Clarke. London, 1717.

Studies
Le Rossignol, J. E. *The Ethical Philosophy of Samuel Clarke*. Leipzig, 1892.
Zimmermann, R. *Clarkes Leben und Lehre*. Vienna, 1870.

2. Toland

Texts
Christianity not Mysterious. London, 1696.
Pantheisticon. London, 1720.

3. Tindal

Text
Christianity as Old as the Creation. London, 1730.

4. Collins

Texts
A Discourse of Free-thinking. London, 1713.
Philosophical Enquiry concerning Human Liberty and Necessity. London, 1715.
A Discourse of the Grounds and Reasons of the Christian Religion. London, 1724.
A Dissertation on Liberty and Necessity. London, 1729.

5. Dodwell

Text
An Epistolary Discourse, proving from the Scriptures and the First Fathers that the Soul is a Principle naturally Mortal. London, 1706.

6. Bolingbroke

Texts
The Philosophical Works of the Right Hon. Henry St. John, Lord Viscount Bolingbroke. Edited by D. Mallet. London, 1754 (5 vols.), 1778, 1809; Philadelphia (4 vols.), 1849.
Letters on the Study and Use of History. London, 1738 and 1752.

Studies
Brosch, M. *Lord Bolingbroke.* Frankfurt a M., 1883.
Hassall, A. *Life of Viscount Bolingbroke.* London, 1915 (2nd edition).
James, D. G. *The English Augustans: I, The Life of Reason: Hobbes, Locke, Bolingbroke.* London, 1949.
Merrill, W. McIntosh. *From Statesman to Philosopher. A Study of Bolingbroke's Deism.* New York, 1949.
Sichel, W. *Bolingbroke and His Times.* London, 1902.

7. Deism in General

Carrau, L. *La philosophie religieuse en Angleterre depuis Locke jusqu'à nos jours.* Paris, 1888.

Farrar, A. S. *A Critical History of Free Thought.* London, 1862.

Lechler, G. V. *Geschichte des englischen Deismus.* 2 vols. Stuttgart, 1841.

Leland, J. *A View of the Principal Deistical Writers.* 2 vols. London, 1837.

Noack, L. *Die englischen, französischen und deutschen Freidenker.* Berne, 1853–5.

Sayous, A. *Les déistes anglais et le christianisme rationaliste.* Paris, 1882.

Stephen, L. *History of English Thought in the Eighteenth Century.* 2 vols. London, 1876.

8. Butler

Texts

Works. Edited by J. H. Bernard. 2 vols. London, 1900.

Works. Edited by W. E. Gladstone. 2 vols. London, 1910 (2nd edition).

The analogy of Religion, natural and revealed, to the Constitution and Cause of Nature, with an introduction by R. Bayne. London (*E.L.*).

Fifteen Sermons upon Human Nature, or Man considered as a Moral Agent. London, 1726, 1841, etc.

Fifteen Sermons (and *Dissertation on Virtue*). Edited by W. R. Matthews. London, 1949.

Studies

Broad, C. D. *Five Types of Ethical Theory.* (Chapter III, 'Butler', pp. 53–83.) London, 1930.

Collins, W. L. *Butler.* Edinburgh and London, 1889.

Duncan-Jones, A. *Butler's Moral Philosophy.* Penguin Books, 1952.

Mossner, E. C. *Bishop Butler and the Age of Reason.* New York, 1936.

Norton, W. J. *Bishop Butler, Moralist and Divine.* New Brunswick and London, 1940.

Chapter Ten: Problems of Ethics

1. Shaftesbury

Text

Characteristics. Edited by J. M. Robertson. 2 vols. London, 1900.

Studies

Brett, R. L. *The third Earl of Shaftesbury: A Study in Eighteenth-Century Literary Theory*. London, 1951.

Elson, C. *Wieland and Shaftesbury*. New York, 1913.

Fowler, T. *Shaftesbury and Hutcheson*. London, 1882.

Kern, J. *Shaftesburys Bild vom Menschen*. Frankfurt a M., 1943.

Lyons, A. *Shaftesbury's Principle of Adaptation to Universal Harmony*. New York, 1909.

Meinecke, F. *Shaftesbury und die Wurzeln des Historismus*. Berlin, 1934.

Osske, I. *Ganzheit, Unendlichkeit und Form. Studien zu Shaftesburys Naturbegriff*. Berlin, 1939.

Rand, B. *Life, Unpublished Letters and Philosophical Regimen of Anthony, Earl of Shaftesbury*. London, 1900.

Spicker, G. *Die Philosophie des Grafen von Shaftesbury*. Freiburg i. B., 1871.

Zani, L. *L'etica di Lord Shaftesbury*. Milan, 1954.

2. Mandeville

Texts

The Grumbling Hive or Knaves turned Honest. London, 1705.

The Fable of the Bees or Private Vices Public Benefits. London, 1714, and subsequent editions.

The Fable of the Bees. Edited by F. B. Kaye. Oxford, 1924.

Studies

Hübner, W. *Mandevilles Bienenfabel und die Begründung der praktischen Zweckethik der englischen Aufklärung* (in *Grundformen der englischen Geistesgeschichte*. Edited by P. Meissner. Stuttgart, 1941, pp. 275–331).

Stammler, R. *Mandevilles Bienenfabel*. Berlin, 1918.

3. Hutcheson

Text
Works. 5 vols. Glasgow, 1772.

Studies
Fowler, T. *Shaftesbury and Hutcheson.* London, 1882.
Rampendal, R. *Eine Würdigung der Ethik Hutchesons.* Leipzig, 1892.
Scott, W. R. *Francis Hutcheson, His Life, Teaching and Position in the History of Philosophy.* London, 1900.
Vignone, L. *L'etica del senso morale in Francis Hutcheson.* Milan, 1954.

4. Butler

For *Texts* and *Studies* see Bibliography under Chapter Nine.

5. Hartley

Text
Observations on Man, His Frame, His Duty and His Expectations. Edited by J. B. Priestley. 3 vols. London, 1934 (3rd edition).

Studies
Bower, G. S. *Hartley and James Mill.* London, 1881.
Heider, M. *Studien über David Hartley.* Bonn, 1913.
Ribot, T. *Quid David Hartley de consociatione idearum senserit.* Paris, 1872.
Schoenlank, B. *Hartley und Priestley, die Begründer des Assoziationismus in England.* Halle, 1882.

6. Tucker

Text
The Light of Nature Pursued. Edited, with a Life, by H. P. St. John Mildmay. 7 vols. London, 1805 and reprints.

Study
Harris, W. G. *Teleology in the Philosophy of Joseph Butler and Abraham Tucker.* Philadelphia, 1942.

7. Paley

Texts
Paley's Works, first published in 8 vols., 1805–8, have been

republished several times, the number of volumes varying from eight to one (1851).

The Principles of Moral and Political Philosophy. London, 1785, and subsequent editions.

Natural Theology, or Evidences of the Existence and Attributes of the Deity collected from the Appearances of Nature. London, 1802, and subsequent editions.

Study

Stephen, L. *History of English Thought in the Eighteenth Century.* 2 vols. London, 1876. (For Paley see I, pp. 405 f., and II, pp. 121 f.)

8. General Works

Texts (Selections)

Rand, B. *The Classical Moralists. Selections.* London, 1910.

Selby-Bigge, L. A. *British Moralists.* 2 vols. Oxford, 1897.

Studies

Bonar, J. *Moral Sense.* London, 1930.

Mackintosh, J. *On the Progress of Ethical Philosophy, chiefly during the XVIIth and XVIIIth Centuries.* Edited by W. Whewell. Edinburgh, 1872 (4th edition).

Martineau, J. *Types of Ethical Theory.* 2 vols. Oxford, 1901 (3rd edition, revised).

Moskowitz, H. *Das moralische Beurteilungsvermögen in der Ethik von Hobbes bis J. S. Mill.* Erlangen, 1906.

Raphael, D. Daiches. *The Moral Sense.* Oxford, 1947. (This work deals with Hutcheson, Hume, Price and Reid.)

Sidgwick, H. *Outlines of the History of Ethics for English Readers.* London, 1931 (6th edition).

NOTES

1 W. Molesworth edited two collections of Hobbes's writings: *Opera philosophica quae latine scripsit* in five volumes (1839–45) and *The English Works of Thomas Hobbes* in eleven volumes (1839–45). In the references given in this and in the next chapter the letters O.L. and E.W. refer respectively to these editions.

2 *Concerning Body*, 1, 1, 6; E. W., I, p. 7.

3 *Concerning Body*, 1, 1, 7; E.W., I, p. 8.

4 *Concerning Body*, 1, 1, 2; E.W., I, p. 3.

5 *Concerning Body*, 1, 1, 2; E.W., I, p. 3.

6 *Leviathan*, 1, 9; E.W., III, p. 71.

7 *Ibid.*

8 *Ibid.*

9 *Ibid.*

10 *Leviathan*, 1, 7; E.W., III, p. 52.

11 *Concerning Body*, 1, 1, 8; E.W., I, p. 10.

12 *Ibid.*, p. 11.

13 *Concerning Body*, 1, 6, 5; E.W., I, pp. 69–70.

14 *Concerning Body*, 1, 1, 10; E.W., I, p. 12.

15 *Leviathan*, 1, 3; E.W., III, p. 17.

16 *Leviathan*, 1, 4; E.W., III, p. 27.

17 *Leviathan*, 1, 5; E.W., III, pp. 34–5.

18 *Ibid.*, pp. 32–3.

19 *Leviathan*, 1, 11; E.W., III, p. 92.

20 *Ibid.*, p. 93.

21 *Leviathan*, 1, 3; E.W., III, p. 17.

22 *Leviathan*, 1, 12; E.W., III, p. 97.

23 *Leviathan*, 3, 34; E.W., III, p. 383.

24 E.W., IV, p. 306.

25 *Ibid.*, p. 309.

26 *Ibid.*

27 *Ibid.*, p. 313.

28 *Concerning Body*, 1, 1, 9; E.W., I, p. 11.

29 *Ibid.*

30 *Concerning Body*, 1, 6, 6; E.W., I, p. 71.

31 *Ibid.*, p. 72.

32 Cf. *Leviathan*, 1, 9; E.W., III, pp. 72–3.

33 The study of the consequences from the qualities of men in particular includes, besides ethics, study of the functions of speech. Study of, for example, the technique of persuading gives us rhetoric, while study of the art of reasoning gives us logic.

34 *Concerning Body*, 1, 1, 2; E.W., I, p. 3.
35 *Concerning Body*, 1, 6, 1; E.W., I, p. 66.
36 *Ibid.*
37 *Concerning Body*, 1, 6, 12; E.W., I, p. 81.
38 *Concerning Government and Society*, dedicatory epistle; E.W., II, p. iv.
39 *Ibid.*
40 *Concerning Body*, 1, 6, 6; E.W., I, p. 73.
41 *Concerning Body*, 4, 1, 1; E.W., I, pp. 387-8.
42 For example, given a certain definition of motion or a certain definition of body, motion or body will necessarily possess certain properties. But it does not follow immediately that there is motion or body. What follows is that if there is motion or if there is body, it will have these properties.
43 *Ibid.*, p. 388.
44 *Concerning Body*, 1, 6, 7; E.W., I, p. 74.
45 Hobbes is here referring to the conventional character of language. Names are conventional marks and signs.
46 *Concerning Body*, 1, 2, 4; E.W., I, p. 16.
47 *Concerning Body*, 1, 2, 9; E.W., I, p. 20.
48 *Leviathan*, 1, 4; E.W., III, p. 21.
49 For an account of Ockham's doctrine on this point, see vol. III of this *History*, p. 56.
50 *Concerning Body*, 1, 2, 6; E.W., I, p. 17.
51 *Concerning Body*, 1, 2, 5; E.W., I, p. 17.
52 *Leviathan*, 1, 4; E.W., III, p. 19.
53 *Leviathan*, 1, 1; E.W., III, p. 1.
54 *Human Nature*, 1, 4, 10; E.W., IV, p. 18.
55 *Leviathan*, 1, 4 and 5; E.W., III, pp. 24 and 33.
56 *Concerning Body*, 1, 6, 14; E.W., I, pp. 83-4.
57 *Concerning Body*, 1, 3, 9; E.W., I, p. 37.
58 *Objection*, IV; O.L., pp. 257-8.
59 *Concerning Body*, 1, 3, 8; E.W., I, p. 36.
60 Hobbes insists that truth and falsity are predicable of propositions, never of things. Truth 'is not any affection of the thing, but of the proposition concerning it' (*Concerning Body*, 1, 3, 7; E.W., I, p. 35).
61 *Ibid.*
62 *Concerning Body*, 1, 5, 7; E.W., I, p. 60.
63 The 'essence' of a thing is 'that accident for which we give a certain name to a body, or the accident which denominates its subject . . . as extension is the essence of a body' (*Concerning Body*, 2, 8, 23; E.W., I, p. 117).
64 *Concerning Body*, 2, 8, 24; E.W., I, p. 118.
65 *Ibid.*
66 *Ibid.*
67 *Concerning Body*, 1, 6, 10; E.W., I, p. 77.
68 *Concerning Body*, 2, 8, 2; E.W., I, p. 104.
69 *Ibid.*, p. 103.
70 *Concerning Body*, 2, 9, 3; E.W., I, pp. 121-2.
71 *Concerning Body*, 2, 10, 7; E.W., I, pp. 131-2.
72 *Concerning Body*, 2, 9, 5; E.W., I, p. 123.

73 *Ibid.*

74 *Leviathan*, 1, 5; E.W., III, p. 33.

75 *Concerning Body*, 2, 7, 2; E.W., I, p. 94.

76 *Ibid.*, p. 95.

77 *Concerning Body*, 2, 7, 3; E.W., I, p. 94.

78 *Concerning Body*, 2, 7, 13; E.W., I, p. 100.

79 *Concerning Body*, 2, 8, 1; E.W., I, p. 102.

80 *Ibid.*

81 *Concerning Body*, 2, 8, 2; E.W., I, p. 103.

82 *Ibid.*

83 *Concerning Body*, 2, 8, 3; E.W., I, p. 104.

84 *Concerning Body*, 2, 8, 5; E.W., I, p. 105.

85 *Ibid.*

86 *Concerning Body*, 4, 25, 10; E.W., I, p. 405.

87 *Concerning Body*, 4, 25, 3; E.W., I, pp. 391–2.

88 *Concerning Body*, 4, 25, 10; E.W., I, p. 405.

89 *Concerning Body*, 4, 25, 2; E.W., I, p. 391.

90 *Concerning Body*, 2, 8, 10; E.W., I, p. 109.

91 *Concerning Body*, 2, 8, 18; E.W., I, p. 115.

92 *Ibid.*

93 *Concerning Body*, 2, 9, 9; E.W., I, p. 126.

94 *Concerning Body*, 4, 25, 12; E.W., I, p. 407.

95 *Leviathan*, 1, 6; E.W., III, p. 31.

96 *Ibid.*

97 *Ibid.*

98 *Ibid.*

99 *Ibid.*, p. 4.

100 *Ibid.*

101 *Concerning Body*, 4, 25, 13; E.W., I, pp. 409–10.

102 *Human Nature*, 8, 1; E.W., IV, p. 34.

103 *Ibid.*

104 Hobbes distinguishes between pleasures and displeasures of sense and pleasures and displeasures of the mind. The latter arise from expectation of an end or of consequences. Pleasures of the mind are called *joy*, while displeasures of the mind are called *grief* (in distinction from displeasures of sense, which are called *pain*).

105 *Leviathan*, 1, 6; E.W., III, p. 44.

106 *Ibid.*, p. 46.

107 *Human Nature*, 7, 1; E.W., IV, p. 31.

108 *Leviathan*, 1, 6; E.W., III, p. 48.

109 *Ibid.*

110 *Concerning Body*, 4, 25, 13; E.W., I, p. 409.

111 *Leviathan*, 1, 8; E.W., III, p. 57.

112 *Human Nature*, 10, 3; E.W., IV, p. 55.

113 *Leviathan*, 1, 8; E.W., III, p. 61.

CHAPTER TWO

1 *Leviathan*, 1, 13; E.W., III, p. 112.

2 *Ibid.*, p. 113.

3 *Ibid.*

4 *Ibid.*, p. 114.

5 *Ibid.*, p. 115.

6 *Ibid.*

7 *Ibid.*, p. 114.

8 *Leviathan*, 1, 14; E.W., III, p. 116.

9 Right reason, Hobbes explains, means here 'the peculiar and

true ratiocination of every man concerning those actions of his, which may either redound to the damage or benefit of his neighbours'. 'Peculiar', because in the 'state of nature' the individual's reason is for him the only rule of action.

10 *Philosophical Elements of a True Citizen*, 2, 1; E.W., II, p. 16.

11 *Leviathan*, 1, 14; E.W., III, pp. 116–17.

12 *Ibid.*, p. 117.

13 *Ibid.*, p. 118.

14 *Ibid.*, p. 120.

15 *Ibid.*

16 *Ibid.*

17 *Ibid.*, p. 121.

18 *Leviathan*, 1, 15; E.W., III, p. 130.

19 *Ibid.*

20 *Ibid.*, p. 131.

21 *Ibid.*, p. 147.

22 *Ibid.*, p. 145.

23 *Ibid.*, p. 146.

24 *Ibid.*

25 *Ibid.*

26 *Leviathan*, 2, 17; E.W., III, p. 154.

27 *Ibid.*, p. 157.

28 *Leviathan*, 1, 16; E.W., III, p. 147.

29 *Ibid.*, p. 151.

30 *Leviathan*, 2, 17; E.W., III, p. 158.

31 *Ibid.*

32 *Leviathan*, 1, 18; E.W., III, p. 161.

33 *Leviathan*, 2, 19; E.W., III, p. 173.

34 *Leviathan*, 1, 20; E.W., III, p. 185.

35 *Ibid.*

36 *Ibid.*, p. 186.

37 *Leviathan*, 2, 18; E.W., III, p. 161.

38 *Ibid.*, p. 163.

39 *Ibid.*, p. 165.

40 *Leviathan*, 2, 29; E.W., III, p. 310.

41 *Ibid.*, p. 311.

42 *Leviathan*, 3, 32; E.W., III, p. 359.

43 *Leviathan*, 4, 47; E.W., III, pp. 697–8.

44 *Leviathan*, 3, 39; E.W., III, p. 459.

45 E.W., IV, p. 339.

46 *Ibid.*

47 *Leviathan*, 2, 21; E.W., III, pp. 196–7.

48 *Ibid.*, p. 201.

49 *Ibid.*, p. 203.

50 *Ibid.*, p. 199.

51 *Ibid.*, p. 142.

52 *Ibid.*, p. 204.

53 *Ibid.*, p. 208.

54 *Ibid.*, p. 202.

55 *Leviathan*, 2, 18; E.W., III, p. 168.

56 E.W., IV, p. 413.

57 *Ibid.*, p. 415.

58 *Ibid.*

59 For the political theories of St. Augustine and St. Thomas Aquinas, Chapters VIII and XL of vol. II of this *History* may be consulted.

60 For Machiavelli, pp. 128–34 of vol. III of this *History* may be consulted.

CHAPTER THREE

1 The philosophy of Francis Bacon is discussed in Chapter XIX of vol. III of this *History*.

2 *The Platonic Renaissance in England*, translated by James P. Pettegrove (Edinburgh, Nelson, 1953).

3 *The True Intellectual System*

of the Universe, 1, 5, 1; edit. Harrison, 1845, vol. II, p. 515. All quotations from this work of Cudworth are taken from Harrison's edition.

4 The True Intellectual System of the Universe, 1, 5, 1; II, pp. 537–8.

5 Ibid., p. 635.

6 Ibid., p. 509.

7 Ibid., III, pp. 49–50.

8 Ibid., p. 54.

9 Ibid., 3, 37; I, p. 217.

10 Ibid., 5, 1; II, p. 616.

11 Ibid., 5, 4; III, p. 441.

12 Ibid., p. 440.

13 Ibid.

14 Œuvres de Descartes, A.T., v, pp. 249 f.

15 The True Intellectual System of the Universe, 5, 4; III, p. 438.

16 Ibid.

17 This treatise is included in vol. III of Harrison's edition of The True Intellectual System of the Universe. And references are given according to pagination in this edition.

18 4, 1, 7; III, p. 582.

19 Ibid., 4, 2, 2; III, p. 587.

20 Ibid., 4, 3, 1; III, pp. 601–2.

21 Ibid., 4, 5, 9; III, p. 637.

22 Ibid.

23 Ibid., 4, 5, 12; III, pp. 638–9.

24 Ibid., 4, 6, 2; III, p. 639.

25 Ibid., 5, 1; II, p. 533.

26 Selected sermons, 1773, pp. 6–7.

27 1, 4, 2.

28 Ibid.

29 Ibid.

30 Ibid., 1, 4, 4.

31 De legibus naturae, 1.

32 Ibid.

33 Ibid., 5.

CHAPTER FOUR

1 References to this work by volume and page are to the edition by A. C. Fraser.

2 Essay, 'Epistle to the Reader'.

3 E., Introduction, 8; I, p. 32.

4 Ibid., 2; I, p. 26.

5 Ibid., 3; I, p. 27.

6 Ibid., p. 28.

7 E., 3, 2, 2; II, p. 9.

8 E., Introduction, 3; I, p. 28.

9 E., 1, 1, 1; I, p. 37.

10 E., 1, 2, 15 f.; I, p. 80.

11 E., 1, 1, 2; I, p. 39.

12 E., 1, 1, 5; I, p. 40.

13 E., 1, 1, 12; I, p. 45.

14 E., 1, 1, 27; I, p. 62.

15 E., 1, 2, 1; I, p. 64.

16 E., 1, 2, 3; I, pp. 66–7.

17 E., 1, 2, 3; I, p. 67.

18 E., 1, 1, 18; I, p. 51.

19 Ibid., p. 53.

20 E., 1, 1, 22; I, p. 56.

21 E., 2, 1, 2; I, pp. 121–2.

22 E., 2, 1, 3; I, pp. 122–3.

23 E., 2, 1, 4; I, p. 124.

24 E., 2, 1, 8; I, p. 127.

25 E., 2, 1, 24; I, p. 142.

CHAPTER FIVE

1 E., 2, 5; I, p. 158.

2 E., 2, 6; I, p. 159.

3 E., 2, 7, 1; I, p. 160.

4 E., 2, 7, 7; I, p. 163.

5 E., 2, 1, 25; I, p. 142.

6 E., 2, 2, 2; I, p. 145.

7 E., 2, 12, 1; I, p. 214.

8 Edit. Rand, p. 120.

9 E., 2, 12, 1; I, p. 213.

10 Ibid., p. 214.

[11] E., 2, 12, 8; I, p. 217.
[12] E., 2, 12, 4; I, p. 215.
[13] E., 2, 12, 5; I, pp. 215–16.
[14] Ibid., p. 216.
[15] E., 2, 18, 2; I, p. 294.
[16] Locke insists, against Descartes and his followers, that extension and body are not the same thing. The idea of body involves, for example, the idea of solidity, but the idea of extension does not.
[17] E., 2, 13, 3; I, p. 220.
[18] E., 2, 13, 4; I, p. 220.
[19] E., 2, 14, 3; I, p. 239.
[20] E., 2, 14, 31; I, p. 256.
[21] E., 2, 15, 6; I, p. 262.
[22] E., 2, 17, 1; I, p. 277.
[23] Ibid., p. 276.
[24] E., 2, 17, 4; I, p. 278.
[25] E., 2, 17, 8; I, pp. 281–2.
[26] E., 2, 17, 9; I, p. 283.
[27] E., 2, 22, 8; I, p. 385.
[28] E., 2, 22, 9; I, p. 385.
[29] Ibid.
[30] Ibid.
[31] E., 2, 8, 8; I, p. 169.
[32] E., 2, 8, 9; I, p. 170.
[33] E., 2, 8, 10; I, p. 170.
[34] E., 2, 8, 23; I, p. 179.
[35] E., 2, 8, 15; I, p. 173.
[36] E., 2, 8, 17; I, p. 174.
[37] E., 2, 8, 16; I, p. 174.
[38] E., 2, 8, 19; I, p. 176.
[39] E., 2, 8, 20; I, p. 176.
[40] See vol. 3, Part II of this History, p. 98.
[41] See vol. 1, Part I of this History, pp. 145–6.
[42] E., 2, 8, 8; I, p. 169.
[43] E., 2, 23, 1; I, pp. 390–1.
[44] E., 2, 23, 2; I, p. 391.
[45] Ibid., p. 392.
[46] E., 2, 23, 6; I, p. 396.
[47] Ibid., p. 397.
[48] E., 2, 23, 37; I, p. 422.
[49] E., 4, 3, 6; II, p. 192.
[50] E., 2, 23, 33; I, p. 418.
[51] Ibid.
[52] E., 2, 23, 37; I, p. 422.
[53] E., 2, 12, 1; I, pp. 213–14.
[54] E., 2, 25, 1; I, p. 427.
[55] E., 2, 25, 3; I, p. 428.
[56] E., 2, 25, 5; I, p. 428.
[57] E., 2, 25, 7; I, pp. 429–30.
[58] E., 2, 25, 8; I, p. 430.
[59] E., 3, 10, 33; II, p. 145.
[60] E., 2, 26, 1; I, p. 433.
[61] Ibid., p. 434.
[62] E., 2, 26, 2; I, p. 435.
[63] E., 2, 21, 3; I, p. 310.
[64] E., 2, 21, 4; I, p. 312.
[65] E., 2, 21, 5; I, p. 313.
[66] E., 2, 27, 4; I, pp. 441–2.
[67] E., 2, 27, 5; I, p. 443.
[68] E., 2, 27, 4; I, p. 442.
[69] E., 2, 27, 7; I, p. 444.
[70] Ibid., p. 445.
[71] E., 2, 27, 11; I, p. 448.
[72] Ibid., p. 449.
[73] Ibid.
[74] E., 2, 27, 20; I, p. 461.
[75] E., 3, 1, 1; II, p. 3.
[76] E., 3, 2, 1; II, p. 9.
[77] E., 3, 7, 1; II, p. 98.
[78] E., 3, 9, 6; II, p. 106.
[79] Ibid., p. 107.
[80] E., 3, 9, 8; II, p. 108.
[81] E., 3, 10, 2; II, p. 123.
[82] E., 3, 10, 34; II, p. 147.
[83] E., 4, 21, 4; II, p. 462.
[84] E., 3, 3, 6; II, p. 16.
[85] Ibid., pp. 16–17.
[86] E., 3, 3, 11; II, p. 21.
[87] E., 3, 3, 12; II, p. 22.
[88] E., 3, 3, 13; II, p. 23.
[89] E., 4, 7, 9; II, p. 274.
[90] E., 3, 3, 17; II, p. 27.
[91] Ibid., pp. 27–8.
[92] E., 3, 3, 12; II, p. 23.
[93] E., 3, 3, 14; II, 9, 25.
[94] E., 3, 3, 18; II, p. 29.
[95] Ibid., p. 29.

CHAPTER SIX

1 Rand, p. 85.
2 E., 4, 1, 1; II, p. 167.
3 E., 4, 1, 7; II, p. 171.
4 E., 4, 2, 1; II, p. 176.
5 Ibid., p. 177.
6 Ibid.
7 E., 4, 2, 14; II, p. 185.
8 Ibid., p. 186.
9 E., 4, 3, 1; II, p. 190.
10 E., 4, 3, 6; II, p. 191.
11 E., 4, 3, 9; II, p. 199.
12 Ibid.
13 E., 4, 3, 11; II, p. 200.
14 E., 4, 3, 14; II, p. 203.
15 E., 4, 3, 16; II, p. 206.
16 E., 4, 3, 26; II, p. 218.
17 Ibid.
18 E., 4, 3, 24; II, p. 215.
19 E., 4, 3, 25; II, p. 217.
20 E., 4, 3, 26; II, pp. 217–18.
21 Ibid.
22 E., 4, 3, 18; II, p. 207.
23 E., 4, 3, 21; II, p. 212.
24 E., 4, 9, 3; II, p. 305.
25 E., 4, 4, 3; II, p. 228.
26 E., 4, 4, 6; II, p. 231.
27 E., 4, 4, 8; II, p. 233.
28 E., 4, 4, 4; II, p. 230.
29 E., 4, 4, 5; II, p. 230.
30 E., 4, 4, 12; II, p. 237.
31 E., 4, 10, 1; II, p. 306.
32 E., 4, 10, 3; II, p. 307.
33 E., 4, 10, 4; II, p. 308.
34 E., 4, 10, 6; II, p. 309.
35 E., 4, 11, 1; II, p. 325.
36 E., 4, 11, 2; II, p. 326.
37 E., 4, 11, 10; II, pp. 335–6.
38 E., 4, 14, 4; II, p. 362.
39 Ibid.
40 E., 4, 15, 1; II, p. 363.
41 E., 4, 15, 4; II, p. 365.
42 E., 4, 16, 5; II, p. 374.
43 E., 4, 16, 12; II, p. 380.
44 E., 4, 16, 14; II, p. 383.
45 E., 4, 19, 9; II, p. 434.
46 E., 4, 19, 10; II, p. 436.
47 E., 4, 19, 13; II, p. 438.
48 E., 4, 19, 14; II, p. 438.
49 E., 4, 20, 10; II, p. 450.
50 Catholic theologians would not deny that reason is capable *in principle* of distinguishing between propositions which are contrary to reason and propositions, the truth or falsity of which cannot be decided by reason without the aid of revelation. But in particular cases we may, when left to our own devices, confuse the latter with the former.

CHAPTER SEVEN

1 E., 4, 12, 8; II, p. 347.
2 E., 4, 4, 7; II, p. 232.
3 E., 3, 11, 17; II, p. 157.
4 E., 2, 20, 2; I, p. 303.
5 E., 2, 28, 5; I, p. 474.
6 E., 2, 28, 7; I, p. 475.
7 E., 2, 28, 10; I, p. 477.
8 E., 2, 28, 8; I, p. 475.
9 Ibid.
10 E., 4, 3, 18; II, p. 208.
11 Ibid.
12 For Hooker, vol. 3, Part II of this *History* may be consulted, pp. 135–8.
13 Unless otherwise indicated, 'T.' in references signifies the second *Treatise*.
14 2, 6.
15 T., 2, 5.
16 T., 2, 15.
17 T., 3, 19.
18 T., 2, 6.

19 For Grotius, vol. 3, Part II of this *History* may be consulted, pp. 143-9.
20 *T.*, 5, 29.
21 *T.*, 5, 31.
22 *Ibid.*
23 *T.*, 5, 32.
24 *T.*, 5, 49.
25 *T.*, 16, 190.
26 *T.*, 7, 77.
27 *T.*, 9, 124.
28 *T.*, 9, 127.
29 *T.*, 9, 124.
30 *T.*, 9, 123.
31 *T.*, 7, 89.
32 *T.*, 8, 95.
33 *T.*, 9, 131.
34 *T.*, 8, 99.
35 *T.*, 8, 96.
36 *T.*, 7, 90.
37 *T.*, 8, 101.
38 *T.*, 8, 116.
39 *T.*, 11, 134.
40 *T.*, 11, 136.
41 *T.*, 11, 134.
42 *T.*, 13, 150.
43 *T.*, 12, 143.
44 *T.*, 13, 149.
45 *T.*, 11, 142.
46 *T.*, 12, 146.
47 *T.*, 12, 148.
48 *T.*, 19, 211.
49 *Ibid.*
50 *T.*, 19, 225.
51 *T.*, 19, 240.

CHAPTER EIGHT

1 To explain gravity mechanically, Descartes had postulated that the ethereal medium forms vortices.
2 p. 95.
3 For these Renaissance scientists Chapter XVIII of vol. III of this *History* may be consulted.
4 *Principia mathematica*, preface to first edition.
5 Third edition, 1721, p. 380.
6 II, p. 314, translation by A. Motte.
7 *Ibid.*
8 *Opticks*, 3rd edition, 1721, p. 377.
9 *Principia mathematica*, I, p. 6.
10 *Ibid.*
11 *Opticks*, pp. 108 f.
12 *Ibid.*, p. 344.
13 *Ibid.*, p. 379.
14 p. 344.

CHAPTER NINE

1 The two series of Boyle lectures mentioned were subsequently published together in one volume with the title *A Discourse concerning the Being and Attributes of God, the Obligations of Natural Religion, and the Truth and Certainty of the Christian Revelation*. References are to the 1719 edition of this work.
2 *A Discourse*, 1, p. 9.
3 *Ibid.*
4 *Ibid.*, p. 12.
5 *Ibid.*, p. 15.
6 *Ibid.*, p. 38.
7 *Ibid.*, pp. 41-2.
8 *Ibid.*, p. 44.
9 *Ibid.*, p. 48.
10 *Ibid.*, p. 51.
11 *Ibid.*, p. 64.
12 *Ibid.*, p. 76.
13 *Ibid.*, p. 113.
14 *Ibid.*, p. 119.

15 Cf. the letters printed at the end of *A Discourse*, p. 16.
16 *Ibid.*, pp. 21–2.
17 *Ibid.*, p. 27.
18 *A Collection of Papers which passed between the late learned Mr. Leibniz and Dr. Clarke*, 1717, p. 77.
19 *Ibid.*, p. 125.
20 *Ibid.*, p. 149.
21 *Ibid.*, p. 113.
22 *A Discourse*, 2, p. 47.
23 *Ibid.*, p. 38.
24 *Ibid.*, p. 39.
25 *Ibid.*, p. 5.
26 *Ibid.*, p. 54.
27 *Ibid.*, p. 107.

28 *Ibid.*, p. 284.
29 *Ibid.*, p. 19.
30 Page references are given to Gladstone's edition of Butler's works in two volumes (Oxford, 1896).
31 1, pp. 1–2.
32 Introduction, 8; 1, pp. 9–10.
33 1, 1, 3; 1, p. 22.
34 2, 1, 24; 1, p. 201.
35 2, 8, 17; 1, pp. 362–3.
36 2, 8, 2; 1, p. 354.
37 2, 8, 9; 1, p. 359.
38 2, 7, 62; 1, p. 352.
39 2; 1, p. 388.
40 3; 1, p. 388.
41 5; 1, p. 392.

CHAPTER TEN

1 *Characteristics*, II, p. 15. References to Shaftesbury's writings will be given according to volume and page of the 1773 edition of the *Characteristics of Men, Manners, Opinions, Times*, which contains a number of treatises and pieces on ethical matters.
2 *Characteristics*, II, p. 77.
3 *Ibid.*, p. 23.
4 *Ibid.*, p. 436.
5 *Ibid.*, p. 442.
6 *Ibid.*, p. 227.
7 *Ibid.*, p. 16.
8 *Ibid.*, p. 22.
9 *Ibid.*, p. 77.
10 *Ibid.*, p. 78.
11 *Ibid.*, p. 176.
12 *Ibid.*, pp. 414–15.
13 *Ibid.*, pp. 42–3.
14 *Ibid.*, p. 29.
15 *Ibid.*, p. 28.
16 *Ibid.*, p. 66.
17 *Ibid.*, p. 267.
18 *Ibid.*, p. 76.
19 *Ibid.*, p. 77.
20 *Inquiry*, I, 1.

21 *Ibid.*, I, 2.
22 *Ibid.*, II, Introduction.
23 *System*, 1, 1, 4.
24 *Ibid.*
25 *Inquiry*, II, 7.
26 *System*, 1, 1, 5.
27 It is worth noting that a number of Hutcheson's ideas about aesthetic appreciation (for example, about its disinterested character) reappear in Kant's account of the judgment of taste.
28 *Inquiry*, II, 3.
29 *Ibid.*, II, 7.
30 *Ibid.*
31 References to Butler's writings are given according to volume and page of Gladstone's edition of his works (1896).
32 This dissertation, therefore, was published after the appearance of Hutcheson's *Inquiry* and *Essay on the Passions*.
33 12; 1, p. 407.
34 *Ibid.*, 15; 1, pp. 409–10.

[35] *Ibid.*, 16; I, p. 410.

[36] *Sermons*, 11, 3; II, p. 187.

[37] *Ibid.*

[38] *Sermons*, 11, 11; II, p. 196.

[39] *Sermons*, 11, 6; II, p. 190.

[40] *Sermons*, 11, 18; II, p. 203.

[41] Hutcheson was influenced by such distinctions through his acquaintance with Butler's *Sermons*. But, as we have seen, he went on to identify morality with benevolence to all intents and purposes. And it was this position that Butler criticized in his dissertation on virtue.

[42] *Sermons*, 11, 13; II, p. 199.

[43] *Sermons*, 11, 7; II, p. 57.

[44] *Sermons*, 11, 8; II, p. 57.

[45] *Sermons*, 11, 10; II, p. 59.

[46] 1; I, p. 398.

[47] *Ibid.*, 1, p. 399.

[48] *Sermons*, 2, 16; II, p. 62.

[49] *Sermons*, 3, 11; II, p. 74.

[50] *Sermons*, 3, 12; II, p. 75.

[51] *Sermons*, 3, 13; II, p. 76.

[52] 4; I, p. 400.

[53] *Ibid.*, 4; I, pp. 400–1.

[54] *Ibid.*, 5; I, p. 401.

[55] Preface to *Sermons*, 33; II, p. 25.

[56] *Sermons*, 3, 4; II, p. 70.

[57] 21; II, p. 15.

[58] *Ibid.*, 22; II, p. 16.

[59] *Sermons*, 3, 6; II, p. 71.

[60] *Dissertation of the Nature of Virtue*, 3; I, pp. 399–400.

[61] *Sermons*, 2, 19; II, p. 64.

[62] N.T., 22; *Works*, 1821, IV, p. 297.

[63] N.T., 6; IV, p. 59.

[64] *Principles*, 1, 1; I, p. 1.

[65] *Principles*, 1, 5; I, p. 14.

[66] *Principles*, 1, 6; I, pp. 16–17.

[67] *Ibid.*, p. 18.

[68] *Principles*, 1, 7; I, p. 31.

[69] *Principles*, 2, 2; I, p. 44.

[70] *Ibid.*, p. 45.

[71] *Principles*, 2, 3; I, p. 46.

[72] *Ibid.*, p. 47.

[73] *Ibid.*, p. 46.

[74] *Principles*, 2, 6; I, p. 54.

[75] *Principles*, 6, 1; I, p. 353.

[76] *Principles*, 6, 3; I, p. 375.

[77] *Ibid.*

[78] I do not mean to imply that Butler can properly be called a utilitarian. For the matter of that, it would be misleading to describe Hutcheson in this way.

OTHER IMAGE BOOKS

OTHER IMAGE BOOKS

OTHER IMAGE BOOKS

THE NEW TESTAMENT OF THE JERUSALEM BIBLE: Reader's Edition – Alexander Jones, General Editor

THE NEW TESTAMENT OF THE NEW AMERICAN BIBLE (complete and unabridged)

NO MAN IS AN ISLAND – Thomas Merton

THE NOONDAY DEVIL: Spiritual Support in Middle Age – Bernard Basset, S.J.

THE OLD TESTAMENT OF THE JERUSALEM BIBLE: Reader's Edition – Alexander Jones, General Editor
Volume 1: Genesis – Ruth; Volume 2: 1 Samuel – 2 Maccabees; Volume 3: Job – Ecclesiasticus; Volume 4: The Prophets – Malachi

ORTHODOXY – G. K. Chesterton

THE PAIN OF BEING HUMAN – Eugene Kennedy

THE POWER AND THE WISDOM – John L. McKenzie

POWER TO THE PARENTS! – Joseph and Lois Bird

THE PROTESTANT CHURCHES OF AMERICA – Revised Edition – John A. Hardon, S.J.

THE PSALMS OF THE JERUSALEM BIBLE – Alexander Jones, General Editor

RELIGION AND PERSONALITY – Adrian van Kaam, C.S.Sp.

RELIGION AND WORLD HISTORY – Christopher Dawson. Ed. by James Oliver and Christina Scott

RELIGIONS OF THE WORLD (2 vols.) – John A. Hardon, S.J.

A RELIGIOUS HISTORY OF THE AMERICAN PEOPLE (2 vols.) – Sydney E. Ahlstrom

RENEWING THE EARTH – Ed. by David J. O'Brien and Thomas A. Shannon

THE ROMAN CATHOLIC CHURCH – John L. McKenzie

ST. FRANCIS OF ASSISI – G. K. Chesterton

ST. FRANCIS OF ASSISI – Johannes Jorgensen

SAINT THOMAS AQUINAS – G. K. Chesterton

THE SEVEN STOREY MOUNTAIN – Thomas Merton

SEX: THOUGHTS FOR CONTEMPORARY CHRISTIANS – Ed. by Michael J. Taylor, S.J.

SHALOM: PEACE – The Sacrament of Reconciliation – Revised Edition – Bernard Häring, C.Ss.R.

THE SINAI MYTH – Andrew M. Greeley

THE SOUL AFIRE: REVELATIONS OF THE MYSTICS – Ed. by H. A. Reinhold

SPIRITUAL CANTICLE – St. John of the Cross. Trans. and ed., with an Intro., by E. Allison Peers

THE SPIRITUAL EXERCISES OF ST. IGNATIUS – Trans. by Anthony Mottola, Ph.D. Intro. by Robert W. Gleason, S.J.

OTHER IMAGE BOOKS

THE STORY OF THE TRAPP FAMILY SINGERS – Maria Augusta Trapp
SUFFERING – Louis Evely
SUMMA THEOLOGIAE – Thomas Aquinas. General Editor: Thomas
Gilby, O.P.
   Volume 1: The Existence of God. Part One: Questions 1–13
THE SURVIVAL OF DOGMA – Avery Dulles, S.J.
A THEOLOGY OF THE OLD TESTAMENT – John L. McKenzie
THIS MAN JESUS – Bruce Vawter
A THOMAS MERTON READER – Revised Edition – Ed. by Thomas
P. McDonnell
TOWARD A NEW CATHOLIC MORALITY – John Giles Milhaven
THE TWO-EDGED SWORD – John L. McKenzie
THE VARIETIES OF RELIGIOUS EXPERIENCE – William James
VIPER'S TANGLE – François Mauriac
THE WIT AND WISDOM OF BISHOP FULTON J. SHEEN – Ed. by Bill
Adler
WITH GOD IN RUSSIA – Walter J. Ciszek, S.J., with Daniel L.
Flaherty, S.J.

B 78 – 4